Palgrave Studies in Impact Finance

Series Editor
Mario La Torre
University of Rome "La Sapienza"
Rome, Italy

The *Palgrave Studies in Impact Finance* series provides a valuable scientific 'hub' for researchers, professionals and policy makers involved in Impact finance and related topics. It includes studies in the social, political, environmental and ethical impact of finance, exploring all aspects of impact finance and socially responsible investment, including policy issues, financial instruments, markets and clients, standards, regulations and financial management, with a particular focus on impact investments and microfinance.

Titles feature the most recent empirical analysis with a theoretical approach, including up to date and innovative studies that cover issues which impact finance and society globally.

More information about this series at
http://www.palgrave.com/gp/series/14621

Mario La Torre • Mario Calderini
Editors

Social Impact Investing Beyond the SIB

Evidence from the Market

palgrave
macmillan

Editors
Mario La Torre
University of Rome "La Sapienza"
Rome, Italy

Mario Calderini
School of Management
Politecnico di Milano
Milan, Milano, Italy

Palgrave Studies in Impact Finance
ISBN 978-3-030-08674-9 ISBN 978-3-319-78322-2 (eBook)
https://doi.org/10.1007/978-3-319-78322-2

Cover illustration: ramoncovelo / Getty Images

Printed on acid-free paper

This Palgrave Macmillan imprint is published by the registered company Springer Nature Switzerland AG
The registered company address is: Gewerbestrasse 11, 6330 Cham, Switzerland

Acknowledgements

First and foremost we would like to thank all contributors, whose biographies are provided in this volume, without whom this edited book would not have been possible, and two anonymous referees for their useful comments and suggestions.

Also, we want to express our gratitude to all participants of the 2017 Social Impact Investment International Conference organized by Sapienza University of Rome with its partners: Tiresia of Politecnico di Milano and Casmef Centro Arcelli of Luiss Guido Carli University. We received a great help from the Conference Scientific Committee.

Finally, we show our gratitude to the Palgrave Macmillan team, Tula Weis and Ruth Noble for their support during the publishing process.

Contents

Notes on Contributors

Filippo Addarii is co-founding partner and CEO of PlusValue, research and consultancy company to align public and private interests for public goods. Over the last 15 years, he has advised national and international public institutions, corporations, and not-for-profit organizations on innovation strategies for socio-economic development, including the European Commission, British Foreign Office, and UN Fund for Democracy. Since 2014, his efforts have focused on the scale-up of impact investing as embedded into urban regeneration projects, advising the international developer Lendlease.

Addarii holds a MRes in Urban Studies and Affairs from University College London (UCL) and a MSc in Non-Profit Management from Università degli Studi di Urbino. He has successfully completed executive courses at Harvard Kennedy School (Civil Society Leadership Management), INSEAD (Social Entrepreneurship Programme), and CASS Business School (Centre for Charity Effectiveness, London, UK).

Mario Calderini is Full Professor in Social Innovation at the School of Management of Politecnico di Milano and he is Director of Tiresia, Centre of Research on Social Innovation and Social Impact Investments. He is President of the Scientific Committee of the Social Impact Agenda per l'Italia and he was previously member of the Social Impact Investment Taskforce. His main research areas are social impact investments and social innovation.

Rosella Carè is a postdoctoral research fellow in banking and finance at University Magna Graecia (UMG) of Catanzaro, Italy. She received a PhD in Healthcare Management and Economics from UMG and a Ph.D. in 'Sciences de Gestion' from the Conservatoire National des Arts et Métiers (CNAM), France. During 2012 and 2013, she was a visiting PhD student at ESCP Europe, Paris, and in 2016 she was an invited visiting researcher at Waterloo University, Canada. As temporary professor at UMG she teaches banking and finance disciplines. She is author or co-author of works published by Springer, Routledge and Palgrave Macmillan. Her research interests include social and sustainable finance, alternative finance and sustainability, and reputational risk and reputational crisis in the banking sector.

Rossana Caridà has been a researcher of Italian Public Law at University Magna Graecia (UMG) of Catanzaro, Italy since 2012. She holds a PhD in Administrative Law from the University of Catania (Italy). From 2013 to 2016, she served as Aggregate Professor of Italian Public Law for the degree courses in Business Administration and in Sociology and taught Administrative Law in the degree course in Organization of Public and Private Administrations at UMG. Currently, she is Aggregate Professor of Italian Public Law for the degree course in Business Administration at UMG. She teaches also in many High Training Courses (Postgraduate Schools of Law, Masters, etc.) and she was responsible for various research projects relating to Public and Administrative Law, with a structural link with Constitutional Principles. Caridà has authored more than 30 scientific publications and a book. Her main areas of research concern fundamental fights, citizenship and public administrators' liability.

Helen Chiappini is a postdoctoral research fellow at G. d'Annunzio University of Chieti and Pescara and a teacher assistant in Corporate Finance at Luiss Guido Carli University. She taught in a MBA course and in a MSc course at Link Campus University of Rome and at Pontificia Lateran University of Vatican City. She was Visiting Research Fellow at Centre of Banking and Finance of Regent's University London and she received a Ph.D. *cum laude* in Banking and Finance at Sapienza University of Rome. Her areas of research include social impact investments, socially responsible investments and non-performing loans management strategies. She recently published a book titled *Social Impact Funds. Definition Assessment and Performance* with Palgrave Macmillan (2017).

Giuseppe Ferraro graduated in Law from the University of Calabria with a 110/110 vote with honors. He specialized in legal professions at the LUISS Guido Carli law school in Rome and received a second-level master's degree in Management of Innovation and Information Technologies. Currently, he is a second year Ph.D. student in the School of Theory of Law and European Legal and Economic Systems at the University Magna Graecia of Catanzaro, Italy. His research interests are public private partnerships for innovation and alternative finance for Italian public entities.

Carmen Gallucci is Associate Professor of Corporate Finance at University of Salerno, Italy where she holds courses in Corporate Finance and Business Evaluation. Her research activity focuses on corporate finance, the bank-firm relationship and the interaction between corporate governance models and economic and financial performance.

Lars Hultkrantz is Professor of Economics at Örebro University. He has been doing research in public economics, transportation economics, environmental and resource economics and economics of tourism. He is a member of the Expert Group on Public Economics at the Swedish Ministry of Finance. He has been an advisor to the development of guidelines for benefit-cost analysis in Sweden and Norway.

Mario La Torre is Full Professor in Banking and Finance at the University of Rome "La Sapienza", Rome, Italy. His main research areas are banking and financial intermediaries, financial markets and financial innovation. He is an expert in ethical finance, impact finance and microfinance, as well as audiovisual and art financing. He is editor of the book series Palgrave Studies in Impact Finance published by Palgrave Macmillan. He has been a member of the G8 Social Impact Investment Taskforce.

Fiorenza Lipparini is a Founding Partner and Director of Research at PlusValue. She leads on research activities and focuses on social entrepreneurship, socio-economic impact assessment tools and techniques, digital social innovation and funding, governance and evaluation of multi-stakeholder partnerships for the delivery of societal goods. Before founding PlusValue, Lipparini was EU Policy Senior Analyst at the Young Foundation, and earlier a policy analyst for Intesa Sanpaolo, in Brussels.

She is co-author with Filippo Addarii of *Vision and Trends of Social Innovation for Europe*, and a co-author on a European Commission report titled 'ICT-Enabled Social Innovation to support the Implementation of the Social

Investment Package – Mapping and Analysis of ICT-enabled Social Innovation initiatives promoting social investment in integrated approaches to the provision of social services: IESI Knowledge Map 2015'.

She holds a Ph.D. in Comparative Literature and Linguistics.

Francesca Medda is Professor of Applied Economics and Finance at the University College London (UCL). Since 2010, she has served as Director of the UCL QASER (Quantitative and Applied Spatial Economics Research) Laboratory. Since 2012, she has served as economic adviser to the UK Ministry of Environment and Agriculture (Defra) and in 2014 at the Ministry of Finance (HM Treasury). She is Vice-President of the Parliamentary and Scientific Committee. Her research focuses on project finance, innovative financial mechanisms and risk evaluation in different infrastructure sectors such as transport industry, energy innovation and new technologies, urban investments (smart cities), supply chain provision and optimization, and efficiency. She works actively with the private and public sector including the European Investment Bank, the World Bank, UNESCO, UN-Habitat, WILLIS Re, HALCROW and UITP.

Antonio Minguzzi is Associate Professor of Management at the University of Molise, Italy. His research interests include social finance and small business development. He has published national and international articles on management and small business. Since 2015, he has been General Manager of the Banco di Napoli Foundation, which is a private foundation engaging in philanthropy in the social sector in Southern Italy.

Michele Modina is Associate Professor of Economics and Business Management at the University of Molise, Italy where he holds courses in Corporate Finance and Start-up and Business Planning. His research activity focuses on value creation, the bank-firm relationship and the role of corporate finance, the management of investment and financing techniques, including new methods of the provision of financial resources.

Julio Navío-Marco is a top corporate Spanish executive with more than 20 years experience in the digital & Information & Communication Technologies sector with a thorough understanding of the information technologies industry. Marco holds an MSc. degree in Telecommunications Engineering (UPM), a BA and Ph.D. in Business Administration (UNED), and a Program for Development of Directors from IESE Business School. Marco is also Lecturer in Business Organization and Entrepreneurship (UNED).

Alessandro Rizzello received his Ph.D. in Health Care Management and Economics from the University Magna Graecia (UMG) of Catanzaro, Italy with a dissertation that focused on social impact investing and social impact bonds in healthcare. Currently, he teaches Social and Sustainable Finance at UMG. His research interests are social impact investing, social impact bonds, social and sustainable finance and crowdfunding of social ventures. Previously, he worked as a head of a financial office in the Italian public administration. He received his master's degree in Economics from the LUISS University in Rome.

Elisabetta Scognamiglio has a Ph.D. in Economics from the Federico II University of Naples. She discussed a Ph.D. thesis on social risk in impact investing with specific focus on social impact bonds. Research interests concern the risks and returns in social impact investment. Previously, she worked as a project manager for an Italian microfinance institution and currently works as an impact analyst for an Italian company.

Marta Solórzano-García is Senior Lecturer in Business Administration in the Organisation Studies Department at The National University of Distance Education (UNED) Business School (Spanish Distance Teaching University). She is the director of the Social Entrepreneurship and Social Innovation Postgraduate Program. She also teaches in the doctoral program and in executive education offerings. Her research focuses on organizational design and change, social entrepreneurship, social enterprise, and social impact. García has participated in several research projects with the Chamber of Commerce of Madrid, the Ministry of Employment and Immigration, the Department of Finance and Public Administration, and several European projects.

Annarita Trotta is Full Professor of Banking and Finance at University Magna Graecia (UMG) of Catanzaro, Italy. She holds a Ph.D. in Business Administration from the University of Naples Federico II, where she was an assistant professor of Banking on the Faculty of Economics from 1995 to 2001. From 2001 to 2006, she was an associate professor at the University of Catanzaro. Since 2006, she has been a professor of Economics and Management of Financial Institutions and Markets at UMG, where she teaches Banking, Financial Markets, and Corporate Finance. Over her 20-year academic career, Trotta has authored (or co-authored) more than 50 scientific publications and four books. Her primary areas of research are social and sustainable finance; impact investing; alternative finance and sustainability; reputational risk and reputational crisis in the banking sector; corporate social responsibility in the banking sector; subprime crisis and credit rating agencies; local banking and information asymmetries; credit risk; small business, venture capital and informal venture capital; bank-small business relationships; and finance and medicine.

Mercedes Valcárcel-Dueñas is the managing director at Fundación Tomillo, advisor, and board member in various social entities and foundations; she also has extensive experience in multinational projects with abilities to lead multidisciplinary teams. Valcárcel-Dueñas is a lecturer in Finance for social businesses, social innovation, and social impact measurement. She has authored several publications on social entrepreneurship and social finance, impact investments, social economy, and social impact assessment. She has recently been appointed to the European Commission Advisory group on innovation for Small and Medium Enterprises for Horizon 2020 as expert in social innovation, and to the Advisory Group on Gender.

Karen Wendt is external lecturer at Modul Vienna University. She has more than 20 years of experience in investment banking with UniCredit and has been sitting on the board of the Equator Principles Financial Institutions Association (EPFI Association) for more than seven years. She is also an investment banker and consultant on responsible investment banking and positive impact investment. Her anthology *Responsible Investment Banking* was published by Springer International in 2015 and she contributes to publications for Springer and Taylor and Francis (Routledge) on a permanent basis, including on topics such as organizational development, change management, rating, conflict resolution mechanisms and project management. Her new anthology *Positive Impact Investing and Organizational Culture* will be published in 2018 as well as *Creating Ecosystems of Ethical Culture in Business and Non Business Organizations* and *Sustainable Financial Innovation.*

List of Figures

List of Tables

1

Introduction

Mario La Torre and Mario Calderini

Social impact investments (SIIs) are those that intentionally aim at social impact and financial returns. The term SII is relatively new in the investment panorama, since it was coined in 2007 at the Rockefeller Bellagio Centre in Italy (Harji and Jackson 2012). However, the underlying idea of investing in order to support projects and organizations meeting social needs is well anchored in most of the world's cultures.

To date, the SII market is estimated in 114 billion worldwide (Mudaliar et al. 2017) and it is characterized by many actors, generally grouped into supply-side and demand-side organizations. Demand-side-organizations demand funding to support their high-impact activities, while supply-side organizations offer funding to impact-oriented institutions. Instead of this general taxonomy, the SII market faces differences in terms of types of

M. La Torre (✉)
University of Rome "La Sapienza", Rome, Italy
e-mail: mario.latorre@uniroma1.it

M. Calderini
School of Management, Politecnico di Milano, Milan, Milano, Italy
e-mail: mario.calderini@polimi.it

M. La Torre, M. Calderini (eds.), *Social Impact Investing Beyond the SIB*, Palgrave Studies in Impact Finance, https://doi.org/10.1007/978-3-319-78322-2_1

organizations involved in any country as well as in the development of financial instruments and regulations as recognized by the Social Impact Investment Taskforce (SIIT 2014).

The SIIT (2014) classifies some financial instruments and sub-markets as mature—like the microcredit market—and emerging—like social impact bonds (SIBs).

SIBs have gained the consideration of many public bodies due to their structure based on a public-private partnership and on the payment of financial return subordinated to the achievement of the expected social impact. The pay-for-success approach utilized for SIBs, has inspired, over the last several years, different and variegated financial impact-oriented financial structures.

This book aims at analyzing case studies of impact investments going beyond SIBs. With this perspective in mind, the volume firstly recalls literature of SIIs and some opening points in the architectures of SIBs; secondly, the book analyzes specific case studies of public-private partnerships, of crowdfunding platforms, and of social impact measurement models.

The book contains nine chapters structured as follows.

Chapter 2, "Investing with Impact: An Integrated Analysis between Academics and Practitioners" by Rosella Carè and Karen Wendt, introduces the theme of SII from the scholars' and practitioners' perspective. Indeed, the chapter summarizes literature on social impact investments and assesses what drives impact investors' decisions.

Chapter 3, "Social Risk and Financial Returns: Evidences from Social Impact Bonds" by Elisabetta Scognamiglio, Alessandro Rizzello and Helen Chiappini, provides an empirical insight into factors characterizing social risk of social impact bonds (SIBs) and explores the correlation between social risk and financial return by implementing a social risk score and analyzing a sample of 34 SIBs sharing information publically.

Chapter 4, "The Use of Payment by Results in Healthcare: A Review and Proposal" by Alessandro Rizzello, Rossana Caridà, Anna Rita Trotta, Giuseppe Ferraro and Rosella Carè, aims to clarify opportunities and challenges of the SIB development in the Italian context, from economic and legal perspectives. This conceptualization is based on literature review and on the assessment of SIBs in multiple case studies.

Chapter 5, "Impact Investing Innovation: Bringing Together Public, Private, and Third Sectors to Create Greater Value: The Case of the Public Private Partnership Initiative for the New Public Hospital of Treviso" by Filippo Addari, Fiorenza Lipparini and Francesca Medda, describes the Public Private Partnership (PPP) implemented to finance the new hospital in Treviso, Italy and explains how to reach the goal promoters have made recourse to the Shared Value framework developed by Porter and Kramer (2011). This case study represents one of the first cases of large infrastructure realized in Europe within the framework of impact investments.

Chapter 6, "The Evolution of a Social Service Crowdfunding Platform towards an Investing Logic: The Meridonare Case Study" by Carmen Gallucci, Michele Modina and Antonio Minguzzi, analyzes the Meridonare crowdfunding platform and its features. The chapter proposes a Social Bond Crowdfunding-based (SBCb) model as an innovative financial structure, shifting the role of the Banco di Napoli Foundation, which created Meridonare, from impact facilitator to impact generator. The new model platform moves from the needs of strengths investment perspectives and from the pay-by-results rewarding mechanism.

Chapter 7, "Benefit-Cost Evaluation of Prevention and Early Intervention Measures for Children and Youth in Sweden" by Lars Hultkrantz, reports on an on-going effort to create a societal benefit-cost model for evaluation of causal effects of social programmes that target individuals and groups in Sweden; the model supports the knowledge of "ex ante" priority decision making and "ex post" follow-up of local interventions funded by municipalities and regional authorities according to an impact investment approach.

Chapter 8, "Impact Measurement for Social Innovation: Analysis of the Spanish Third Sector" by Marta Solórzano-García, Julio Navío-Marco and Mercedes Valcárcel Dueñas, assesses a range of social impact monitoring and evaluation practices used by organizations working in the Spanish third sector.

Finally, Chap. 9, "Social Impact Investments Beyond Social Impact Bonds: A Research and Policy Agenda" by Helen Chiappini, concludes the book and assesses some research and policy points still open in the impact investment field, like the need for: a hard and soft regulation; a transparent governance; reliable social and financial performance; and the market development.

References

Harji, K., & Jackson, E. T. (2012). *Accelerating impact: Achievements, challenges and what's next in building the impact investment industry*. New York: The Rockefeller Foundation.

Mudaliar, A., Schiff, H., Bass, R., & Dithrich, H. (2017). *Annual impact investor survey 2017*. New York: Global Impact Investment Network. https://assets.rockefellerfoundation.org/app/uploads/20120707215852/Accelerating-Impact-Full-Summary.pdf; https://thegiin.org/research/publication/annual-survey2017.

Porter, M. E., & Kramer, M. R. (2011). The big idea: Creating shared value – How to reinvent capitalism and unleash a wave of innovation and growth. *Harvard Business Review, 89*(1–2), 62–77.

SIIT. (2014). *Impact investment: The invisible hearth of markets*. London. http://www.socialimpactinvestment.org/reports/Impact%20Investment%20Report%20FINAL%5B3%5D.pdf

2

Investing with Impact: An Integrated Analysis Between Academics and Practitioners

Rosella Carè and Karen Wendt

1 Introduction

Since the 2007/2008 financial crisis, many questions have been posed about how financial markets operate and how they are able to benefit society (Shiller 2013; Zingales 2015). The contribution made by financial markets and financial institutions to the prosperity of society has been questioned, and the need to develop new investment opportunities able to create blended returns and shared value has emerged (Porter and Kramer 2011; Lehner 2016; Weber and Feltmate 2016; Jacobs and Mazzucato 2016). Around the globe, new investment models able to reflect responsible behaviour have been claimed in order to keep financial markets in tune with the development of society.

R. Carè (✉)
University Magna Graecia of Catanzaro, Catanzaro, Italy
e-mail: care@unicz.it

K. Wendt
Modul Vienna University, Wien, Austria

M. La Torre, M. Calderini (eds.), *Social Impact Investing Beyond the SIB*, Palgrave Studies in Impact Finance, https://doi.org/10.1007/978-3-319-78322-2_2

In this vein, impact investments have become one of the most important and most talked about market approaches. Impact investors go beyond the traditional socially responsible investments because their ambitions are to actively place capital in business or projects with the aim to promote environmental or social objectives (Nicholls 2010a, b; Hummels et al. 2016).

The Canadian Task Force on Social Finance (2010, p. 5) defines impact investing as "the active investment of capital in businesses and funds that generate positive social and/or environmental impacts, as well as financial returns (from principal to above market rate) to the investor."

Further specification on what impact investing entails is provided by the World Economic Forum (2013, p. 6), which describes impact investing "as an investment approach that intentionally seeks to create both financial return and positive social or environmental impact that is actively measured." This definition highlights two major characteristics of impact investing (World Economic Forum 2013; Brandstetter and Lehner 2015):

1. impact investing is an investment approach and not a stand-alone asset class. In the wide range of impact investing opportunities, financial instruments span from equity to bonds;
2. outcomes must be measured in order for the investment to be considered an impact investment.

At the same time, impact investing differs from Socially Responsible Investing (SRI) because this latter technique screens investment moving from environmental, social, and government factors (the most well-known ESG factors), while impact investors seek to make positive and measurable impacts in addition to traditional financial returns (Geobey and Weber 2013; Weber 2016).

Nicholls (2010a, p. 81) encloses impact investments in the area of social investments and explains how they reflect systemic investor rationality that typically aims at balancing means-ends and values-driven rationalities by seeking returns that benefit both the investor and the investee/beneficiary.

Many authors have tried to clarify the boundaries of this emerging investing approach.

However, the academic literature shows significant variations in the conceptualization of impact investing, and many authors highlight that the same method of impact investing goes by many names (Hebb 2013; Höchstädter and Scheck 2015; Trotta et al. 2015; Rizzello and Carè 2016), including double and triple bottom line, mission-related investing, program-related investment, blended-value, and economically targeted investing. The 2017 "Annual Impact Investor Survey" provided by GIIN highlighted that one of the major challenges to the growth of the impact investing industry is related to a common understanding of definition and segmentation of the impact investing market (GIIN 2017a).

Höchstädter and Scheck (2015) investigate a large number of academic and practitioner works by highlighting several inconsistencies in definitional and terminological aspects. By analyzing only peer-reviewed work, Rizzello et al. (2016) depict the academic landscape of impact investing by providing a useful map of contributions, areas of inquiries, and future research directions. However, these two works—Rizzello et al. (2016) and Höchstädter and Scheck (2015)—are actually the only two works that have tried to shed light on this research area. They do not provide an assessment of financial instruments and investment opportunities that are actually available in the impact investment market. Moving from these considerations, this work aims 1) to provide a deeper understanding of the impact investing landscape through a systematic literature review, by providing an assessment of the instruments and actors involved; 2) to analyze the investors' preferences by using a pilot survey; 3) to discuss the major trends and challenges that have emerged, both in theory and practice. To clarify the variety of concepts, instruments, and approaches around the term "impact investment," this research—through an exploratory analysis—is based on a qualitative approach including both a systematic literature review (Tranfield et al. 2003) and a research survey (Baker et al. 2011). In particular, we performed a systematic literature review and examined the content of the different research subfields in impact investing studies. Then, we scrutinized the results of our literature review with the aim to identify the instruments and current practices that can be enclosed in the impact investing landscape. To perform this second objective, we enclosed technical reports in our review and conducted a survey in order to capture practitioners' perception of impact investing. The chapter is organized as follows. Section 2 highlights our methodological approach, while Sect. 3 describes the main results of our literature review. Section 4 shows the results of our exploratory survey on impact investors. Section 5 provides insights and implications that may be useful for the development of the impact investing market, and Sect. 6 focuses on limitations and the main conclusion.

2 Research Design and Methodological Approach

In this work, a two-pronged methodology was undertaken: a systematic literature review approach (Tranfield et al. 2003) in order to perform a selection of the most relevant works published to date in the field of impact investing, and an investors' survey (Baker et al. 2011) in order to provide a preliminary analysis of the participants in the impact investing market. In the next sections, we discuss our search method, inclusion and exclusion criteria, sample characteristics, and data analysis process.

2.1 Systematic Literature Review: Methodological Details

A systematic literature review can be defined as an objective, replicable, and comprehensive method to assess relevant studies on a specific topic (Tranfield et al. 2003; Thorpe et al. 2005; Weed 2005). To perform our systematic literature review, we followed the three-stage procedure suggested by Tranfield et al. (2003): planning, execution, and reporting.

Our review entailed extensive searches of relevant databases with the aim to ensure that all literature on impact investing was identified while maintaining the focus of greatest pertinence with our research objective. To avoid bias and errors in the process of literature identification, a research protocol has been developed (Tranfield et al. 2003).

Considering the explorative nature of our study, we have considered more than only the most important journals of the field. We opted to scrutinize the following databases for the investigation: ISI WoS, Scopus, and Google Scholar and considered all journals in each database. The same search criteria were used for all databases and the databases analyses were performed in August 2017 and included all works published as of that date. Database searches were performed by using only two strings—"impact investing" and "impact investment."

The analysis of the results allowed us to detect, as expected, a large overlap between databases. The greater number of results is attributable to Google Scholar, which, for its search algorithmic structure, also returns results that do not perfectly match with the search expression (Mikki 2009, p. 42). However, the use of Google Scholar helped us to capture both academic and practitioners' work. Due to the exploratory nature of our work and moving from our research objective, we decide to scrutinize both academic and practitioners' works. In particular, with regard to the academic works, we decide to include in our sample only works published into international scientific journals, books, and book chapters, as they are considered "certified knowledge." Consequently, conference proceedings, working papers, and non-peer-reviewed journal articles have been excluded from our sample of analysis. The abstracts of all the articles obtained were analyzed in order to verify the relevance with the object abstracts. This step significantly reduced the results of the search. Finally, with regard to the practitioners' literature, in order to be sure that all published reports were captured through our search strings, we scrutinized the Global Impact Investing Network (GIIN) database (Höchstädter and Scheck 2015) and manually added missing reports. In this step, both GIIN-authored reports and third-party reports were selected. Reports have been further analyzed in order to remove duplicates and non-relevant results. Our final sample is composed of 215 works that are distributed as highlighted in Fig. 2.1.

2.2 Review Results

In recent years the number of works published about impact investing has growth. Figure 2.2 show their distribution by year.

Practitioners' contributions represent 58% of the entire sample. Table 2.1 provides an overview of the works enclosed in our analysis.

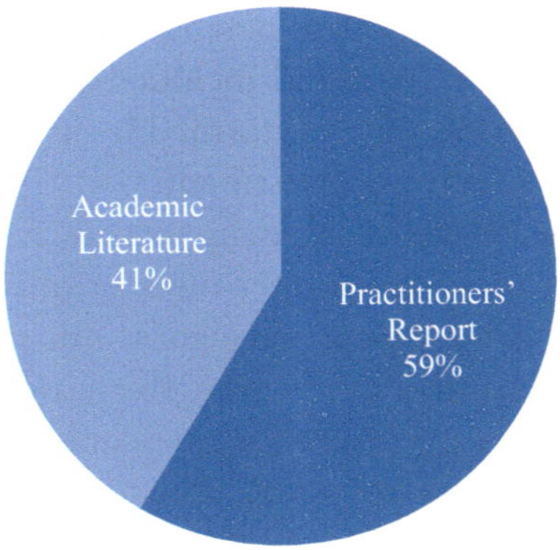

Fig. 2.1 Sample distribution. Source: Author

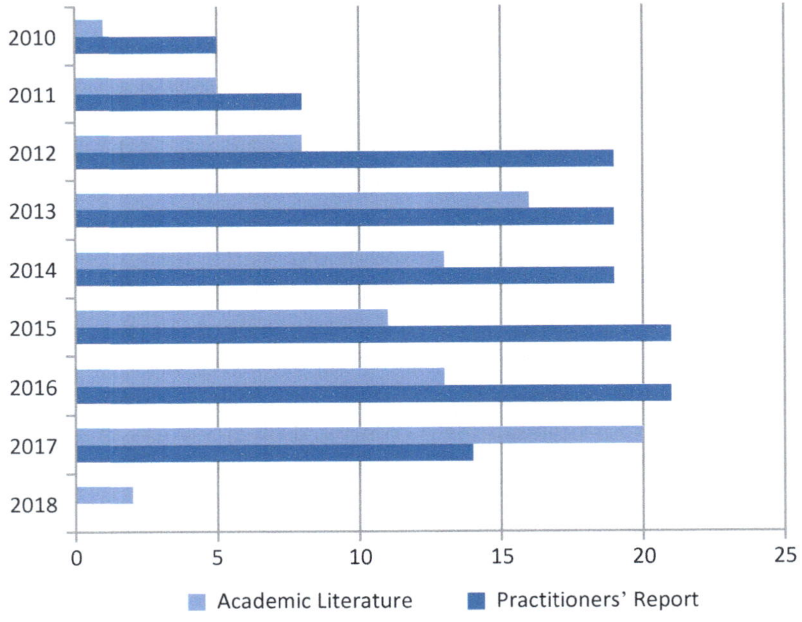

Fig. 2.2 Sample distribution by year. Source: Author

Table 2.1 Reports enclosed in the sample

Commissioner/consultant	Title	Year
GIIN	Annual Impact Investor Survey	2017
GIIN	Impact Measurement in the Health Sector	2017
GIIN	Scaling the use of guarantees in U.S. community investing	2017
Business & Sustainable Development Commission and Convergence	The state of blended finance	2017
Nesta Impact Investments	Nesta Impact Investments—Annual Report	2017
GIIN & Cambridge Associates	The financial performance of real assets impact investments	2017
Council of Development Finance Agencies (CDFA)	Urban revitalization & impact investing	2017
The ImPact and CREO Syndicate	Water: An Impact Investment Primer For Family Offices and Foundations	2017
Cornerstone Capital Group	Colorado Impact Report	2017
Federal Reserve Bank of St. Luis	Impact Investing: Survey of Missouri Nonprofits	2017
OXFAM	Impact investing: who are we serving?	2017
Athena Capital Advisor	Impact Investing: History & Opportunity	2017
Mckinsey&Company	Impact investing: purpose-driven finance finds its place in India	2017
UK Government	Growing a culture of Social Impact Investing in UK	2017
Impact Investing Australia	2016 Investor Report	2016
Toniic Institute Report & BNP Paribas	Millennials & Impact Investment	2016
Responsible Investment Association	2016 Canadian Impact Investment—Trends Report	2016
UBS	Doing well by doing good	2016
GIIN	Impact Investing Trends: Evidence of a Growing Industry	2016
GIIN	Annual Impact Investor Survey	2016
CECP	Investing with purpose	2016
Bertha Centre for Social Innovation and Entrepreneurship	Innovative Finance in Africa Review	2016

(*continued*)

Table 2.1 (continued)

Commissioner/consultant	Title	Year
BRIDGES VENTURE	Better Outcomes, Better Value: The evolution of social impact bonds in the UK	2016
Bertelsmann Stiftung	Social Impact Investment in Germany: From momentum to implementation	2016
Purpose Capital, Canadian Credit Union Association (CCUA)	A Guidebook for Canadian Credit Unions	2016
GIIN	Annual Impact Investor Survey	2016
Social Finance UK	Social Impact Bonds: The Early Years	2016
GIIN	The Business Value of Impact Measurement	2016
Big Society Capital	Corporate social investment—Gaining traction	2016
ANDE, Latin American Private Equity & Venture Capital Association (LAVCA), and LGT Impact Ventures	The Impact Investing Landscape in Latin America	2016
GIIN	Achieving the Sustainable Development Goals: The Role of Impact Investing	2016
Investisseurs & Partenaires (I&P) and The Foundation for International Development Study and Research (Ferdi)	Investing in Development in Africa: How Impact Investment can contribute to meeting the Sustainable Development Goals (SDGs) in Africa	2016
Intellecap	Mapping Philanthropy and Impact Investing Opportunities in India	2016
GIIN & Open Capital Advisors	The Landscape for Impact Investing in Southern Africa	2016
Barclays	The Value of Being Human: A Behavioural Framework for Impact Investing and Philanthropy	2015
OECD	Social Impact Bonds: state of play & lessons learnt	2016
OECD	Social Impact Investment: Building the Evidence Base	2015
ABN-AMRO	Social Impact Bonds: Opportunities and Challenges in the Netherlands	2015

(continued)

Table 2.1 (continued)

Commissioner/consultant	Title	Year
GIIN & University of New Hampshire	Scaling U.S. community investing	2015
Omidyar Network	Frontier Capital: Early Stage Investing for Financial Returns and Social Impact in Emerging Markets	2015
Mission Investors Exchange	Essentials of Impact Investing: A Guide for Small-Staffed Foundations	2015
The Impact Programme	Survey of the Impact Investment Markets 2014 Challenges and Opportunities in Sub-Saharan Africa and South Asia	2015
City of London Corporation	Developing a Global Financial Centre for Social Impact Investment	2015
Money Management Institute	Bringing Impact Investing Down to Earth: Insights for Making Sense, Managing Outcomes, and Meeting Client Demand	2015
GIIN	ImpactBase Snapshot: An Analysis of 300+ Impact Investing Funds	2015
JP MORGAN & GIIN	Eyes on the Horizon. The Impact Investor Survey	2015
GIIN & Cambridge Associates	Introducing the Impact Investing Benchmark	2015
GRI, IRIS, and Triodos	GRI, IRIS, and the Investor Perspective IRIS Standards Series	2015
The Lemelson Foundation and Enclude	Catalyzing Capital for Invention: Spotlight on India	2015
Brookings Institution	Policy recommendations for the applications of impact bonds	2015
Merrill Lynch's Wealth Management Institute	Impact Investing: The Performance Realities	2015
GIIN & Dalberg Global Development Advisors	The Landscape for Impact Investing in West Africa	2015
The Center for Effective Philanthropy	Investing and Social Impact: Practices of Private Foundations	2015
Clifford Chance	Impact Investing Private Equity Fund Industry: Legal Considerations	2015

(continued)

Table 2.1 (continued)

Commissioner/consultant	Title	Year
GIIN & Dalberg Global Development Advisors	The Landscape for Impact Investing in South Asia	2015
Social Finance UK	Technical Guide: Designing outcome metrics	2015
Social Finance UK	The Global Impact Bond Market	2014
Bank of America Merrill Lynch, Bridges Ventures	A De-risking Toolkit for Impact Investment	2014
Bridges Ventures & The Parthenon Group	Investing for Impact—case studies across asset classes	2014
Social Ventures Australia (SVA)	How to Grow Impact Investing	2014
Bank of America Merrill Lynch and Bridges Ventures	Choosing Social Impact Bonds. A practitioner' s Guide	2014
Social Impact Investment Task Force	Impact investment: The invisible heart of markets	2014
Social Finance	Foundations for Social Impact Bonds: How and Why Philanthropy Is Catalyzing the Development of a New Market	2014
UK National Advisory Board to Social Impact Taskforce	Building a social impact investment market. The UK experience	2014
The Impact Programme	The Impact Programme—Market Baseline Study: Impact investment in Sub-Saharan Africa and South Asia in 2013	2014
Intellecap	Invest. Catalyze. Mainstream: The Indian Impact Investing Story	2014
The Impact Programme	The Impact Programme: Annual Report 2013	2014
RAND Europe	Phase 2 report from the payment by results Social Impact Bond pilot at HMP Peterborough	2014
US National Advisory Board on Impact Investing	Private Capital, Public Good: How Smart Federal Policy Can Galvanize Impact Investing—and Why It's Urgent	2014
Social Impact Investment Taskforce, established by the G8	Reports from the Social Impact Investment Taskforce, established under the UK's presidency of the G8	2014
MARS, Purpose capital	State of the Nation Impact investing in Canada	2014

(*continued*)

Table 2.1 (continued)

Commissioner/consultant	Title	Year
LGT Venture Philanthropy, Aspen Network of Development Entrepreneurs (ANDE), Quintessa Partners, University of St. Gallen Hub São Paulo	Mapping the impact investing sector in Brazil	2014
Big Lottery fund	SIBs. The State of Play. Full Report	2014
Impact Economy	Serving Client Demand for Impact Investing: A Hands-On Guide for Financial Advisors and Senior Management	2014
JP MORGAN & GIIN	Spotlight on the Market	2014
GIIN	Catalytic First-Loss Capital	2013
Toniic	E-Guide to Early-Stage Global Impact Investing	2013
World Economic Forum	From Ideas to Practice, Pilots to Strategy. Practical Solutions and Actionable Insights on How to Do Impact Investing	2013
Keystone Accountability	Impact Investment What Investees Think	2013
World Economic Forum	Bringing Impact Investing From the Margins to the Mainstream	2013
Mission Investors Exchange, the Council on Foundations	Community Foundation Field Guide to Impact Investing: Reflections from the Field and Resources for Moving Forward	2013
Sonen Capital	Evolution of an Impact Portfolio: From Implementation to Results	2013
Center for Global Development, Social Finance	Investing in Social Outcomes: Development Impact Bonds	2013
InSight at Pacific Community Ventures, Case at Duke University, ImpactAssets	Impact Investing 2.0: The Way Forward	2013
Impact Economy	Making Impact Investible	2013
Rosemary Addis, John McLeod, Alan Raine	IMPACT—Australia: Investment for social and economic benefit	2013
FEDERAL RESERVE BANK OF SAN FRANCISCO	Social Impact Bonds: Using Impact Investment to Expand Effective Social Programs	2013
UKSIF	The Future of Investment: Impact Investing	2013

(*continued*)

Table 2.1 (continued)

Commissioner/consultant	Title	Year
Cambridge Associates	Impact Investing: A Framework for Decision Making	2013
Purpose Capital	Guidebook for Impact Investors: Impact Measurement	2013
The European Venture Philanthropy Association	A Practical Guide to Measuring and Managing Impact—2015	2013
D. Capital Partners	Impact Investing in Education: An Overview of the Current Landscape	2013
MARS, Purpose capital (commissioned by TD)	The Landscape for Social Impact Investing—a White Paper	2013
MARS	Mission Possible	2013
PCV Insight, CASE at Duke, ImpactAssets	A Market Emerges: The Six Dynamics of Impact Investing	2012
Boston Consulting Group	The First Billion: A forecast of social investment demand	2012
City of London Corporation	A brief handbook on social investment	2012
Global Alliance for Banking on Values	Strong and Straightforward: The Business Case for Sustainable Banking	2012
Impact Assets	Risk, return and impact: understanding diversification and performance within an impact investing portfolio	2012
Social Finance, Finethic	Microfinance, Impact Investing, and pension fund investment policy survey	2012
Nesta Impact Investments	Standards of Evidence for Impact Investing	2012
J.P. MORGAN	A Portfolio Approach to Impact Investment: A Practical Guide to Building, Analyzing and Managing a Portfolio of Impact Investments	2012
E.T. Jackson, Associates Ltd.	Accelerating Impact: Achievements, Challenges and What's Next in Building the Impact Investing Industry	2012

(continued)

Table 2.1 (continued)

Commissioner/consultant	Title	Year
Bridges Ventures	The Power of Advice in the UK Sustainable and Impact Investment Market	2012
The Rockefeller Foundation, United Nations Global Compact	A Framework for Action: Social Enterprise and Impact Investing	2012
Godeke Consulting	Building a Healthy & Sustainable Social Impact Bond Market: The Investor Landscape	2012
Cambridge Associates Limited	The U.K. Social Investment Market: The Current Landscape and a Framework for Investor Decision Making	2012
Social Finance	A New Tool for Scaling Social Impact: How Social Impact Bonds Can Mobilize Private Capital To Advance Social Good	2012
Pacific Community Ventures et. Al	Impact at Scale: Policy Innovation for Institutional Investment with Social and Environmental Benefit	2012
Pacific Community Ventures et. Al	The Impact Investor: The Need for Evidence and Engagement	2012
McKinsey	From Potential to Action: Bringing Social Impact Bonds to the U.S.	2012
Monitor Inclusive Markets, Acumen Fund	From Blueprint to Scale: The Case for Philanthropy in Impact Investing	2012
NCIF, the IRIS initiative	Collaborating to Harmonize Standardized Metrics for Impact Investors	2012
The Social Investment Business	Making Good in Social Impact Investment: Opportunities in an Emerging Asset Class	2011
Responsible Research	Impact Investing in Emerging Markets	2011
UK Government—Ministry of Justice	Lessons learned from the planning and early implementation of the Social Impact Bond at HMP Peterborough	2011

(continued)

Table 2.1 (continued)

Commissioner/consultant	Title	Year
J.P. Morgan, the GIIN	Insight into the Impact Investment Market. An In-Depth Analysis of Investor Perspectives and Over 2200 Transactions	2011
Dalberg Global Development Advisors	Impact Investing in West Africa	2011
Insight at Pacific Community Ventures & Initiative for Responsible Investing at Harvard University	Impact Investing: A Framework for Policy Design and Analysis	2011
Grantmakers in Health	Grantmakers in Health: Guide to Impact Investing	2011
GIIN	Impact-based incentive structures	2011
3lg	From Faith to Faith Consistent Investing: Religious Institutions and their Investment Practices	2010
FSG Social Impact Advisors	Maximizing Impact: An Integrated Strategy For Grantmaking and Mission Investing in Climate Change	2010
Center for Global Development	More than Money: Impact Investing for Development	2010
The Parthenon Group, Bridges Ventures	Investing for Impact: Case Studies Across Asset Classes	2010
J.P. Morgan, Rockefeller Foundation, GIIN	Impact Investments: An Emerging Asset Class	2010

The academic interest in this field of research has grown exceptionally in 2017 as described in Fig. 2.2. Literature about impact investing shows a significant variation by sub-theme of focus with works that discuss only Social Impact Bonds (SIBs), social finance, or social entrepreneurship and other works that provide a general overview on impact investing. A classification is provided in Table 2.2.

2.3 Portfolio Strategies and Impact Investing: An Investors' Survey

Despite the growing number of works published in the field of impact investing, only a few studies have tried to explore the main characteristics

Table 2.2 Academic literature by sub-theme

Literature about impact investing
Antadze and Westley (2012), Bozesan (2013), Brandstetter and Lehner (2015), Brest and Born (2013), Bugg-Levine and Emerson (2011), Burand (2015), Clarkin and Cangioni (2016), Cronin (2017), Evans (2013), Farley and Bush (2016), Geczy et al. (2015), Gilligan (2017), Glänzel and Scheuerle (2016), Grieco (2015), Hangl (2014), Hebb (2013), Höchstädter and Scheck (2015), Jackson (2013a, b), Koshovets and Frolov (2015), Lane (2014), Liern and Pérez-Gladish (2018), Martin (2016), McGoey (2014), Meade (2017), Mendell and Barbosa (2013), Nicholls (2010a), Ormiston et al. (2015), Phillips (2016), Pretorius and Giamporcaro (2012), Rizzello et al. (2016), Roundy et al. (2017), Salamon (2014), Sardy and Lewin (2016), Scherer et al. (2012), Schrötgens and Boenigk (2017), Shulman and George (2012), Spiess-Knafl and Scheck (2017), Suetin (2011), Thillai Rajan et al. (2014), Trotta et al. (2015), Urban and George (2018), Vecchi et al. (2015, 2017), Viviers and Firer (2013), Viviers et al. (2011), Walker et al. (2016), Weber (2016), Wilburn and Wilburn (2014)
Literature about social impact bonds, pay-for-performance, and pay-for-success instruments
Bafford (2014), Baliga (2013), Crowley (2014), Deering (2014), Dowling (2017), Erickson and Andrews (2011), Fitzgerald (2013), Fox and Albertson (2011, 2012), Giacomantonio (2017), Hedderman (2013), Jackson (2013a, b), Joy and Shields (2013), Kim and Han (2015), McGoey (2014), McHugh et al. (2013), Meade (2017), Mohamad et al. (2016), Quinn and Munir (2017), Rizzello and Carè (2016), Roundy et al. (2017), Scherer et al. (2012), Schinckus (2017a, b), Stoesz (2014), Trotta et al. (2015), Ward (2012)
Literature with a focus on social innovation and/or community development
Bhatt and Ahmad (2017), Erickson and Andrews (2011), Farley and Bush (2016), Geobey et al. (2012), Lehner and Nicholls (2014), Phillips (2016), Tekula and Shah (2016), Winget et al. (2017)
Literature with a focus on impact investing instruments and approaches
Cetindamar and Ozkazanc-Pan (2017), Chiappini (2017), Cronin (2017), EMPEA (2015), Fanconi and Scheurle (2017), Geczy et al. (2015), Gilligan (2017), Glänzel and Scheuerle (2016), Hummels and de Leede (2014), Hummels and Millone (2014), La Torre and Chiappini (2016), Roundy et al. (2017), Schrötgens and Boenigk (2017), Silby and Nicholas (2015), Spiess-Knafl and Scheck (2017), Thillai Rajan et al. (2014), Vecchi et al. (2015), Weber (2013)
Impact investing in the space of social finance
Geobey and Harji (2014), Geobey and Weber (2013), Geobey et al. (2012), Hangl (2014), Lehner and Nicholls (2014), Mendell and Barbosa (2013), Mohamad et al. (2016), Weber (2016)
Social enterprise financing
Lehner and Nicholls (2014), Lyons and Kickul (2013), Roundy et al. (2017), Shulman and George (2012), Silby and Nicholas (2015), Spiess-Knafl and Scheck (2017), Tekula and Shah (2016), Wilburn and Wilburn (2014)

and attitudes of impact investors (Roundy et al. 2017; GIIN 2017a), and much remains to be done. This work attempts to address this void by providing the investors' perspective on impact investing through a research survey. Research surveys are considered as a way of bridging the gap between financial theory and practice (Weaver 1993), and the continuing dialogue between academics and practitioners could be helpful in designing research agendas by working from the considerations that the practice of finance can contribute to financial theory, and vice versa (Weaver 1993; Kent Baker and Mukherjee 2007). In contrast, Aggarwal (1993) describes five main reasons why researchers interested in understanding the forces underlying financial practice should consider a series of limitations of information obtained through surveys. In particular, interviewees are reluctant to divulge their reasons and other details about their strategies and actions, may not be fully aware of all the reasons for their firm's strategies and actions, and are not easily accessible (Aggarwal 1993). In designing our survey, we considered that one of the main challenges in conducting a survey of institutional investors is to find an effective distribution channel to reach the relevant individuals. We also considered the fact that investors have very busy schedules and might not be willing to spend time to finish a lengthy survey. Moving from these considerations, we attempted to strike a balance between the topics to be covered in the survey and the time investors are willing to spend to answer questions. We assumed that they would at most devote approximately 15 minutes to an online survey. The survey was conducted online with the aim to open the possibility of reaching investors outside of one geographical region and was distributed to the following categories of participants: Development Financial Institutions (DFIs), institutional investors (pension fund, insurance, bank, or other), asset managers, other service providers or advisors (investment bank or broker, investment consultant, financial analyst, proxy advisor, accountant or auditor, credit rating agency, or other), private companies, associations (investor association, association of beneficiaries of institutional investors, association of asset managers, business federation, trade union, NGO, or other), private persons (qualifying as professional investors), retail investors, and academic researchers active in the field of impact investing. To attract investors to participate, we described our research project before starting questions.

We included questions about the participants' demographic data, such as age and gender, questions about the participants' portfolio strategies and compositions, and then we asked a series of questions aimed at discovering how investors became interested in and decided to include impact investments in their portfolio.

3 The Impact Investing Landscape: A Theoretical Analysis

3.1 Terminological Clarifications and Conceptual Assessment

Impact investing is a growing field of practice and research. From a conceptual point of view, Bugg-Levine and Emerson (2011, p. 10) highlight that the idea behind impact investing is that investors can pursue financial returns while also intentionally addressing social and environmental challenges. Definitions of impact investing are based on two common principles: (1) the blended value principle and (2) the principle of sustainable financial return (Weber 2016). In this sense, Weber (2016) clarifies that these two principles distinguish impact investment from conventional investment because the latter does not strive for positive social impact but only financial return (Weber 2016, p. 86). However, the precise conceptual boundaries and terminology are still under discussion (Glänzel and Scheuerle 2016), and other terms such as "social investment" (Dowling 2017) are used to describe widely similar approaches. Some authors use the term "social impact investing" (Martin 2013; Joy and Shields 2013; Hangl 2014; Glänzel and Scheuerle 2016; Schrötgens and Boenigk 2017; Chiappini 2017). In this sense, Salamon (2014, p. 14) highlights that the term "impact investing" itself provides little clue about what the content of such "positive impact" is supposed to be, and suggests the use of the terms "social and environmental impact investing" or "social impact investing" in order to put attention not only on the financial return but also on the type of positive effect that investors may have. In particular, Glänzel and Scheuerle (2016) use the term social impact investing to clearly distinguish from the finance-first approaches of impact investing that have a stronger commercial orientation. Hummels and de Leede (2014) enclose impact investing in the wider category of responsible investing, of which impact investing is only a part while Hebb (2013), Pretorius and Giamporcaro (2012), Viviers and Firer (2013), and Viviers et al. (2011) consider impact investing as "responsible investing." Shulman and George (2012) consider impact investing as a form of Socially Responsible Investing (SRI), while Geobey and Weber (2013) clarify that SRI screens out investments for social, environmental, or governance reasons, while impact investing is based on the assumption that investments can create financial returns and address social and environmental challenges simultaneously. Impact investing is also included by many authors in the social finance landscape (Suetin 2011; Geobey and Weber 2013; Geobey et al. 2012; Mendell and Barbosa 2013; Weber 2013, 2016). Finally, Roundy et al. (2017) underline that impact investing is a phenomenon conceptually close to other types of investments in early-stage for-profit and non-profit organizations, such as angel investors, venture capitalists, philanthropists, and philanthropic foundations.

3.2 Instruments and Investment Approaches

In recent years, diverse impact investment opportunities have emerged across multiple asset classes (Lyons and Kickul 2013). The term impact investment provides a broad rhetorical umbrella under which a wide range of investors could huddle (Bugg-Levine and Emerson 2011, p. 12). Hummels and de Leede (2014) define microfinance as an exemplary case of impact investing. Grieco (2015) lists as examples of impact investments: Social Impact Bond, Developmental Impact Bond, Cash on Delivery Aid, Microfinance, and Green Bonds. Microfinance (Hummels and de Leede 2014; Hummels and Millone 2014; Koshovets and Frolov 2015; La Torre and Chiappini 2016; Fanconi and Scheurle 2017), Private Equity, Venture Capital, Social Venture Capital, and Developmental Venture Capital are enclosed in the impact investing landscape by many authors (Lane 2014; EMPEA 2015; Silby and Nicholas 2015; Martin

2016; Bhatt and Ahmad 2017). Moreover, our sample shows a high number of authors that focus only on SIBs as a way of supporting the public funding for social programmes in specific areas of intervention (such as health or criminal justice) (Erickson and Andrews 2011; Fox and Albertson 2011, 2012; Ward 2012; Fitzgerald 2013; Hedderman 2013; Jackson 2013a; McHugh et al. 2013; Crowley 2014; Deering 2014; Social Finance UK 2014, 2016; Stoesz 2014; Tan et al. 2015; Bridges Venture 2016; Dowling 2017; Giacomantonio 2017; Schinckus 2017a, b) while others focus on Islamic Social Impact Bonds or Developmental Impact Bonds (Center for Global Development & Social Finance 2013; Mohamad et al. 2016).

In the impact investing landscape, the 2017 survey proposed by the GIIN (2017a) highlights the following main investment opportunities: deposits & cash equivalents; private debt; public debt: publicly traded bonds or loans; equity-like debt; private equity; public equity; real assets; pay-for-performance instruments. By highlighting the role and the opportunities related to real assets impact investing funds, Cambridge Associates (2017) point out that risk-adjusted market rates of return are achievable in impact investing and that the selection process is key to success.

Moreover, our analysis shows that in recent years, current macro drivers such as climate change, demographic shifts, and resource scarcity have heightened interest in real assets impact investments (Cambridge Associates 2017). In this sense, sustainable infrastructure investing and real assets impact investing strategies are crucial for achieving the Sustainable Development Goals (SDGs), particularly by bridging the gap between patient capital and venture capital, and can be transformative in scaling up sustainable energy investments, especially through climate change mitigation projects and land restoration projects (The New Climate Economy 2016). The role of impact investing—and in particular of the entire spectrum of blended finance—in closing the SDG funding gap is further highlighted in a recent report provided by Business & Sustainable Development Commission and Convergence (2017).

Furthermore, terms such as "community investing" and "community development investing" are considered subsets of impact investing that are distinguished by a focus on marginalized areas or communities that conventional market activity does not reach (GIIN & University of New Hampshire 2015). In the field of community investing, investors can access a wide range of asset classes, including fixed-income investments (e.g., debt in nonprofit loan funds), cash investments (e.g., deposits in community development banks and credit unions), and equity investments in real estate—often accompanied by government tax credits—and in private equity impact funds (GIIN & University of New Hampshire 2015). A 2017 report of GIIN focuses on the role of credit-enhancement tools as a way to stimulate private-sector investment in solutions to social and environmental problems. In the growing impact investing market, many projects and enterprises may have interesting prospects for positive social and/or environmental impact while lacking a risk-return profile that meets the needs of conventional investors seeking risk-adjusted, market-rate returns. For such opportunities, credit enhancement can unlock private capital to help solve a wide range of pressing challenges. In particular, guarantees offer a way to leverage relatively small amounts of capital to address the real and perceived risks that keep many investors from participating in impactful deals (GIIN 2017b).

3.3 Impact Investing: Actors

Weber (2016) and Geobey and Harji (2014) highlight that the current players in the field of impact investing are foundations, high-net-worth individuals, banks, institutional investors, and asset managers such as pension funds, asset management firms, and other financial institutions. Nevertheless, Weber (2016) clarifies that these different types of investors have different motivations to engage in impact investment. In this sense, bigger banks and financial institutions see impact investing as a business opportunity, while foundations see impact investing as a way to employ capital comparable to granting donations (Weber 2016). A classification of the relevant players in impact investing is provided by Harji and Jackson (2012) who proposed the following categories: (1) Asset owners (high-net-worth individuals/families; corporations; governments; employees; retail investors; foundations); (2) Asset managers (investment advisors; fund managers; family offices; foundations; banks; corporations;

venture funds; impact investment funds/intermediaries; pension funds; sovereign wealth funds; development finance institutions; government investment programs); (3) Demand side-actors (corporations; small and growing businesses; social enterprises; cooperatives; microfinance institutions; community development finance institutions); and (4) Service providers (government programs; capacity development providers; universities; non-governmental organizations; consulting firms; networks; standard-setting bodies).

Impact investors can operate as individuals, as groups of investors, or as institutional venture capital funds (Roundy et al. 2017). In this vein, Jackson (2013b) clarifies that actors can be divided into four broad categories: asset owners who actually own capital, asset managers who deploy capital, demand-side actors who receive and utilize the capital, and service providers who help make this market work.

3.4 The Impact Investors' Categories and Preferences: A Preliminary Assessment

New investors in impact investment have emerged all over the globe over the last decade, and the market has moved from a stage of "uncoordinated innovation" to "market building" as early stage infrastructure has emerged in order to catalyze increased activity (Ormiston et al. 2015). Impact investors seek to allocate their capital where it can generate the more integrated, blended value (Bugg-Levine and Emerson 2011, p. 10). This particular category of investors is described as "blended investors" seeking an investment that both makes a financial return and delivers a certain degree of environmental or social return (Harold et al. 2007; Antadze and Westley 2012). Freireich and Fulton (2009) provided—for the first time—a preliminary categorization of impact investors distinguishing between "impact-first" and "financial-first." In particular, based on their primary objective, impact-first investors seek to optimize social or environmental impact with a floor for financial returns, while financial-first investors seek to optimize financial returns with a floor for social or environmental impact. In this scheme, financial-first investors are typically commercial investors who seek out sub-sectors that offer market-rate returns while achieving some social or environmental good (Freireich and Fulton 2009, p. 31).

The distinction between impact-first and financial-first is also used by Bozesan (2013), Freireich and Fulton (2009), and Hebb (2013). The last annual impact investor survey provided by the GIIN (2017a) highlighted that:

- impact investing assets are allocated to a range of geographies, sectors, and stage of business;
- the predominant instruments are private debt, real assets, and private equity;
- during 2016 investments have either met or exceeded the expectations for both impact and financial performance;
- the majority of impact investors principally target risk-adjusted market rate returns.

Liern and Pérez-Gladish (2018) divide the decision-making process into two stages. The first involves the applications of filters to four main critical issues (target geography, impact theme, asset class, and target return category). The second considers the classical financial criteria (risk and return) and tries to maximize the social impact of the portfolio.

From a behavioural point of view, Schrötgens and Boenigk (2017) investigated—through a web survey involving 145 private investors—the effects of three potential influences on impact investment: return, age, and social impact. The authors conclude some interesting insights. First, the study provides indication on a potential age range of social impact investors and highlights that the perceived innovativeness of an impact project increases the probability of investment. Finally, the study provides some interesting considerations with regard to the impact investors' characteristics (such as optimism and self-confidence).

Roundy et al. (2017) provide an interesting survey based on 31 impact investors and highlight that:

- impact investors seek both financial ROI that social ROI;
- angel investors are similar to impact investors because they can also make investments for reasons that are not only related to purely financial returns;
- the motivations of impact investors are more complex and often are related to personal values and values that prioritize societal change and the creation of social good;
- impact investors are motivated by a "slow money" or "patient capital" approach that differs from traditional angel or venture capital investment.

4 The Impact Investing Landscape: Survey Results

4.1 Study Units and Response Rate

In their study, Harji and Jackson (2012) mainly differentiate between the supply-side investors—asset owners and their managers—and the demand-side investors—business owners and social entrepreneurs seeking funds and service providers. Starting from our literature review, we developed a questionnaire tailored to impact investors. Our study units therefore were: family office and private investors, asset managers including financial institutions and DFIs, investors' associations, investment consultants and advisors as they influence the decisions of impact investors in a comparable manner as asset managers, and academic researchers active in the field of impact investing. The questionnaire was beta tested by one member of a private equity association and one member of a financial institution working in impact investing. The institutions of the beta testers were not included in the survey. Despite a quite short response time of three weeks, 20% of the 100 supply-side providers responded. The non-response bias is mitigated by the fact that late responders show a similar response behaviour as non-responders. The breakdown of responders is summarized in Table 2.3.

The split of Table 2.3 shows that 75% of responses were from practitioners on the supply side, whereas 25% of responses came from academic researchers that advise on impact investing.

Table 2.3 Response rate by categories

Supply side	
Banks	18.75%
Asset managers	6.25%
Investment consultants	6.25%
Investment advisors	6.25%
Investor associations	6.25%
Family offices	6.25%
Private investors	25%
Academia	
Academic researchers	12.50%
Educators in impact investing	6.25%
Professors of finance	6.25%

Source: Our elaboration

4.2 Survey Evidence: Risk Aversion Versus Risk Affinity

More than half of respondents disagree with the statement that stability (low fluctuation) is worth foregoing profits. Of those who agreed that profit can be waived for stability, 75% came from the academic sphere. Moreover, participants were asked whether they disagree or agree with the following statement:

> Generally, I prefer investments with little or no fluctuation in value, and I'm willing to accept the lower return associated with these investments.

Responses are summarized in Fig. 2.3.

To see whether investors and advisors put their money where their mouth is, the survey wanted to know what the investors focus on. Putting private capital or even fiduciary money into start-ups and ventures could be seen as a risk-taking strategy with high investment risk and high return potential. For this reason, we asked the following question:

> When I invest my money, I am. (Fig. 2.4)

As summarized in Fig. 2.4, 81.25% of all respondents were equally concerned about financial, environmental, and social returns.

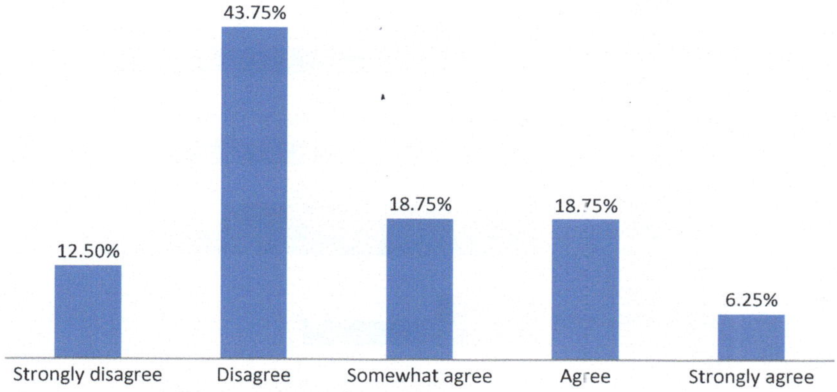

Fig. 2.3 Responses to question 1. Source: Author

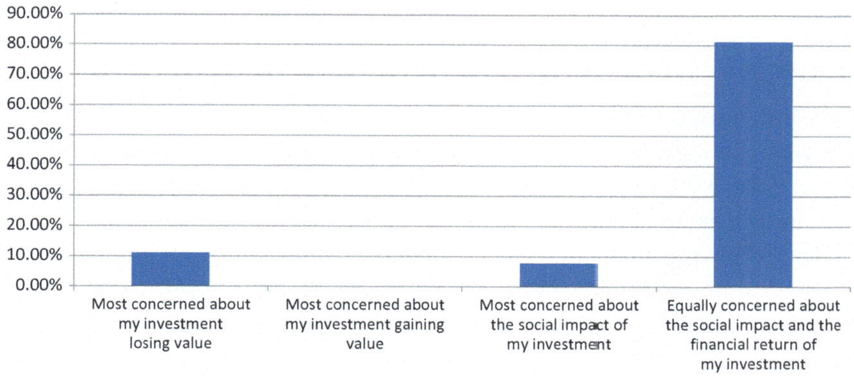

Fig. 2.4 Responses to question 2. Source: Author

When asked to "Enter the current allocation in whole numbers for the savings used to answer question 10. Your percentages must total 100%. If you don't enter any data, the questionnaire will assume 100% of your assets are in short-term reserves" it appeared that 36.9% of all assets are in short-term reserves and that the supply side does not seem to be entirely invested but is still looking for opportunities. An asset allocation quota of 22.4% seems to suggest that investors accept asset fluctuation and—as far as private debt and equity is concerned—also counterparty

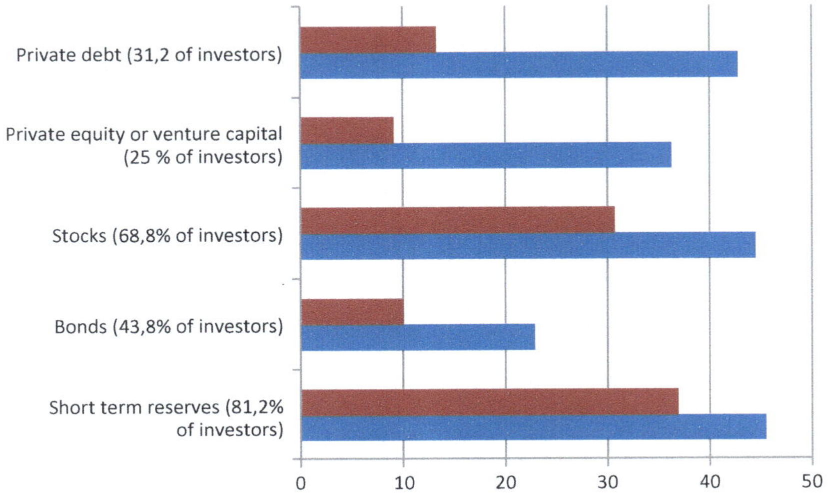

Fig. 2.5 Asset allocation. Source: Author

risk and start-up risk. Overall, 22% of assets are invested in high-risk asset classes, which is aligned with the statement in question 1, where more than 55% of investors were discarding the option of stable, low-fluctuation assets. Figure 2.5 provides an overview of the responses.

The following questions were targeted at finding out about the main themes in impact investing: the questions of how investors consider impact in investing and how they make sure they include it in the equation. Most investors see the intention to create positive societal impact as the main drive in impact investing. Most of those who value that intention also want the impact to be measured and achieved (more than 60%). The second criterion in impact investing was found to have a long-term investment horizon (42% of investors). Having a responsible investment strategy was considered and valued by 40% of investors, which was followed in popularity by the intention to make a financial return and being an active manager. None of the investors regarded impact investing as a separate asset class, while a small fraction from academia did (Fig. 2.6).

Also surprising was the fact that pressure from clients was not considered as the main driver of impact investing. The main reasons for impact investing were noted to be as follows:

1. seeking a social return,
2. reducing the risk of assets,
3. aligning internal policies with the long-term interests of beneficiaries,
4. ethical considerations,
5. pressure from clients, and
6. legal and regulatory constraints (Fig. 2.7).

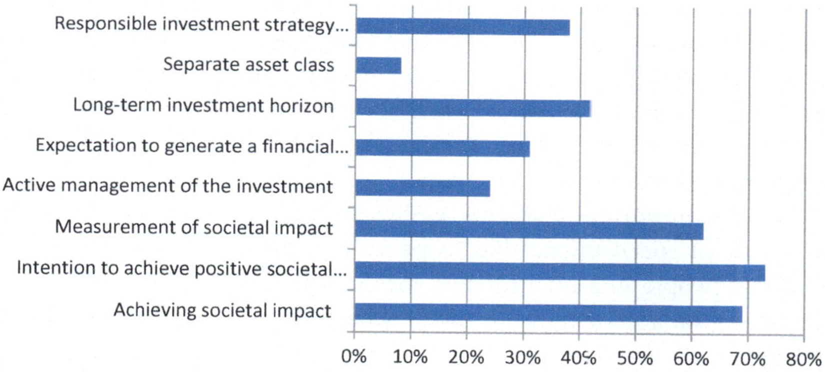

Fig. 2.6 Fundamental characteristics of impact investing. Source: Author

Fig. 2.7 Main rationale in impact investing. Source: Author

A small fraction of 8% considers all of these factors to be equally relevant. The control question—what other reasons exist for impact investing?—showed that only a small fraction of 8% found other reasons relevant. These other reasons can be explored better in follow-up research.

4.3 Impact Investing: Converging Definitions

The last sections of our survey intended to get at the various and slightly different definitions of impact investing and to determine whether or not impact investing is still in search of a commonly shared definition in the world of practitioners and researchers. The definitions provided in Table 2.4 were provided in response to the question: "Can you provide a definition of impact investing?"

The most important elements as shown in Fig. 2.7 are that the environmental or social impact has to provide positive effects and improve the life of people in a quantifiable, measurable way, one that allows the calculation of a return on impact, where impact can be measured, reported, and compared to a benchmark. GIIN has stressed the importance of applying a theory of change, which investors regarded as a building block in impact investing, together with ethical leadership. Some respondents also acknowledge that impact investing is extending the investment universe by creating funding for new market players that potentially would not have had access to funding otherwise. They appear to state that this cannot be done in the mainstream model, and therefore highlight the aspect that funds are provided to companies that would not have gotten funding under the mainstream model. Thus, impact investing is addressing the investment gap by providing capital to such companies. We assumed that the investment gap is mainly addressed by providing venture capital and private debt. However, this aspect has to be further investigated in detail. Whereas private investors invest for themselves, the survey was inclined to also understand the attitude of institutional investors who have additional aspects to consider. For this reason, we decided to ask: "What is the main rationale for institutional investors and asset managers to take impact investment opportunities into account in their investment decisions?" Responses to this question are summarized in Fig. 2.7.

Table 2.4 Definitions of impact investing

#1	One investment that has a meaningful effect on people and the environment, improving their current situation and preferably for those with less opportunities.
#2	Investments intended to generate positive, measurable social and environmental benefits as well as financial returns.
#3	Creation of measurable impact on society and ecology and the environment/climate as an element of intended outcome.
#4	Recommendations on investments I can rely on regarding the return on investment as well as the social component (what will be done with my money).
#5	Impact investing is the deployment of capital to pursue both returns and positive socioeconomic and/or environmental benefits, which are measured and reported.
#6	Ethical investments for which the pathway to impact is clear and metrics for impact objectives exist.
#7	Invest in companies that are concerned with social impact issues.
#8	The application of capital market solutions to create social good. Creating market demand out of social need.
#9	Doing good while doing well.
#10	Projects that yield a social or environmental return which can be quantified and where there is a benchmark and/or preset objective regarding such returns.
#11	In impact investing the return on impact (thus impact—or creating good for society—) is maximised rather than financial profits.
#12	Triple bottom line investing pursuing financial plus ecosocial return, measuring impact, applying a theory of change, creating additionality. Make investments happen that would not have got funds under a mainstream approach and address the 2 trillion investment gap.

Source: Our elaboration

The last question was mainly a control question to see whether respondents understand the differences between SRI, ESG, and impact investing.

The respondents were asked to provide answers in their own words to the question: "How does impact investing differ from PRI, SRI and ESG?"

Most respondents found positive differentiators from the SRI, CSR, and ESG approaches.

The following elements were mentioned:

- impact investing is *a positive approach* to *generating favourable outcomes for targeted beneficiaries*, whereas PRI, SRI, and ESG tend to be negative filters about what investments to avoid;
- impact must be *measurable*;
- creation of measurable impact on society and ecology and the environment;
- *positive quantifiable and measured* social and environmental objectives, and therefore a *strategic component in the theory of change of the enterprise and investment*;
- it covers all *capital market innovation*;
- environmental and social returns and risk are made explicit;
- *enlarges the investment universe instead of reducing it* helps to *create new assets and influence the market through theory of change* mainly used for start-ups, VC, and equity investments plus private debt *addressing the 2 trillion USD investment gap (found by the World Bank)*;
- in comparison to SRI, ESG, and PRI, impact investing is *actively creating a positive social and environmental impact*;
- impact investing builds on the fundamentals of exclusionary, positive, and ESG screens to deploy capital in profitable companies that intentionally identify and seek positive social and/or environmental benefits and that commit to *actively measuring, reporting, and improving impact performance over time.*

Two of the respondents held the view that impact investing is a journey that builds on SRI and ESG as well as disclosure and reporting, all attributes that are more connected to the SRI approach and that do not necessarily reflect impact investing.

5 Future Research Directions

Impact investing offers a very broad range of future research directions that could be potentially interesting for academics, policymakers, and practitioners.

This work offers a preliminary assessment of investor attitudes in considering impact investing opportunities in their asset allocation strategies.

Recent works (GIIN 2017a; Roundy et al. 2017; Schrötgens and Boenigk 2017; Liern and Pérez-Gladish 2018) highlight that this is a research area that has not been completely explored. Future studies need to deeply analyze investors' attitudes in terms of financial returns required, risk perceived, risk tolerance, and risk exposure.

Moreover, the most cited definition of impact investing, provided by the Canadian Task Force on Social Finance (2010, p. 5) defines impact investing as "the active investment of capital in businesses and funds that generate positive social and/or environmental impacts, as well as financial returns (from principal to above market rate) to the investor." However, during the last years, certain segments of the impact investing industry have seen strong returns and a high positive impact as conflicting objectives, while others argue that strong performance across both objectives can be simultaneously achieved (Evans 2013). Evans (2013) raised principal-agent problems resulting from asymmetric information in pursuing the agreed goals and the generation of both financial and social returns in impact investing strategies. The themes of principal-agent problems and asymmetric information are also dealt with by Rizzello and Carè (2017) with regard to the SIB model. Future theoretical investigation in this research area is needed and could be tested moving from actual impact investing experiences.

Finally, many investment opportunities areas—such as VC, PE, and Angel Impact Investing—are actually under-explored. Only a few works (see among others, Lane 2014; EMPEA 2015; Silby and Nicholas 2015; Martin 2016; Bhatt and Ahmad 2017) try to shed light on the opportunities that these kinds of investments may offers to social enterprises. Future work, especially qualitative and quantitative research, should analyze both the supply side and the demand side of this growing impact investing segment.

6 Conclusions

This work offered a pilot analysis of the impact investing landscape by using both theoretical and practical perspectives. Our survey provides interesting insights for future studies. Investors' attitudes and behaviours represent one of the most important fields of research (see among others: GIIN 2017a; Roundy et al. 2017; Schrötgens and Boenigk 2017; Liern and Pérez-Gladish 2018). Moreover, to our knowledge this is the first comprehensive literature review that has tried to assess both actors and financial instruments and approaches that can be included in the impact investing landscape. The review confirms that there are several instruments and approaches that can be used to make a positive impact in society. A close connection between social enterprises and impact investing has been detected. With regard to investors' behaviour, our review retrieved only two works that try to explain what drives impact investors' decisions. For this reason, our survey offers several important insights for future studies.

Many differences between the academic and practitioners' definitions about impact investing have been found. In this sense, while in the academic sectors many academics considers impact investing as a form of SRI, practitioners do not consider the concepts to be the same. Interviewees focuses their attentions on the measurability of impact and are equally concerned about social/positive impact and financial return. Although the current study has extended our understanding about impact investments, it also suffers from a number of limitations. As with all reviews, it was limited by the search terms used and the exclusion criteria. Several working papers and conference proceedings have been excluded from our review because they do not represent "scientific knowledge" assessed through peer review. However, the papers discussed in this literature review provide a snapshot of research on impact investing that is representative of the state of the art at the time. From a policy/practitioners' perspective, three main conclusions may be drawn from this work: (1) impact investing has a great potential for the growth of social enterprises by offering a wide range of financial instruments that span from equity to debit; (2) social impact bonds represent the most talked about instruments in the impact investing industry by representing useful instruments to fund many kinds of public programmes in time of budget constraints; and (3) investors look with great interest at this market. Finally, the results of this work have implications for the development of the impact investing market both if we consider the market from the supply side and from the demand side. Only with a better understanding of the entire impact investing landscape and the related investment opportunities is it possible to ensure an effective market development.

References

Aggarwal, R. (1993). Theory and practice in finance education: Or why we shouldn't just ask them. *Financial Practice & Education, 3*(2), 15–18.

Antadze, N., & Westley, F. R. (2012). Impact metrics for social innovation: Barriers or bridges to radical change? *Journal of Social Entrepreneurship, 3*(2), 133–150.

Bafford, B. (2014). The feasibility and future of social impact bonds in the United States. *Sanford Journal of Public Policy, 3*, 12–19.

Baker, H. K., Singleton, J. C., & Veit, E. T. (2011). *Survey research in corporate finance: Bridging the gap between theory and practice*. New York: Oxford University Press.

Baliga, S. (2013). Shaping the success of social impact bonds in the United States: Lessons learned from the privatization of US prisons. *Duke Law Journal, 63*, 437.

Bhatt, P., & Ahmad, A. J. (2017). Financial social innovation to engage the economically marginalized: Insights from an Indian case study. *Entrepreneurship & Regional Development, 29*(5–6), 391–413.

Bozesan, M. (2013). Demystifying the future of investing. *Journal of Integral Theory and Practice, 8*(1–2), 19–56.

Brandstetter, L., & Lehner, O. M. (2015). Opening the market for impact investments: The need for adapted portfolio tools. *Entrepreneurship Research Journal, 5*(2), 87–107.

Brest, P., & Born, K. (2013). When can impact investing create real impact? *Stanford Social Innovation Review, 11*(4), 22–31.

Bridges Venture. (2016). *Better outcomes, better value: The evolution of social impact bonds in the UK*. Retrieved from https://thegiin.org/knowledge/publication/better-outcomes,-better-value-the-evolution-of-social-impact-bonds-in-the-uk.

Bugg-Levine, A., & Emerson, J. (2011). Impact investing: Transforming how we make money while making a difference. *Innovations, 6*(3), 9–18.

Burand, D. (2015). Resolving impact investment disputes: When doing good goes bad. *Washington University Journal of Law & Policy, 48*, 55.

Business & Sustainable Development Commission, & Convergence. (2017). *The state of blended finance*. Retrieved from http://businesscommission.org/our-work/working-paper-the-state-of-blended-finance.

Cambridge Associates. (2017). *The financial performance of real assets impact investments*. Retrieved from https://thegiin.org/assets/The%20Financial%20

Performance%20of%20Real%20Assets%20Impact%20Investments_web-file.pdf.

Canadian Task Force on Social Finance. (2010). *Mobilizing private capital for public good*. Retrieved from https://www.marsdd.com/wp-content/uploads/2011/02/MaRSReport-socialfinance-taskforce.pdf.

Center for Global Development & Social Finance. (2013). *Investing in social outcomes: Development impact bonds. The report of the development*. Impact Bond Working Group. Retrieved from https://www.cgdev.org/publication/investing-social-outcomes-development-impact-bonds.

Cetindamar, D., & Ozkazanc-Pan, B. (2017). Assessing mission drift at venture capital impact investors. *Business Ethics: A European Review, 26*(3), 257–270.

Chiappini, H. (2017). *Social impact funds*. Springer International Publishing.

Clarkin, J. E., & Cangioni, C. L. (2016). Impact investing: A primer and review of the literature. *Entrepreneurship Research Journal, 6*(2), 135–173.

Cronin, M. J. (2017). Impact investing at the base of the pyramid: Unitus seed fund. In M. Cronin & T. Dearing (Eds.), *Managing for social impact: Management for professionals*. Cham: Springer.

Crowley, D. M. (2014). The role of social impact bonds in pediatric health care. *Pediatrics, 134*(2), e331–e333.

Deering, J. (2014). A future for probation? *The Howard Journal of Criminal Justice, 53*(1), 1–15.

Dowling, E. (2017). In the wake of austerity: Social impact bonds and the financialisation of the welfare state in Britain. *New Political Economy, 22*(3), 294–310.

EMPEA. (2015). How private equity models and practitioners can advance impact investing in emerging markets. In K. Wendt (Ed.), *Responsible investment banking CSR, sustainability, ethics & governance*. Cham: Springer.

Erickson, D., & Andrews, N. (2011). Partnerships among community development, public health, and health care could improve the well-being of low-income people. *Health Affairs, 30*(11), 2056–2063.

Evans, M. (2013). Meeting the challenge of impact investing: How can contracting practices secure social impact without sacrificing performance? *Journal of Sustainable Finance & Investment, 3*(2), 138–154.

Fanconi, P., & Scheurle, P. (2017). Microfinance – The concept. In *Small money-big impact: Fighting poverty with microfinance* (pp. 11–32). Hoboken, NJ: John Wiley & Sons.

Farley, K. W., & Bush, C. B. (2016). Using relationships as resources in social impact investing: Examining a local food movement in Appalachia. *Journal of Appalachian Studies, 22*(2), 224–244.

Fitzgerald, J. L. (2013). Social impact bonds and their application to preventive health. *Australian Health Review, 37*(2), 199–204.

Fox, C., & Albertson, K. (2011). Payment by results and social impact bonds in the criminal justice sector: New challenges for the concept of evidence-based policy? *Criminology and Criminal Justice, 11*(5), 395–413.

Fox, C., & Albertson, K. (2012). Is payment by results the most efficient way to address the challenges faced by the criminal justice sector? *Probation Journal, 59*(4), 355–373.

Freireich, J., & Fulton, K. (2009). *Investing for social and environmental impact.* New York, NY: Monitor Institute.

Geczy, C., Jeffers, J. S., Musto, D. K., & Tucker, A. M. (2015). Institutional investing when shareholders are not supreme. *Harvard Business Law Review, 5*, 73.

Geobey, S., & Harji, K. (2014). Social finance in North America. *Global Social Policy, 14*(2), 274–277.

Geobey, S., & Weber, O. (2013). Lessons in operationalizing social finance: The case of Vancouver City savings credit union. *Journal of Sustainable Finance & Investment, 3*(2), 124–137.

Geobey, S., Westley, F. R., & Weber, O. (2012). Enabling social innovation through developmental social finance. *Journal of Social Entrepreneurship, 3*(2), 151–165.

Giacomantonio, C. (2017). Grant-maximizing but not money-making: A simple decision-tree analysis for social impact bonds. *Journal of Social Entrepreneurship, 8*(1), 47–66.

Gilligan, M. (2017). Catalyzing social impact investments. In *Managing for social impact* (pp. 205–216). Cham: Springer.

Glänzel, G., & Scheuerle, T. (2016). Social impact investing in Germany: Current impediments from investors' and social entrepreneurs' perspectives. *Voluntas: International Journal of Voluntary and Nonprofit Organizations, 27*(4), 1638–1668.

Global Impact Investing Network. (2017a). *Annual impact investor survey.* Retrieved from https://thegiin.org/assets/GIIN_AnnualImpactInvestorSurvey_2017_Web_Final.pdf.

Global Impact Investing Network. (2017b). *Scaling the use of guarantees in U.S. community investing.* Retrieved from https://thegiin.org/assets/GIIN_Issue_Brief_Guarantees_final%20for%20web.pdf.

Global Impact Investing Network, & University of New Hampshire. (2015). *Scaling U.S. community investing.* Retrieved from https://thegiin.org/assets/

images/pub/GIIN_Scaling%20US%20Community%20Investing%20The%20Investor-Product%20Interface.pdf.

Grieco, C. (2015). Is doing good, good enough? In *Assessing social impact of social enterprises* (pp. 37–59). Springer International Publishing.

Hangl, C. (2014). A literature review about the landscape of social finance. *Journal of Finance and Risk Perspectives, 3*(4), 64–98.

Harji, K., & Jackson, E. T. (2012). Accelerating impact: Achievements, challenges and what's next in building the impact investing industry. E.T. Jackson and Associates Ltd and The Rockefeller Foundation. Retrieved from https://thegiin.org/knowledge/publication/accelerating-impact-achievements-challenges-and-whats-next-in-building-the-imp.

Harold, J., Spitzer, J., & Emerson, J. (2007). *Blended value investing: Integrating environmental risks and opportunities into securities valuation.* Oxford: Skoll Centre for Social Entrepreneurship.

Hebb, T. (2013). Impact investing and responsible investing: What does it mean? *Journal of Sustainable Finance & Investment, 3*(2), 71–74.

Hedderman, C. (2013). Payment by results: Hopes, fears and evidence. *British Journal of Community Justice, 11*(2–3), 43–58.

Höchstädter, A. K., & Scheck, B. (2015). What's in a name: An analysis of impact investing understandings by academics and practitioners. *Journal of Business Ethics, 132*(2), 449–475.

Hummels, H., & de Leede, M. (2014). The emergence of impact investments: The case of microfinance. In *Socially responsible investment in the 21st century: Does it make a difference for society?* (pp. 91–115). Bingley: Emerald Group Publishing Limited.

Hummels, H., & Millone, M. (2014). The social function of asset classes in microfinance. In *Microfinance institutions* (pp. 162–186). London: Palgrave Macmillan.

Hummels, H., Vecchi, V., Balbo, L., Brusoni, M., & Caselli, S. (2016). Impact investments. The emergence of a new beacon in investing. In *Principles and practice of impact investing: A catalytic revolution* (pp. 1–25). Saltaire: Greenleaf Publishing.

Jackson, E. T. (2013a). Evaluating social impact bonds: Questions, challenges, innovations, and possibilities in measuring outcomes in impact investing. *Community Development, 44*(5), 608–616.

Jackson, E. T. (2013b). Interrogating the theory of change: Evaluating impact investing where it matters most. *Journal of Sustainable Finance & Investment, 3*(2), 95–110.

Jacobs, M., & Mazzucato, M. (Eds.). (2016). *Rethinking capitalism: Economics and policy for sustainable and inclusive growth*. Hoboken, NJ: John Wiley & Sons.

Joy, M., & Shields, J. (2013). Social impact bonds: The next phase of third sector marketization? *Canadian Journal of Nonprofit and Social Economy Research, 4*(2), 39–55.

Kent Baker, H., & Mukherjee, T. K. (2007). Survey research in finance: Views from journal editors. *International Journal of Managerial Finance, 3*(1), 11–25.

Kim, J., & Han, M. (2015). Education financing and public–private partnership development assistance model. *Procedia-Social and Behavioral Sciences, 177*, 100–103.

Koshovets, O., & Frolov, I. E. (2015). Impact investing as a 'basic innovation' for the global economy and finance system post-crisis transformation. *Economy & Business, 9*, 769–780.

La Torre, M., & Chiappini, H. (2016). Microfinance investment vehicles: How far are they from OECD social impact investment definition? In *Bank funding, financial instruments and decision-making in the banking industry* (pp. 145–191). Springer International Publishing.

Lane, M. J. (2014). *The mission-driven venture: Business solutions to the world's most vexing social problems*. Hoboken, NJ: John Wiley & Sons.

Lehner, O. M. (Ed.). (2016). *Routledge handbook of social and sustainable finance*. New York: Routledge.

Lehner, O. M., & Nicholls, A. (2014). Social finance and crowdfunding for social enterprises: A public–private case study providing legitimacy and leverage. *Venture Capital, 16*(3), 271–286.

Liern, V., & Pérez-Gladish, B. (2018). Fuzzy degree of geographic appropriateness for social impact investing. In *Soft computing for sustainability science* (pp. 163–178). Cham: Springer.

Lyons, T. S., & Kickul, J. R. (2013). The social enterprise financing landscape: The lay of the land and new research on the horizon. *Entrepreneurship Research Journal, 3*(2), 147–159.

Martin, M. (2013). *Making impact investible*. Impact economy working papers, 4. Lausanne, CH: Impact Economy.

Martin, M. (2016). Growing the ecosystem of impact investment. In *Building the impact economy* (pp. 175–185). Springer International Publishing.

McGoey, L. (2014). The philanthropic state: Market–state hybrids in the philanthrocapitalist turn. *Third World Quarterly, 35*(1), 109–125.

McHugh, N., Sinclair, S., Roy, M., Huckfield, L., & Donaldson, C. (2013). Social impact bonds: A wolf in sheep's clothing? *Journal of Poverty and Social Justice, 21*(3), 247–257.

Meade, L. (2017). Impact investing and public private partnerships. *Public Sector, 40*(2), 24.

Mendell, M., & Barbosa, E. (2013). Impact investing: A preliminary analysis of emergent primary and secondary exchange platforms. *Journal of Sustainable Finance & Investment, 3*(2), 111–123.

Mikki, S. (2009). Google Scholar compared to Web of Science: A literature review. *Nordic Journal of Information Literacy in Higher Education, 1*(1), 41–51.

Mohamad, S., Lehner, O. M., & Khorshid, A. (2016). A case for an Islamic social impact bond. *ACRN Oxford Journal of Finance and Risk Perspectives, 5*(2), 65–74.

Nicholls, A. (2010a). The institutionalization of social investment: The interplay of investment logics and investor rationalities. *Journal of Social Entrepreneurship, 1*(1), 70–100.

Nicholls, A. (2010b). *The landscape of social investment in the UK*. Birmingham: Third Sector Research Center & Health Services Management Centre.

Ormiston, J., Charlton, K., Donald, M. S., & Seymour, R. G. (2015). Overcoming the challenges of impact investing: Insights from leading investors. *Journal of Social Entrepreneurship, 6*(3), 352–378.

Phillips, R. (2016). Impact investing and community development. *Maine Policy Review, 25*(1), 63–71.

Porter, M. E., & Kramer, M. R. (2011). Creating shared value. *Harvard Business Review, 89*(1–2), 62–77.

Pretorius, L., & Giamporcaro, S. (2012). Sustainable and responsible investment (SRI) in South Africa: A limited adoption of environmental criteria. *Investment Analysts Journal, 75*, 1–19.

Quinn, Q. C., & Munir, K. A. (2017). Hybrid categories as political devices: The case of impact investing in frontier markets. In *From categories to categorization: Studies in sociology, organizations and strategy at the crossroads* (pp. 113–150). Emerald Publishing Limited.

Rizzello, A., & Carè, R. (2016). Insight into the social impact bond market: An analysis of investors. *ACRN Oxford Journal of Finance and Risk Perspectives, 5*, 145–171.

Rizzello, A., & Carè, R. (2017). Managing principal agent conflicts in social impact bonds: A theoretical approach. In *Proceedings of the 16th FRAP and 2nd SSFII Conference 2017 – Cambridge, UK.*

Rizzello, A., Carè, R., Migliazza, M. C., & Trotta, A. (2016). Social impact investing: A model and research agenda. In O. Lehner (Ed.), *Routledge handbook of social and sustainable finance*. London: Routledge.

Roundy, P., Holzhauer, H., & Dai, Y. (2017). Finance or philanthropy? Exploring the motivations and criteria of impact investors. *Social Responsibility Journal, 13*(3), 419–512.

Salamon, L. M. (2014). *New frontiers of philanthropy: A guide to the new tools and new actors that are reshaping global philanthropy and social investing*. New York: Oxford University Press.

Sardy, M., & Lewin, R. (2016). Towards a global framework for impact investing. *Academy of Economics and Finance Journal, 7*, 73–79.

Scherer, J., Schenk, L., & Finance, S. (2012). Advancing social impact measurement to build an asset class: The appeal of social impact bonds. *Community Investments, 24*(1), 10–13.

Schinckus, C. (2017a). Financial innovation as a potential force for a positive social change: The challenging future of social impact bonds. *Research in International Business and Finance, 39*, 727–736.

Schinckus, C. (2017b). The valuation of social impact bonds: An introductory perspective with the Peterborough SIB. *Research in International Business and Finance*. https://www.sciencedirect.com/science/article/pii/S0275531917303677?via%3Dihub

Schrötgens, J., & Boenigk, S. (2017). Social impact investment behavior in the nonprofit sector: First insights from an online survey experiment. *Voluntas: International Journal of Voluntary and Nonprofit Organizations, 28*(6), 2658–2682.

Shiller, R. J. (2013). *Finance and the good society*. Oxford: Princeton University Press.

Shulman, J. M., & George, B. (2012). Growing jobs and getting returns: Impact investing through entrepreneurs. *Journal of Global Business Management, 8*(1), 123–132.

Silby, W., & Nicholas, J. (2015). Angel impact investing. In *Angels without borders: Trends and policies shaping angel investment worldwide*. World Scientific Publishing.

Social Finance. (2014). *The global social impact bond market*. London: Social Finance.

Social Finance UK. (2016). *Social impact bonds: The early years*. Retrieved from http://www.socialfinance.org.uk//uploads/2016/07/SIBs-Early-ears_SocialFinance_2016_Final-003.pdf.

Spiess-Knafl, W., & Scheck, B. (2017). *Impact investing: Instruments, mechanisms and actors*. Cham: Palgrave Macmillan.

Stoesz, D. (2014). Evidence-based policy reorganizing social services through accountable care organizations and social impact bonds. *Research on Social Work Practice, 24*(2), 181–185.

Suetin, A. (2011). Post-crisis developments in international financial markets. *International Journal of Law and Management, 53*(1), 51–61.

Tan, S., Fraser, A., Giacomantonio, C., Kruithof, K., Sim, M., Lagarde, M., et al. (2015). *An evaluation of social impact bonds in health and social care: Interim report*. London: Policy Innovation Research Unit (PIRU).

Tekula, R., & Shah, A. (2016). Impact investing: Funding social innovation. *Routledge Handbook of Social and Sustainable Finance*, 125.

The New Climate Economy. (2016). *The sustainable infrastructure imperative: Financing for better growth and development*. Retrieved from http://newclimateeconomy.report/wp-content/uploads/sites/4/2014/08/NCE_2016Report.pdf.

Thillai Rajan, A., Koserwal, P., & Keerthana, S. (2014). The global epicenter of impact investing: An analysis of social venture investments in India. *The Journal of Private Equity, 17*(2), 37–50.

Thorpe, R., Holt, R., Macpherson, A., & Pittaway, L. (2005). Using knowledge within small and medium-sized firms: A systematic review of the evidence. *International Journal of Management Reviews, 7*(4), 257–281.

Tranfield, D., Denyer, D., & Smart, P. (2003). Towards a methodology for developing evidence-informed management knowledge by means of systematic review. *British Journal of Management, 14*(3), 207–222.

Trotta, A., Caré, R., Severino, R., Migliazza, M. C., & Rizzello, A. (2015). Mobilizing private finance for public Good: challenges and opportunities of Social impact bonds. *European Scientific Journal, ESJ*, 11(10), 259–279.

Urban, B., & George, J. (2018). An empirical study on measures relating to impact investing in South Africa. *International Journal of Sustainable Economy, 10*(1), 61–77.

Vecchi, V., Casalini, F., Balbo, L., & Caselli, S. (2015). Impact investing: A new asset class or a societal refocus of venture capital? In *Public private partnerships for infrastructure and business development* (pp. 275–293). New York: Palgrave Macmillan.

Vecchi, V., Balbo, L., Brusoni, M., & Caselli, S. (Eds.). (2017). *Principles and practice of impact investing: A catalytic revolution*. Routledge.

Viviers, S., & Firer, C. (2013). Responsible investing in South Africa – A retail perspective. *Journal of Economic and Financial Sciences, 6*(1), 217–242.

Viviers, S., Ratcliffe, T., & Hand, D. (2011). From philanthropy to impact investing: Shifting mindsets in South Africa. *Corporate Ownership and Control, 8*, 25–43.

Walker, T., Kibsey, S. D., & Lee, S. (2016). Impact investing. *Sustainable Investing: Revolutions in Theory and Practice, 17*.

Ward, J. E. (2012). New money for chronic diseases: Can clinicians and entrepreneurs deliver outcomes eluding governments? *The Medical Journal of Australia, 197*(5), 268–270.

Weaver, S. C. (1993). Why don't we just ask them? *Financial Practice & Education, 3*(2), 11–13.

Weber, O. (2013). Impact measurement in microfinance: Is the measurement of the social return on investment an innovation in microfinance? *Journal of Innovation Economics & Management, 11*, 149–171.

Weber, O. (2016). Impact investing. In O. M. Lehner (Ed.), *Routledge handbook of social and sustainable finance*. Routledge.

Weber, O., & Feltmate, B. (2016). *Sustainable banking: Managing the social and environmental impact of financial institutions*. Toronto: University of Toronto Press.

Weed, M. (2005). "Meta Interpretation": A Method for the Interpretive Synthesis of Qualitative Research. *Forum Qualitative Sozialforschung / Forum: Qualitative Social Research, 6*(1). doi: http://dx.doi.org/10.17169/fqs-6.1.508

Wilburn, K., & Wilburn, R. (2014). The double bottom line: Profit and social benefit. *Business Horizons, 57*(1), 11–20.

Winget, M., Lamb, N. H., & Wheatley, K. K. (2017). Root capital measuring the effects of impact investing on impoverished rural communities. *Journal of Case Studies, 35*(2), 88–113.

World Economic Forum. (2013). *From ideas to practice, pilots to strategy – Practical solutions and actionable insights on how to do impact investing*. Retrieved from http://www3.weforum.org/docs/WEF_II_SolutionsInsights_ImpactInvesting_Report_2013.pdf.

Zingales, L. (2015). *Does finance benefit society?* (No. w20894). National Bureau of Economic Research.

3

Social Risk and Financial Returns: Evidences from Social Impact Bonds

Elisabetta Scognamiglio, Alessandro Rizzello, and Helen Chiappini

1 Introduction

Social Impact Bonds (SIBs) have recently piqued the interest of governments, investors and researchers. They have also been known as Payment for Success bonds or Pay for Benefit bonds, even though such innovative financing instruments are not real bonds in financial terms, but rather contracts on future social results (Clifford and Jung 2016). Therefore, SIBs involve contracts in which socially motivated investors—like high net worth individuals and institutional investors—provide working capital to social sector service providers, allowing them to scale up high-impact social programs. Investors receive financial returns in relation to

E. Scognamiglio
Federico II University of Naples, Naples, Italy

A. Rizzello
University Magna Graecia of Catanzaro, Catanzaro, Italy

H. Chiappini (✉)
G. d'Annunzio University of Chieti and Pescara, Pescara, Italy
e-mail: helen.chiappini@unich.it

M. La Torre, M. Calderini (eds.), *Social Impact Investing Beyond the SIB*, Palgrave Studies in Impact Finance, https://doi.org/10.1007/978-3-319-78322-2_3

the social impact achieved and they do not obtain payback if the social goals have not been achieved. This mechanism transfers the risk of not achieving social goals from public administration and taxpayers to investors. SIBs constitute forms of collaboration where commissioners, providers and investors share the risk and pool knowledge and experience in the delivery of services (Maier and Meyer 2017). SIBs demand commissioners, investors and providers to work collaboratively and flexibly, rather than in the classic public procurement manner (Warner 2013).

The financial architecture of SIBs involves different stakeholders including: (a) *commissioner*: one or more public sector bodies (central or local administrations) seeking an outcomes-based solution to a social problem and that commit to paying for pre-determined outcomes; (b) *a provider*: a charity or not-for-profit organization that implements the program and delivers social outcomes for the target populations defined by the SIB; (c) *a specialized intermediary*: organization that facilitates the creation of the deal, brings the service providers, outcome payers and investors together to make the deal possible and provides advice on how the SIB should be structured; (d) *socially motived investors*: they provide the up-front capital to scale social services; (e) *an independent auditor or evaluator*: who determines whether the social outcome has been achieved (Fraser et al. 2016).

Figure 3.1 illustrates the dynamics of the SIB model.

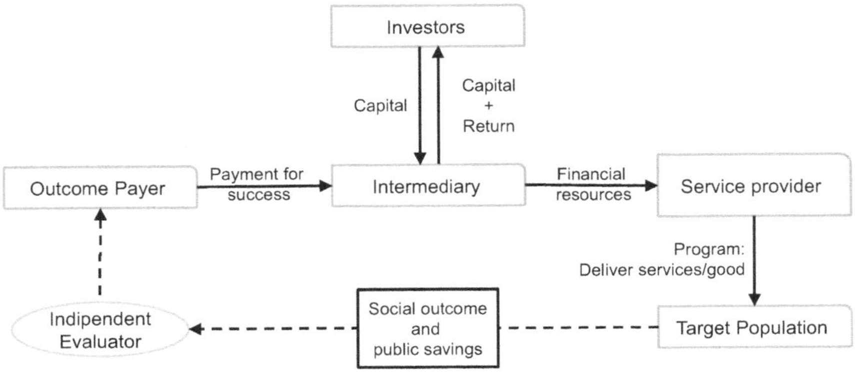

Fig. 3.1 The SIB model. Source: Authors elaboration adapted from Chiappini (2017)

SIBs were pioneered in the United Kingdom (2010) and have grown to become a global phenomenon. There are now 89 SIBs worldwide: 33 located in the United Kingdon, with the second biggest market in the United States (16 SIBs) and 20 more across Continental Europe (Gustafsson-Wright et al. 2015; Dear et al. 2016). Applications of SIBs span several social areas ranging from employment to education and social welfare (Arena et al. 2016).

The achievement of a pre-determined social outcome is key for the success of a SIB, because it triggers payout to the impact investors involved in such schemes. The risk of not achieving the desired outcome is labeled social risk.

Thus, the study sought to explore the relationship between social risk and financial return within the context of SIBs. In more detail, this chapter: (1) provides a scoring model of SIBs social risk; (2) provides empirical insight by measuring the social risk in a sample of SIBs; and (3) explores the relationship between social risk and financial return.

Social risk scoring was determined by adapting and improving the early version contained in Scognamiglio (2017), while financial return was identified in terms of Internal Rate of Return (IRR). The sample is composed of 34 SIBs launched worldwide by analyzing publicly available data and previous works on SIBs. The chapter is organized as follows: Sect. 2 introduces the concept of social risk and describes determinants of SIBs' social risk factors; Sect. 3 presents methodology and data, while Sect. 4 provides empirical results. Sect. 5 analyzes the correlation between social risk and financial return, while Sect. 6 discusses results and Sect. 7 concludes.

Findings provide useful insights enriching the literature on SIBs, which is still in its infancy, and it contributes to the ongoing debate on the role of SIBs in the design and delivery of social welfare interventions.

2 Social Impact Bonds and Social Risk: From Theory to Practice

SIBs represent one of the most debated form of financial innovation within the impact investing field (Fraser et al. 2016). Similar to impact investors, SIB investors expect both social and financial returns. (O'Donohoe et al. 2010). Financial returns are generally, but not exclusively, expressed in terms of IRR that may be fixed or variable in relation to the social performance achieved with the SIB intervention. Social returns are expressed in terms of pre-determined levels of expected *social impact*. An independent evaluator measures the achievement of these thresholds, which determine outcome payments to investors. Financial returns are obtained by the SIB investors, *only if* social impact has been achieved (Nicholls and Tomkinson 2015). Thus, the central element to the concept of social risk is whether social outcomes are achieved.

This type of risk has been recently explored by academics and practitioners in the impact investing field. More in detail, there is not a common understanding of the concept of social risk[1] in the impact investing literature (Lehner 2016). Recent contributions suggested that social risk is expressed in terms of not reaching the intended impact (Brandstetter and Lehner 2014) or as the likelihood that a given allocation of capital will generate the expected social outcomes irrespective of any financial returns or losses (Nicholls and Tomkinson 2015).

In the specific context of SIBs, the term *social risk* is used to identify the possibility that the expected social outcome is not achieved (Arena et al. 2015; Disley and Rubin 2014; Gustafsson-Wright et al. 2015; Disley et al. 2016) due to unpredictable events (Chiappini 2017) that may occur during the implementation of SIBs. However, the financial architecture of SIBs is peculiar and thus requires a more in-depth investigation of financial and social risk. In this vein, the systematic study of Scognamiglio (2017) explored and segmented the concept of social risk in the specific field of SIBs. This study provided an identification of social risk factors that could affect the success of a SIB. Scognamiglio (2017) identified those social risk factors by performing literature review and organizing them in a preliminary model, based on a methodology introduced by Serrano-Cinca et al. (2013). For the purpose of this study, the original scoring model was updated by the authors as explained in the following sections.

---

[1] The academia is not unanimous also under the use of definitions. For instance, sometimes the term impact risk is used interchangeably to identity social risk like in Brandstetter and Lehner (2014).

3 Methodology and Data

3.1 Methodology

This chapter aims to analyze the correlation between financial return and social risk of the SIBs included in our sample. In order to achieve this research objective the methodology is organized in three steps:

1. definition of the social risk scoring model starting from the preliminary version contained in Scognamiglio (2017);
2. data collection and measurement of social risk scores across the sample;
3. test of correlation between social risk and IRR of SIBs.

3.1.1 Modeling the SIB Social Risk Score

As introduced in Sect. 2, the early version of the model produced by Scognamiglio (2017) has been implemented by the authors to re-organize the sub factors identified in the previous work and by removing redundancies. Then, each social risk sub-factor has been grouped under three main categories: program process, players and social outcome evaluation. Table 3.1 shows the new version of the scoring model.

As reported in Table 3.1 each category of risk is characterized by different factors, further divided into sub-factors. Each sub-factor is weighted on the basis of key questions and related options corresponding to different levels of risk ranging from 1 (low) to 5 (high). Some of the sub-factors are intuitively identifiable as more or less risky, while others require further considerations.

Within the program feature, the risk of the duration of program sub-factor has been identified on a range from lower (more than five years) to higher risk (less than three years). Long duration of a program is considered less risky than short duration, because a social program in nature needs longer periods to obtain social results (Dear et al. 2016). Furthermore, the presence of a SIB pilot phase may influence the risk of not meeting desired social outcomes because the SIB design take into account lessons learnt (Dear et al. 2016). For these reasons, the presence of a pilot phase was considered a factor that reduces the level of social risk. Similarly, the availability of previous evidence from the intervention design was considered a less risky sub-factor.

Table 3.1 SIB social risk scoring model

Risk category	Risk factor	Sub-factor	Key question	Options	Score
Program process	Program features	Duration of program	How long is the project?	More than 5 years	1
				From 3 to 5 years	2
				Less than 3 Years	3
		Pilot phase	Is there a pilot phase?	Yes	1
				No	2
		Empirical evidence	Is it an evidence-based program? On which scale?	Evidence on large scale	1
				Evidence on small scale	2
				No evidence	3
		Policy variation	Does the contract permit the ongoing variation consequent to a policy change?	Yes	1
				No	2
Players	Service provider	Number of service providers	How many service providers are involved?	From 3 to 5	1
				From 1 to 3	2
				More than 5	3
		Worker/target number relation	How many workers are present for each target group?	One-to-one	1
				Not more than one to ten	2
				More than one to ten	3
		Number of similar projects developed	How many similar projects has the service provider involved in this program developed that present more experience in the same area of intervention?	More than 10	1
				From 5 to 10	2
				Not more than 5	3
		Years of experience of service provider	How many years of experience does the older service provider involved in the program have?	More than 10	1
				From 5 to 10	2
				Not more than 5	3
	Intermediary	Intermediary present	Is there an intermediary involved?	Yes	1
				No	2
		Years of experience	How many years of experience does the intermediary have?	More than 10	1
				From 5 to 10	2
				Not more than 5	3
	Independent evaluator	Independent evaluator present	Is there an independent evaluator involved?	Yes	1
				No	2

Social outcome evaluation	Evaluation	Methodology	Which methodology is used?	Experimental design that controls for bothobserved and unobserved variables	1
				Live but non-experimental counterfactual	2
				'Constructed' counterfactual with no live control	3
				Multiple	4
				No counterfactual	5
		Number of outcomes	How many outcomes are measured?	From 1 to 3	1
				From 3 to 5	2
				More than 5	3

Source: Authors elaboration

Concerning the risk category of players, the presence of a specialized intermediary and of an independent evaluator was scored as less risky because they can respectively ensure a compliant design and the reliability of measurement.

Regarding the risk category of outcome evaluation we attributed low risk scoring to SIBs with small numbers of outcome measures because this reduces the complexity of data and resources required for the measuring activities. The evaluation methodology considered the adoption of a counterfactual method less risky for success in social outcomes. Furthermore, the use of a counterfactual group in the evaluation phase may be time consuming, although this risk could be managed through appropriate evaluation methodology and a more rigorous SIB intervention design (Dear et al. 2016). The absence of a benchmark program outcome could produce an over- or under-valuation of the expected social return (Dear et al. 2016).

Finally, the aggregate measure of social risk for SIBs was obtained by an average of these values.

3.2 Data

The sample originally included 64 SIBs sharing information publically and established until August 30, 2017 when we collected data on social risk categories and IRRs. Those SIBs have been identified through desk research and literature review. However, 30 SIBs have been excluded from this list because they do not disclose one of the following elements: program, players, social outcome evaluation and financial return. Thus, the final sample included 34 SIBs. Details are summarized in Table 3.2.

Data showed that 10 SIBs have been implemented to support youth employment, 10 for homeless people, four to help family and children, two to reduce the recidivism, two to support the health sector, two for education, one for the environment and three to favor immigrant inclusion. Even if the highest number of SIBs have been established in the United Kingdom, the highest total amount was invested in the United States (with $46,000,000 invested), despite the £19,992,000, invested in the United Kingdom (Table 3.2).

Referring to the IRR, the minimum IRR is 0.01% while the maximum is 0.65% (Table 3.2).

Table 3.2 The sample of SIBs in a nutshell

No	SIB country	Social issue	Amount invested	Expected IRR
1	UK	Healthcare	2,020,000 (GBP)	0.30750962
2	UK	Justice—recidivism	5,000,000 (GBP)	0.125
3	UK	Youth unemployment	3,000,000 (GBP)	0.03228012
4	UK	Youth unemployment	900,000 (GBP)	0.36650505
5	UK	Youth unemployment	370,000 (GBP)	0.43492838
6	UK	Youth unemployment	1,500,000 (GBP)	0.44224957
7	UK	Youth unemployment	900,000 (GBP)	0.91697118
8	UK	Youth unemployment	ND	0.33005732
9	UK	Youth unemployment	800,000 (GBP)	0.60376716
10	UK	Youth unemployment	420,000 (GBP)	0.65387026
11	UK	Youth unemployment	ND	0.54297471
12	UK	Homeless	884,000 (GBP)	0.39189693
13	UK	Homeless	ND	0.39189693
14	UK	Homeless	550,000 (GBP)	0.17402075
15	UK	Homeless	620,000 (GBP)	1.51645065
16	UK	Homeless	498,000 (GBP)	0.22465984
17	UK	Homeless	620,000 (GBP)	0.12382061
18	UK	Homeless	310,000 (GBP)	0.283345
19	UK	Welfare—family and children	1,200,000 (GBP)	0.19300798
20	UK	Welfare—family and children	1,000,000 (GBP)	0.15829219
21	USA	Justice—recidivism	9,600,000 (USD)	0.05193473
22	UK	Youth unemployment	900,000 (GBP)	0.49380158
23	ASIA	Education	270,000 (USD)	0.04551592
24	USA	Homeless	6,900,000 (USD)	0.029914
25	USA	Homeless	8,600,000 (USD)	0.05593824
26	Continental Europe	Education	10,000,000 (SEK)	0.03696223
27	Australia	Homeless	9,000,000 (AUD)	0.08281706
28	South Korea	Welfare—family and children	10,000,000 (WON)	0.08546933
29	USA	Environment	25,000,000 (USD)	0.00417568
30	USA	Welfare—family and children	ND	0.08697582
31	USA	Justice—recidivism	4,600,000 (USD)	0.04377177
32	USA	Immigrant wellness	12,400,000 (USD)	0.03216324
33	Finland	Immigrant wellness	ND	0.01370886
34	Australia	Mental health	7,000,000 (AUD)	0.15211241

4 Financial Returns and Social Risk of SIBs: Evidences from the Field

This section presents findings of the empirical analysis conducted on a sample of SIBs currently under implementation. In particular, Sect. 4.1 analyzes results obtained in terms of program process, while Sect. 4.2 analyzes scores of players and Sect. 4.3 analyzes results of social outcome evaluation.

4.1 Program Process

Program process is analyzed according to four sub-factors of risk: duration of program, presence of a pilot phase, empirical evidence and contract clauses relative to ex-post policy variations. Thus, most SIBs have a duration from three to five years (82.4%) (Table 3.3). No SIB requires a pilot

Table 3.3 Program process

Risk category	Risk factor	Sub-factor	Key question	Options	Score	No SIB	% SIB
Program process	Program features	Duration of program	How long is the project?	More than 5 years	1	6	17.6%
				From 3 to 5 years	2	28	82.4%
				Less than 3 Years	3	0	0.0%
		Pilot phase	Is there a pilot phase present?	Yes	1	0	0.0%
				No	2	34	100.0%
		Empirical evidence	Is it an evidence-based program? On which scale?	Evidence on large scale	1	4	11.8%
				Evidence on small scale	2	26	76.5%
				No evidence	3	4	11.8%
		Policy variation	Does the contract permit the ongoing variation consequent to a policy change?	Yes	1	18	52.9%
				No	2	16	47.1%

Source: Authors elaboration

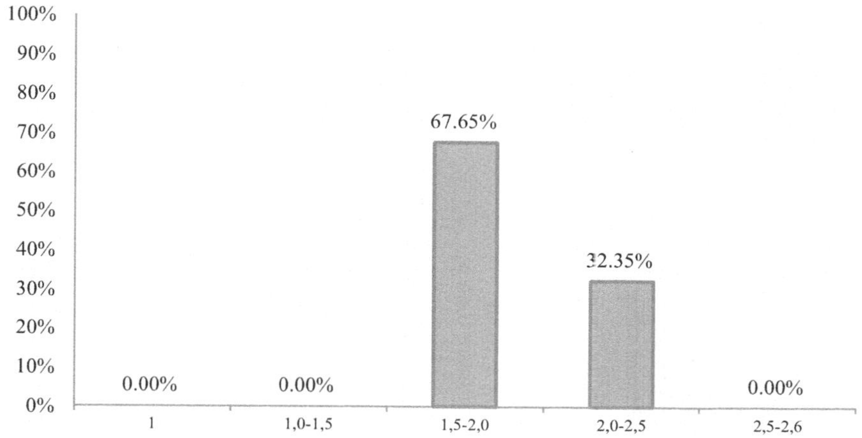

Fig. 3.2 Synthesis of score: Program process. Source: Authors elaboration

phase, while most SIBs show small-scale evidence (76.5%). Furthermore, 52.9% of SIBs consent the program variation after policy revisions.

The analysis shows that most SIBs (67.6%) are characterized by a medium level of program process risk (1.5–2%), while 32.4% of SIBs present higher scores than others, ranging from 2% to 2.5% (Fig. 3.2).

4.2 Players

Players are analyzed according to three risk factors: service provider, intermediary and independent evaluator. Empirical analysis of SIBs included in our sample shows that 94.1% of them have involved between one and three service providers and 55.9% of SIBs have engaged a service provider employing a range of one to 10 workers. Service providers are involved in at least five similar projects (47.1%) or in more than 10 similar projects (47.1%). Furthermore, service providers have long experience in SIBs, showing an expertise from five to 10 years (44.1%) or longer than 10 years (55.9%) (Table 3.4).

Table 3.4 Players

Risk category	Risk factor	Sub-factor	Key question	Options	Score	No SIB	% SIB
Players	Service provider	Number of service providers	How many service providers are involved?	From 3 to 5	1	0	0.0%
				From 1 to 3	2	32	94.1%
				More than 5	3	2	5.9%
		Worker/target number relation	How many workers are present for each target group?	One-to-one	1	13	38.2%
				Not more than one to ten	2	19	55.9%
				More than one to ten	3	2	5.9%
		Number of similar projects developed	How many similar projects has the service provider involved in this program developed that present more experience in the same area of intervention?	More than 10	1	16	47.1%
				From 5 to 10	2	16	47.1%
				Not more than 5	3	2	5.9%
		Years of experience of service provider	How many years of experience have the older service provider involved in the program?	More than 10	1	19	55.9%
				From 5 to 10	2	15	44.1%
				Not more than 5	3	0	0.0%
	Intermediary	Intermediary presents	Is there an intermediary involved?	Yes	1	24	70.6%
				No	2	10	29.4%
		Years of experience	How many years of experience does the intermediary have?	More than 10	1	13	38.2%
				From 5 to 10	2	19	55.9%
				Not more than 5	3	2	5.9%
	Independent evaluator	Independent evaluator present	Is there an independent evaluator involved?	Yes	1	24	70.6%
				No	2	10	29.4%

Source: Authors elaboration

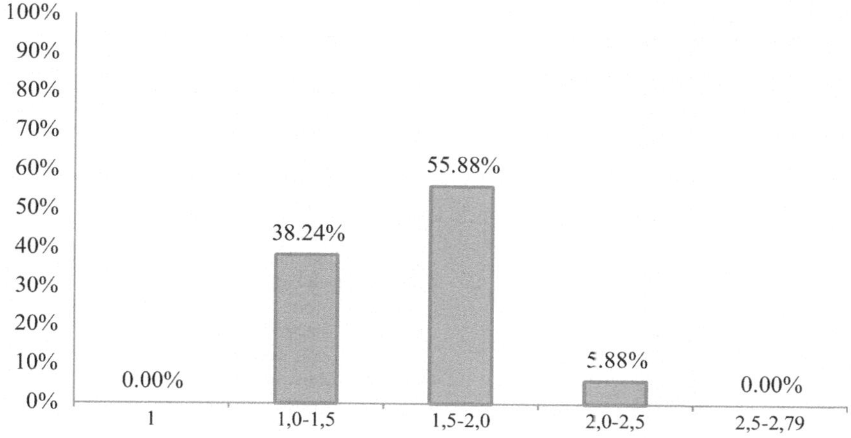

Fig. 3.3 Synthesis of score: Players. Source: Authors elaboration

Most architectures of a SIB include a financial intermediary (70.6%) with an experience from five to 10 years (55.9%). Moreover, 70.6% of SIBs show the presence of an independent evaluator of social impact (Table 3.4).

Most SIBs (55.9%) show a medium level of the players risk factor, while 38.2% of them show a risk ranging from 1% to 1.5% (Fig. 3.3).

4.3 Social Outcome Evaluation

Most SIBs use no counterfactual evaluation methodology, while 14.7% use multiple methodologies (Table 3.5). Few SIBs have implemented controls for both observed and unobserved variables (2.9%).

Among the SIBs, 73.5% measure a range from one to three outcomes, while 17.6% measure more than five outcomes (Table 3.5).

Evaluation represents one of the riskier factors for SIBs. This is derived from the non-counterfactual evaluation method applied and by the number of outcomes measured (Fig. 3.4).

Table 3.5 Social Outcome Evaluation

Risk category	Risk factor	Sub-factor	Key question	Options	Score	No SIB	% SIB
Social outcome evaluation	Evaluation	Methodology	Which methodology is used?	Experimental design that controls for both observed and unobserved variables	1	1	2.9%
				Live but non-experimental counterfactual	2	3	8.8%
				'Constructed' counterfactual with no live control	3	2	5.9%
				Multiple	4	5	14.7%
				No counterfactual	5	23	67.6%
		Number of outcomes	How many outcomes are measured?	From 1 to 3	1	25	73.5%
				From 3 to 5	2	3	8.8%
				More than 5	3	6	17.6%

Source: Authors elaboration

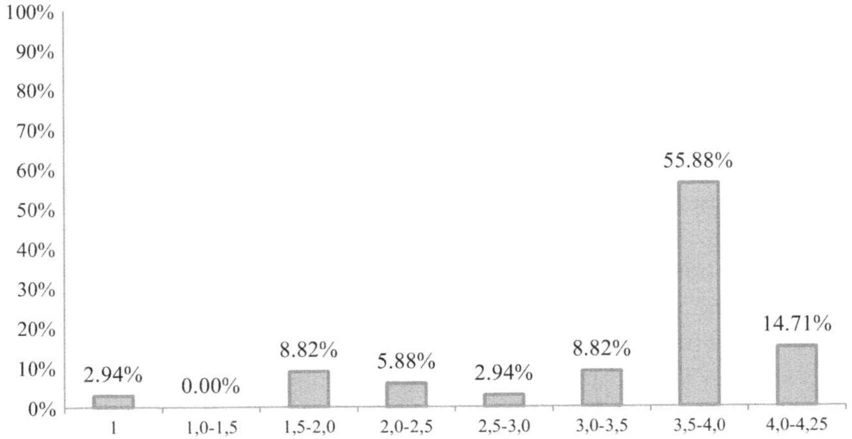

Fig. 3.4 Synthesis of score: Evaluation. Source: Authors elaboration

5 Financial Returns and Social Risk: A Correlation Analysis

This section assesses the correlation between financial return and social risk factors. Program process and players are not significantly correlated with financial return (Table 3.6). The correlation between program process and IRR accounts for −0.00072, while correlation between players and IRR accounts for −0.28035. Thus, it is close to zero.

The correlation between social outcome evaluation and IRR is positive, and it is close to zero (0.35691) like the other factors (Table 3.6).

Table 3.7 shows the correlation between IRR and any risk factor and risk sub-factor. No correlation is relevant. Thus, the financial return of SIBs is uncorrelated to social risk, both in an aggregate sense (social-risk category) and disaggregate sense (social risk factors and sub-factors).

However, some results can be highlighted as showing signs of correlation, for example, program duration is positively correlated with IRR. On the other hand, the presence of an intermediary demonstrates a negative relationship with IRR, while the presence of an independent evaluator shows a positive sign of correlation.

The analysis suggests that the level of social risk does not affect financial return of SIBs, thus other factors appear driving the level of expected financial return of SIBs.

Table 3.6 Correlation between financial return and category of social risk

	IRR	Program process	Players	Social outcome evaluation
IRR	1			
Program process	−0.00072	1		
Players	−0.28035	0.405362	1	
Social outcome evaluation	0.35691	0.127428	−0.2521	1

Source: Authors elaboration

Table 3.7 Correlation between IRR and sub-factors of social risk

	IRR	Duration of program	Pilot Phase	Empirical evidence	Policy variation	Program futures mean	Number of service providers	Worker/target number relation
IRR	1							
Duration of program	0.335784	1						
Pilot phase			1					
Empirical evidence	−0.02553	−0.15905		1				
Policy variation	−0.34868	−0.49099		0	1			
Program futures mean	−0.00072	0.25352		0.764835	0.262336	1		
Number of service providers	−0.16191	0.115728		−0.25769	0.014731	−0.13692	1	
Worker/target number relation	−0.2285	−0.39117		0.4181	0.424246	0.351128	0.139431	1
Number of similar projects developed	0.088936	0.453921		0.202152	−0.13868	0.405371	0.379975	0.039774
Years of experience of service provider	−0.09668	0.411306		0.244232	−0.00698	0.491846	0.029617	0.087097
Service provider mean	−0.12716	0.215817		0.337021	0.121484	0.515692	0.430269	0.527486
Presence of an intermediary	−0.33399	−0.03984		0.133073	0.16736	0.189302	−0.16137	0.137458
Years of experience	−0.40012	−0.12518		0	0.119506	−0.01433	0.139431	0.03856
Intermediary mean	−0.48285	−0.12263		0.058515	0.173943	0.071205	0.046124	0.092823
Independent evaluator	0.247875	0.298807		−0.26615	−0.47926	−0.31474	−0.16137	−0.53019
Methodology	0.31567	0.077801		0.328248	−0.1939	0.224098	−0.1924	0.040365
Number of outcomes	0.22181	0.164122		−0.07831	−0.385	−0.18657	−0.14245	−0.5335
Evaluation	0.35691	0.128035		0.258023	−0.3103	0.127428	−0.22019	−0.16006

Source: Authors elaboration

Number of similar projects developed	Years of experience of service provider	Service provider mean	Presence of an intermediary	Years of experience	Intermediary mean	Independent evaluator	Methodology	Number of outcomes	Evaluation
1									
0.708632	1								
0.832249	0.760976	1							
−0.09494	0.206474	0.064488	1						
0.208813	0.291323	0.253497	0.137458	1					
0.133596	0.335421	0.241224	0.555146	0.900167	1				
0.012659	−0.18353	−0.33416	0.008333	−0.30764	−0.25467	1			
0.041635	−0.17606	−0.06242	−0.32204	−0.18837	−0.29978	0.14389	1		
0.074498	−0.20026	−0.30964	−0.36781	−0.27157	−0.38977	0.715996	0.161291	1	
0.063637	−0.22708	−0.16788	−0.41592	−0.26394	−0.40453	0.387793	0.932451	0.506963	1

6 Discussion

Our findings highlight a non-significant correlation between social risk and the financial return of SIBs. Furthermore, the majority of SIBs examined in the study presented a medium score of social risk. This consideration poses interesting points for discussion.

6.1 Commissioner-Led IRR

One of the main objectives when commissioning SIBs is the ability to produce cost savings in public expenditures (Del Giudice 2015). Moreover, it is a common understanding in literature that the maximum payments are capped in relation to the curve of public expenditure savings calculated in the SIB design by the commissioner (Fraser et al. 2016). In this sense, the maximum level of outcome payments reflects a limitation by taking elements un-related to social risk into consideration. In other words, outcome payments made over the public savings curve could determine a non-positive cost benefit comparison for the commissioner, and therefore, result in a financially unsustainable SIB deal.

Even if our study analyzed some social risk factors that can be considered also a proxy of financial risk factors (i.e., program duration), an in-depth analysis should be conducted in this direction. Specifically, further studies could explore the correlation between financial risk and IRR to investigate if this relationship follows traditional financial trends.

6.2 The SIB Investors' Rationality

The investors' approach to impact investing has been extensively researched in existing literature (Brandstetter and Lehner 2015; Daggers and Nicholls 2016; Chiappini 2017) and it has been observed that SIB investors are mainly social purpose-first oriented (Rizzello and Carè 2016). For impact investors the whole point of investing is not to have a financial return at a given point in the future, but for those funds to produce impact. In other words, financial returns represent—one side of the *unicum* return for this category of investors who are interested in both social and financial returns. Consequently, impact investors assess a tridimensional framework of risk, return and social impact when making their decisions. SIB investments are assessed by their (impact) investors not against the two-dimensional risk-return dichotomy but in a three-dimensional framework to promote value creation. This consideration opens doors for further research in order to explore the role of social risk in the SIB investment decisions.

6.3 Asymmetries of Information

There is an agreement among scholars about the complex nature of contractual arrangements in a SIB (see, among others: Liebman 2011; Warner 2013; Burand 2014; Maier and Meyer 2017). Even if they can differ by national regulatory frameworks, the connection within SIB actors presents multiple differences of governance that can be summarized in managed (typically in United States), direct and intermediated SIBs (typically in United Kingdom) (Gustafsson-Wright et al. 2015).

In a direct SIB, a delivery contract is signed between the outcomes payer and service provider who is responsible for performance management, while the intermediary is responsible for raising capital and determining the feasibility of the deal (Goodall 2014). In an intermediated SIB, the delivery contract is signed between the outcomes payer and the investor or an intermediary that contracts the service provider (Gustafsson-Wright et al. 2015). A managed SIB is signed between the outcomes payer and the intermediary who usually manages the entire process. In such complex governance structure, asymmetries of information may arise between the commissioner, service provider, intermediary and the investors. The public commissioner may also encounter unintended risks or perverse effects in the above-described governance structure. Furthermore, unintended risks may also emerge from events that are out of stakeholder control. Such events may have an impact on determining the amount of social outcomes. These considerations may not enable investors to make correct assessments and pricing of their investments.

The hypothesis of asymmetric information presented a possibility that SIB players did not have a perception of the risks linked to SIBs, especially social risk. In this sense, future research should explore whether the absence of a correlation could be due to other social risk factors or miscategorizing certain factors.

7 Conclusions

This chapter has explored the link between financial return and social risk in a sample of SIBs under implementation and has offered some preliminary insights. This relation was explained in light of investor rationalities, commissioner motivation and asymmetries of information. The chapter also suggested that there is an emergent need for new research in this area to underpin the implications of our results. Future research needs to adopt a three-dimensional assessment of financial returns, social risk and financial risks, by building a holistic risk-return profile adapted for SIBs. Furthermore, researchers should investigate whether these findings can be confirmed by employing ex-post IRR, instead of expected IRR. Such specialized studies will ultimately help inform policymakers and practitioners, contribute to building a successful SIB market and enable commissioners to connect with social and potential investors.

Moreover, the relationship between social risk and financial return can be investigated by distinguishing between promoters in central public administrations and local administrations. Differences in terms of equity and debt structures or social areas (i.e., employment, health, education, housing, justice) could also be assessed. In order to undertake these analyses the SIB market should grow in terms of magnitude and the number of projects.

References

Arena, M., Azzone, G., Bengo, I., & Calderini, M. (2015). *Measuring social impact: The governance issue*. IRIS Network. Retrieved from http://irisnetwork.it/wp-content/uploads/2015/06/colloquio15-arena-azzone-bengo-calderini.pdf.

Arena, M., Bengo, I., Calderini, M., & Chiodo, V. (2016). Social impact bonds: Blockbuster or flash in a pan? *International Journal of Public Administration, 39*(12), 927–939.

Brandstetter, L., & Lehner, O. M. (2014). *Impact investment portfolios: Including social risks and returns*. Retrieved from https://papers.ssrn.com/sol3/papers.cfm?abstract_id=2519671.

Brandstetter, L., & Lehner, O. M. (2015). Opening the market for impact investments: The need for adapted portfolio tools. *Entrepreneurship Research Journal, 5*(2), 87–107.

Burand, D. (2014). Globalizing social finance: How social impact bonds and social impact performance guarantees can scale development. *New York University Journal of Law and Business, 9*, 447.

Chiappini, H. (2017). *Social impact funds: Definition, assessment and performance*. London: Palgrave Macmillan.

Clifford, J., & Jung, T. (2016). Social impact bonds: Exploring and understanding an emerging funding approach. In O. M. Lehner (Ed.), *Routledge handbook of social and sustainable finance*. London: Routledge.

Daggers, J., & Nicholls, A. (2016). The status quo and future research. In Lehner O. M. (2016). Routledge Handbook of Social and Sustainable Finance. Routledge.

Dear, A., Helbitz, A., Khare, R., Lotan, R., Newman, J., Sims, G. C., et al. (2016). Social impact bonds: The early years. *Social Finance*, July. Retrieved from http://socialfinance.org/content/uploads/2016/07/SIBs-Early-Years_Social-Finance_2016_Final.pdf.

Del Giudice, A. (2015). *I social impact bond*. Milan: Franco Angeli.

Disley, E., & Rubin, J. (2014). Phase 2 report from the payment by results social impact bond pilot at HMP peterborough. *Ministry of Justice Analytical Series*. London: Rand Europe.

Disley, E., Giacomantonio, C., Kruithof, K., & Sim, M. (2016). *The payment by results social impact bond pilot at HMP Peterborough: Final process evaluation report*. Ministry of Justice (UK). Retrieved from www.justice.gov.uk/publications/research-and-analysis/moj.

Fraser, A., Tan, S., Lagarde, M., & Mays, N. (2016). Narratives of promise, narratives of caution: A review of the literature on Social Impact Bonds. *Social Policy & Administration*. https://doi.org/10.1111/spol.12260.

Goodall, E. (2014). *Choosing social impact bonds: A practitioner's guide*. London: Bridges Ventures. Retrieved from https://www.bigsocietycapital.com/sites/default/files/attachments/Choosing%20social%20impact%20bonds%20Bridges%20report.pdf.

Gustafsson-Wright, E., Gardiner, S., & Putcha, V. (2015). The potential and limitations of impact bonds: Lessons from the first five years of experience worldwide. *Global Economy and Development at Brookings*. Retrieved from https://www.brookings.edu/wp-content/uploads/2016/07/Impact-Bondsweb.pdf.

Lehner, O. M. (Ed.). (2016). *Routledge handbook of social and sustainable finance*. London: Routledge.

Liebman, J. B. (2011). Social impact bonds: A promising new financing model to accelerate social innovation and improve government performance. *Center for American Progress, 9*. Retrieved from https://cdn.americanprogress.org/wpcontent/uploads/issues/2011/02/pdf/social_impact_bonds.pdf.

Maier, F., & Meyer, M. (2017). Social impact bonds and the perils of aligned interests. *Administrative Sciences, 7*(3), 24.

Nicholls, A., & Tomkinson, E. (2015). Risk and return in social finance: "I am the market". In A. Nicholls, J. Emerson, & R. Patton (Eds.), *Social finance*. Oxford: Oxford University Press.

O'Donohoe, N., Leijonhufvud, C., Saltuk, Y., Bugg-Levine, A., & Brandenburg, M. (2010, November 29). Impact investments: An emerging asset class. *JP Morgan Global Research. Research Note*. Retrieved from https://thegiin.org/assets/documents/Impact%20Investments%20an%20Emerging%20Asset%20Class2.pdf.

Rizzello, A., & Carè, R. (2016). Insight into the social impact bond market: An analysis of investors. *ACRN Oxford Journal of Finance and Risk Perspective, 5*(3), 145–171.

Scognamiglio, E. (2017). *The evaluation of social risk in the social impact investing*. University of Naples Federico II, PhD Thesis.

Serrano-Cinca, C., Gutiérrez-Nieto, B., & Reyes, N. M. (2013). A social approach to microfinance credit scoring. *Working Papers CEB, 13*.

Warner, M. E. (2013). Private finance for public goods: Social impact bonds. *Journal of Economic Policy Reform, 16*(4), 303–319.

4

The Use of Payment by Results in Healthcare: A Review and Proposal

Alessandro Rizzello, Rossana Caridà, Annarita Trotta, Giuseppe Ferraro, and Rosella Carè

1 Introduction

In recent decades, scholars and practitioners worldwide have begun to analyze the use of the Payment by Results (PbR) approach because of its potential to make the use of public funds more efficient (Webster 2016). PbR contracts present a number of challenges, benefits and risks over the current funding models and are discussed in the literature from several perspectives. As stated in Sheil and Breidenbach-Roe (2014: 24), "the principles of paying for impact and commissioning for outcomes are not commonly disputed. However, the way programmes are being designed

This chapter is the result of a collaboration between the authors. In particular, Alessandro Rizzello contributed to Sects. 4, 5.1, 5.2, 5.3, 5.4, 5.5, 5.6, 5.7, 5.8, and 6; Rossana Caridà contributed to Sects. 8 and 9; Giuseppe Ferraro contributed to Sect. 7; and Annarita Trotta contributed to Sects. 1 and 2. Finally, Rosella Carè contributed to Sects. 2.1, 3, and 3.1.

A. Rizzello (✉) • R. Caridà • A. Trotta • G. Ferraro • R. Carè
University Magna Graecia of Catanzaro, Catanzaro, Italy
e-mail: rizzello@unicz.it; trotta@unicz.it

M. La Torre, M. Calderini (eds.), *Social Impact Investing Beyond the SIB*, Palgrave Studies in Impact Finance, https://doi.org/10.1007/978-3-319-78322-2_4

and implemented is leading to questions about the viability of PbR as a method for improving public service delivery and for providing quality outcomes for service users."

These concerns are also linked to issues regarding the variety and complexity of the existing PbR schemes. It therefore appears essential to understand and regulate—in theory and in practice—several innovative types of partnerships that engage investors, governments and service providers in a new way (Wong et al. 2016). These schemes emphasize Social Impact Bonds (SIBs), which are a specific type of outcomes-based, or PbR, contracting. SIBs involve a commissioner buying a service from a service provider, where the payments are conditional on the achievement of a set of pre-specified and measured targets for the outcomes the service achieves (Jackson 2013; Sinclair et al. 2014; Martin 2015).

Applications of such instruments span several social welfare areas, including the healthcare sector (Rizzello and Carè 2016). The healthcare sector seems to represent a particularly promising field for the application of SIBs, in terms of both innovative practice and improvements in outcomes, within the growing financial constraints imposed by austerity measures (Karanikolos et al. 2013). In recent years, SIBs in the healthcare sector have been issued in the United Kingdom, the United States and Israel in several areas of intervention (Tan et al. 2015). However, in many countries, such as Italy, the effective diffusion of such instruments is hampered by market and legal issues (Di Raimo and Mignone 2017; Bengo and Calderini 2016; Blasini 2015).

Based on these considerations, our work aims to provide an overview of the relevant literature regarding PbR models, with SIBs as the main subject, and to perform an explorative multiple case study (MCS) analysis of such schemes in the healthcare sector. To achieve this, our research comprises three phases: (1) a literature overview that conceptualizes the definition of PbR and identifies several different facets related to this issue, with a focus on SIBs; (2) a qualitative analysis of the existing SIBs schemes in healthcare; and (3) a focus on suggestions and implications for scholars, practitioners and policy makers and a discussion—from a law and economic perspective—about the opportunities and obstacles related to the development of PbR instruments in the Italian healthcare sector.

The study is based on a qualitative method (a case study of innovative SIBs in healthcare). The results encourage a refinement of the research in this domain and form a road map for future investigations. The remainder of the work is organized as follows. Section 2 provides a literature overview, outlines the importance of the topic and identifies the key characteristics of PbR schemes, with a focus on SIBs. Section 3 depicts the research design and methods. Section 4 is devoted to analyzing the SIB market, with a focus on the healthcare sector. Section 5 performs the case study analysis, and Sect. 6 presents lessons learned. Section 7 provides reflections and suggestions for future research. Section 8 provides insights about the Italian legislative framework for the development of PbR contracts. Finally, Sect. 9 gives concluding remarks.

2 A Literature Overview

Several academic studies have reported on the systems of payment for productive work (Udal 1924; Leibenstein 1966; Thierry 1987; Heywood et al. 1997) and performance management in both the private and public sectors. This is a very large area of research that analyzes many different topics from several different perspectives. In principle, PbR approaches are recognized as an "abstract ideal" (Baumol 1975). However, from a practical side, at the heart of the debate, there are numerous questions and issues to consider (which involve, among other thing, key outcome variables in defining and measuring the cost and quality of services).

Especially in recent years, a number of scholars have been working on PbR models to examine concrete proposals and experiences for performance management, generally focusing on key public sectors, such as education (Tomlinson 2000) and healthcare (Klein 2006; Farrar et al. 2009; Abbott et al. 2011; Appleby et al. 2012). As stated by Lancefield and Gagliardi (2016: 1), "Paying for results is in vogue. The concept is fairly straightforward: The parties define the result up front, agree on a baseline, work out how confident the organization is in delivering the result, and then specify the expectation and payment in the contract. The idea isn't new —...— but its application is becoming more widespread in the private and public sectors."

After examining a large amount of academic and grey literature to outline the conceptual basis for PbR, Clist and Verschoor (2014: 4) admit that "defining PbR, and related or constituent concepts, is widely noted to be difficult. Different organisations use many different terms, with boundaries between these terms suggesting a variety of different groupings." Researchers, practitioners and policy makers use a range of parallel terms, including pay for performance, performance contracting, outcome commissioning, pay for success, and outcome-based payment schemes (Webster 2016). Farr (2016: 2) notes that outcome-based contracting, defined as a model where service providers have some payment dependent upon the achievement of specific outcomes, includes PbR, performance-based contracts, payment for performance and SIBs.

There is no agreement regarding the use of terminology, and several terms are used interchangeably (Perrin 2013; Olsen 2011; Burand 2014; Tan et al. 2015). However, the different definitions of PbR contain common elements. According to Mason et al. (2015: 1), PbR "is a model for delivering public services where government or the commissioner pays providers for the outcomes they achieve rather than the activities they deliver." Similarly, PbR is defined by Webster (2016: 12) as "a commissioning approach to the delivery of public services where contract payments are wholly or partly dependent on the achievement of specified outcome." Although there are different schemes with different details, three of the most important key characteristics are well understood in the academic and grey literature: (1) contingent payments depend on independent verification of results (Perrin 2013); (2) the legal aspects of PbR contracts should consider both rewards and penalties that are useful for achieving the outcomes (Webster 2016); (3) there is a risk transfer, as payment depends on an outcome (Webster 2016). Beyond the different and overlapping denominations, these models are taking on increasing international significance as models of commissioning in public services reform (Farr 2016). Obviously, evaluating the opportunity to use these models depends on a number of elements (see, among others, Clist and Dercon 2014). As affirmed by Clist and Dercon (2014: 1), "the principle factor that should determine whether PbR is used, and the strength of incentives, is the quality of the performance measure."

Equally important for the practical success of these models are the full understanding of the organizational and legal aspects (including clauses aimed at encouraging the realization of the outcome) as well as the assessment of outcomes and the various related risks. Recent developments in this field have increased in popularity since the 2008 financial crisis, mainly because of their promise to solve specific and pressing social issues in light of financial austerity, although a number of researchers emphasize that there is much less PbR in practice than is claimed (Crowe et al. 2014; Perrin 2013). In this regard, it should be noted that most scientific attention has been devoted to linkages between PbR, social investment and impact investment. Daggers and Nicholls (2016: 69) explain the difference between these concepts:

> Impact Investing concerns the allocation of repayable capital to organizations that have the intention to create specified social or environmental impact. The focus is, therefore, mainly on the investor. Social Investments concerns providing access to repayable capital for social sector organizations (SSOs), where the providers of capital are motivated to create value or environmental impact. There is, therefore, a focus on the investee than in Impact Investing.

It is interesting to note, as affirmed in Mulgan et al. (2011: 13), that "(t)he idea of SIBs has evolved in parallel with the growth of interest in 'impact investing'. Over the last two decades a great deal of work has been done on developing new vehicles and new metrics to apply investment models to social needs. (…) The idea of SIBs has also evolved in parallel with the much longer experience of commissioning for outcomes. Many governments have wanted to be able to contract directly with private or third sector providers which could take the risk of achieving outcomes such as lower unemployment or reoffending." Similarly, Griffiths and Meinicke (2014: 6) affirm that "one of the best known forms of social investment of interest to public sector agencies and their partners is SIBs."

In the social impact investing spheres, SIB is increasingly acknowledged in both academia and public debate, and it is becoming a key point of the political agendas in many countries. Although SIBs present many common characteristics with PbRs, they each have specific features: "they involve bringing in outside (social) investors to finance the provision of the service, rather than having that burden and financial risk placed on the service provider or commissioner" (Griffiths and Meinicke 2014: 6). Therefore, in the SIB model (in contrast to a traditional PbR contract), the financial risks are not placed on the service provider or commissioner; instead, social investors finance the provision of the service (Fox and Albertson 2011; Salamon 2014).

Rizzello et al. (2016) indicated that SIBs play a key role in the social impact investing (SII) sector because they connect the three main "domains" of the SII landscape of research (sustainable finance, impact entrepreneurship and public policy in the social sector).

According to Edmiston and Nicholls (2017: 1), SIBs are "a form of payment by results but extend this by harnessing social investment from capital markets' to cover the up-front costs of service intervention" (McHugh et al. 2013; Sinclair et al. 2014; Nicholls and Tomkinson 2015). The role of private capital in outcome-based commissioning and its relation to more established forms of quasi-marketization has just recently been receiving attention in the literature (see Edmiston and Nicholls 2017). Indeed, SIB-related work is often limited to debating the theoretical aspects or to illustrating the development of the market size (see, among others, Arena et al. 2016; Brandstetter and Lehner 2015; Dear et al. 2016). Regarding the theory, the appeal of SIBs resides in the fact that "private investors can inject capital into traditionally public activities or initiatives, producing more cost-effective practices in both sectors" (Rizzello and Carè 2016).

Moreover, SIBs are considered one of the most interesting financing schemes, and they are garnering increasing attention in the new public management approach (Warner 2013) because they monetize the benefits of social interventions and transfer risks from the public sector to private-sector investors (Warner 2012). Nevertheless, a number of recent studies note problematic aspects (Roy et al. 2017; Edmiston and Nicholls 2017; Cooper et al. 2016) with regard to their possible contribution to the public sector (Warner 2012).

The various concerns about SIBs can be grouped into three main overarching themes: measurement, financialization and governance (Clifford and Jung 2016: 165). These concerns also depend on the variety and complexity of the SIB schemes. Extant literature shows that SIBs can assume various contractual (and organizational) forms:

> despite some attempts at standardization, there is no "one size fits all" formula for SIBs. While with the growing number of SIBs, certain commonalities have started to emerge (Rotheroe 2014; Tomkinson 2015), overall frameworks on SIBs are highly abstract and do not reach into underlying structures and applications required of a more detailed typology (i.e., Palandijan and Hughes 2014). To this end, appears useful to look toward the wider academic and gray literature on social entrepreneurship and social investment, of which SIBs form a part (Clifford and Jung 2016: 165–166)

The typical SIB structure always appears complex because it involves several counterparties (e.g., governments or commissioners, intermediaries, social service providers, investors), often with diverging goals (Maier and Meyer 2017) and different tolerance and preference for risks. These characteristics make SIBs hybrid financial tools, similar to some features of derivatives, bonds and/or equity (Del Giudice 2015; Maier and Meyer 2017). In addition, SIB projects have some similar attributes to Private Finance Initiative or Public Private Partnerships projects (Loxley 2013; Whitfield 2015). As stated by Schinckus (2017: 1): "although the potential of SIBs is theoretically huge, this way of financing is still contested and it does not raise real interest by private investors. This contradictory situation is mainly due to the lack of unified framework for the evaluation of these assets—for drawing the attention of private investors, it is important to explain them opportunities offered by social impact bonds in a language they are familiar with. In other words, the little interest showed by classical investors for SIBs may partly be explained by the absence of a financial formulation of aspects related to social impact bonds."

The financial and social facets of SIBs are two main relevant dimensions (Clifford and Jung 2016) that need further investigation, particularly with regard to the evaluation of risks and the assessment of outcomes. Regarding the assessment of outcomes, many questions lack adequate discussion, such as questions regarding standard impact metrics or a lack of investment track records (Evans 2013; Warner 2013). Jackson (2013) notes that as more SIBs are executed, independent evaluations of their outcomes and impacts are required. In the development of a methodologically robust evaluation model, academics and professionals identify the key driver of the development of the SIB market and indicate that further studies are needed to analyze crucial matters and technical aspects (Brandstetter and Lehner 2014; Social Impact Investment Task Force 2014; Trotta et al. 2015; Rizzello et al. 2016).

Identifying the various types of risk (related guarantee forms) and determining their interrelationship are among the main tasks of future research (Liebman 2011; Pasi 2015; Burand 2014; Maier and Meyer 2017). In summary, several SIB issues require further investigation, and many streams of research are underexplored. The evidence regarding how and whether SIBs work is also limited (Edmiston and Nicholls 2017; Ronicle et al. 2016). Therefore, an in-depth qualitative analysis of extant SIB projects in practice must be undertaken to enhance our understanding of the relationship between various counterparts—such as third-sector organizations (Tan et al. 2015) and the voluntary sector (Sheil and Breidenbach-Roe 2014)—as well as to perform a concrete outcome and risk assessment.

2.1 Understanding Risks in SIB Programmes: A Theoretical Perspective

The SIB scheme is based on the relationship between the involved parties in the commissioning and provisioning of social services (Nicholls and Tomkinson 2013; Palandijan and Hughes 2014; Arena et al. 2016) and on common interests between a wide range of stakeholders, such as governments, private organizations, investors, and financial intermediaries (Kim and Kang 2012; Nicholls and Tomkinson 2013; Arena et al. 2016; Carè 2017). An SIB involves a set of contracts (Nicholls and Tomkinson 2015; Arena et al. 2016) between a set of actors. According to Godeke and Resner (2012: 5), "a SIB is a multi-stakeholder partnership based on contracts that define the targeted outcomes, risk sharing and payment mechanisms among the partners. The government's obligation to pay SIB investors is a contractual obligation; it is distinct from a general obligation, moral obligation or revenue bond," and the contractual level represents one of the main sources of risk to be considered for the development of the market. From a contractual point of view, much of the risks in an SIB project arise from the complexity of the arrangement itself. Carè (2017) classifies the risks into three main levels: (1) the macro level, which comprises external risks; (2) the meso level, which includes risks occurring within the boundaries of the project; (3) and the micro level, which represents risks arising from the relationship between the private and public sectors. The macro level includes regulatory or policy risks that may occur when new policies and new legislation are implemented through changes in the operating setting of the SIB, such as in the case of Peterborough, where the policy reform called "Transforming Rehabilitation" caused the cancellation of the third cohort of the SIB. At the meso level, programmatic, operational and evaluation risks may occur. In particular, programmatic risks may occur when the programme does not work, as in the case of the Rikers Island SIB, where the established parameters make it very difficult to achieve substantial financial savings. Operational risks may occur when the programme is not executed as scheduled in the design phase, and evaluation risks may arise when errors occur in measuring results. Finally, partnership risks (micro level) refer to the possibility that partners do not fulfil their obligations (Carè 2017). Instead, from a portfolio perspective, Saltuk (2012: 27) emphasizes that "the types of risk that arise for impact investments are often the same risks that would arise for a traditional investment in the same sector, region or instrument." Similarly, Emerson (2012: 3) clarifies that impact investors are concerned with risks typical of traditional investments but are additionally concerned with how various aspects of risk play out within the context of impact investing. In particular, these might include the following:

- liquidity risk, which refers to the ease with which an investor may enter or leave a given investment;
- impact risk, which is related to the possibility that what may first be viewed as a good thing may actually end up being not so good;

- manager risk, which refers to shorter track records, with smaller asset bases and portfolio breadth, along with less robust compensation models, which may lead to staff turnover;
- fund development risk, which is related to the manager's ability to close a fund at scale and not get caught in stalled funds or invest in funds that are unable to deploy or are too slow in deploying the capital in suitable impact investments;
- measurement and reporting risk, which refers to the possibility that investors may be exposed to an inaccurate assessment of social and environmental impact;
- social enterprise risk, which is related to the type of underlying business venture that is linked to the investment vehicle and the level of risk it carries;
- subordinate capital risk, which refers to the possibility to rely on grants or subordinate investments from concessionary funders; and
- exit risk, which refers to the greater challenges in realizing investment returns in the future, be it through liquidity events directed to strategic buyers or through IPOs in public stock markets.

Ng et al. (2015) provide an overview of the initiatives that have been developed to address risks and to facilitate the development of the SIB ecosystem.

Reputational risk is conceived as a typology of risk that might affect the commissioner, service provider, intermediaries and social enterprises involved in the project. From the commissioner side, especially when the SIB is commissioned by a public body, reputational risk is tied to both providing services and testing a new approach (Giantris and Pinakiewicz 2013), and there are also risks associated with introducing new policies and practices. The ability to balance these risks is a key element of accessing private capital at no cost to the government until outcomes are achieved (Giantris and Pinakiewicz 2013). Moreover, from a legal point of view, governments (at federal, state or local levels) may not have the legal authority to participate in the SIB scheme as an issuer of SIB or as obligor to pay investors (Ng et al. 2015). In this sense, Ng et al. (2015: 148) clarifies that "to address both legal and reputational risks, special legislative authority, regulatory exemptions, or executive actions can be crafted for government to participate in SIB (e.g., the Massachusetts legislature created a US$ 50 million Social Innovation Financing Trust Fund in July 2012 for the state to fulfil its potential obligations in SIB transactions)." In addition, from a service provider point of view, there is the real risk of an unprepared provider compromising the organization's reputation and the programme's reputation (Giantris and Pinakiewicz 2013). Another risk factor that may affect a SIB scheme is related to the programme's ability to generate a positive impact and to be correctly implemented. Several authors (Emerson 2012; SIIT 2014; Ng et al. 2015) identify implementation and impact risks as some of the most important risks involved in implementing an SIB. It is important to understand how impact risks, which can take various forms, may influence returns (Barby and Gan 2014). A typical example is that it is possible for the programme to create positive change for its target beneficiary but a negative change for other stakeholders (Barby and Gan 2014).

3 Research Design

This work employs an exploratory and qualitative approach based on MCS. The use of a qualitative approach is not uncommon in academic work to reveal the defining features of a phenomenon (Lucas 1974; Eisenhardt 1989; Patton and Appelbaum 2003; Baxter and Jack 2008; Yin 2013), and it seems particularly useful to explore the challenges and opportunities of health impact bonds. The MCS methodology is particularly appropriate to describe complex phenomena within their contexts (Baxter and Jack 2008: 544). An MCS approach offers the ability to (1) navigate a technically distinctive situation that involves many more variables of interest than data points and (2) benefit from the prior development of theoretical propositions to guide data collection and analysis (Yin 2013). In particular, the case study methodology is considered most appropriate in the critical and early phases of a new theory, when key variables and their relationships are being explored (Eisenhardt 1989; Yin 2013). However, a lack of rigor in case studies often occurs in the early stages of the theory development process and therefore may have negative effects in the next stages, when relationships between variables are elaborated and tested (Eisenhardt and Graebner 2007). For this reason, and to ensure the reliability of our study, we designed a research protocol (Yin 2013) that defines the main sources of reliable data, the data analysis techniques, the reporting procedure and the reporting outline.

3.1 Sampling Procedure and Data Collection

In selecting our cases, we considered the following criteria: (1) scientific interest—each case highlights a specific characteristic of the phenomena; (2) transparency—only cases where there is an adequate availability of information are selected; (3) reliability and trustworthiness—only cases where there is certainty of data and information are chosen.

Our sample includes eight existing SIBs in the healthcare sector. We selected the following cases: (1) The Nurse-Family Partnership SIB (US); (2) Social Impact Bond for Prevention of Type II Diabetes (Israel); (3) The Reconnections SIB (UK); (4) The Resolve Social Benefit Bond (Aus); (5) The Heart and Stroke Social Impact Bond (Can); (6) New Zealand Social Bond pilot (New Zealand); (7) Mental Health and Employment SIB (UK); and (8) Ways to Wellness (UK). We excluded the SIBs launched in Japan in April 2017 from our sample because of a lack of data. Table 4.1 provides an overview of the selected case studies.

Table 4.1 Health impact bonds in implementation stage

	SIB name	Country	Healthcare issues
#1	New Zealand Social Bond Pilot	New Zealand	Mental health and employment
#2	The Heart and Stroke Social Impact Bond	Canada	Hypertension
#3	Social Impact Bond for Prevention of Type II Diabetes	Israel	Diabetes prevention
#4	The "Nurse-Family Partnership" SIB	South Carolina (USA)	Early childhood development
#5	Mental Health and Employment Partnership	Haringey, Staffordshire & Tower Hamlets (UK)	Mental health and employment
#6	The "Reconnections" SIB	Worcestershire (UK)	Social isolation
#7	Ways To Wellness	Newcastle	Social prescribing
#8	The Resolve Social Benefit Bond	Australia	Mental health

Source: Authors' elaboration

To confirm the validity of the process, we used multiple sources of information (Yin 2013). We drew data from multiple sources (i.e., websites, reports and secondary sources), with the main aim to increase the construct validity by encouraging convergent lines of inquiry (Yin 1994: 144).

4 The Global Social Impact Bond Market: Scenario and a Focus on Healthcare Sector

SIBs are a small part of the wider market for PbR contracts. While large private companies deliver most PbR contracts, with SIBs, impact investors pay the upfront cost of delivering a social intervention and ultimately receive a return based on the success of that intervention. The idea is that the public sector pays for the service only if the agreed-upon social outcomes are achieved. Moreover, SIBs enable social organizations to manage the financial risks associated with those PbR contracts from which they would otherwise be excluded. SIBs are a growing global phenomenon, having initially been pioneered in the United Kingdom, where the first SIB was launched in 2010. As of 30 September 2017, there are 89 SIBs worldwide. The largest market is the United Kingdom, with 33 SIBs, and the second largest is the United States, with 16; 20 more have been implemented across Europe. Figure 4.1 shows the geographical distribution of SIBs.

Based on the global impact bond online database provided by Social Finance, the total global investment raised is approximately $322 million. SIBs worldwide are currently funding activities in five main categories, and a new issue, the environmental SIB, has launched in the United States. The data per social issue are represented in Fig. 4.2.

The flexibility of SIBs and their potential as a tool for financing new and promising approaches to the challenges faced by public services are demonstrated by the variety of services funded globally through SIB contracts. Such interventions focus on interventions targeted to address different social needs, such as education for young people, employment or training, adoption, children in care and at the edge of care, homelessness,

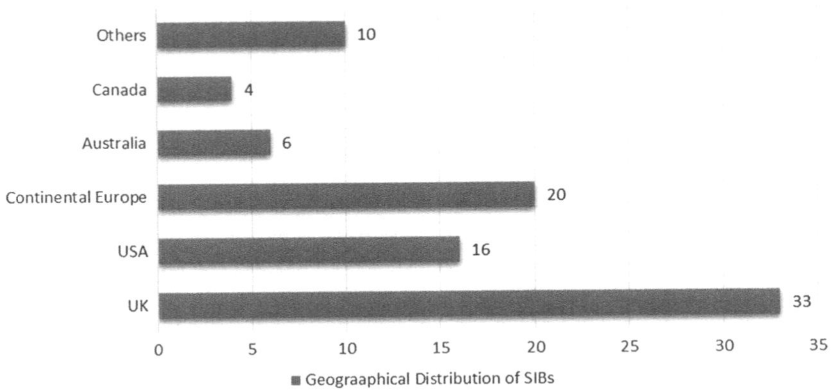

Fig. 4.1 Geographical distribution of SIBs. Source: Authors' elaboration based on Social Impact Bond online database retrieved September 30, 2017, from: www.socialfinance.org.uk/database/

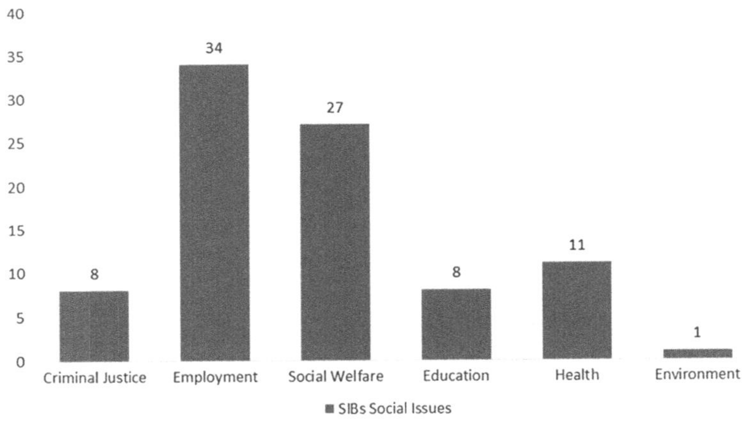

Fig. 4.2 SIBs social issues. Source: Authors' elaboration based on Social Impact Bond online database retrieved September 30, 2017, from: www.socialfinance.org.uk/database/

re-offending and patients suffering with long-term conditions. As reported by Gustafsson-Wright et al. (2015) and by Dear et al. (2016), the SIB market is now developing quickly, and there are considerable opportunities to explore SIB financing of interventions in the healthcare sector in this rapidly growing field (Tan et al. 2015; Rowe and Stephenson

2016). As reported in Fig. 4.2, the healthcare sector represents 13% of the SIBs launched to date, and as of 30 September 2017, we are aware of 36 health impact bonds worldwide, either activated or in the design/negotiation phase (see Table 4.2).

Table 4.2 Health impact bonds under implementation/design/negotiation stage

	State	Status	Intervention area
1	USA—South Carolina	Started	Pregnancy/early childhood
2	USA—California	Pilot phase concluded (under evaluation)	Asthma management
3	Israel	Started	Diabetes prevention
4	UK (New Castle)	Started	Long-term conditions
5	UK (Worcestershire)	Started	Loneliness in older people
6	UK (Manchester)	Started	Home care
7	Canada	Started	Preventing hypertension
8	Australia	Started	Mental health
9	New Zealand	Started	Mental health and employment
10	Japan	Started	Dementia prevention
11	Japan	Started	Diabetes prevention
12	Japan	Started	Cancer screening
13	USA (Connecticut)	Under design/negotiation	Substance abuse
14	USA (Michigan)	Under design/negotiation	Pregnancy
15	USA (New Mexico)	Under design/negotiation	Mental illness
16	USA (New York State)	Under design/negotiation	Maternal and child health
17	USA (Oregon)	Under design/negotiation	Long-term conditions
18	USA (Virginia)	Under design/negotiation	Pregnancy
19	UK (Sandwell)	Under design/negotiation	End-of-life patient care
20	UK (Cornwell)	Under design/negotiation	Long-term conditions
21	UK (Leeds)	Under design/negotiation	Home care
22	South Africa	Under design/negotiation	HIV prevention
23	Japan	Started (pilot phase)	Dementia prevention
24	Netherlands	Under design/negotiation	Home care
25	Brazil	Under design/negotiation	Long-term conditions
26	Cameroon	Under design/negotiation	Maternal and Infant health
27	Cameroon	Under design/negotiation	Eye health

(continued)

Table 4.2 (continued)

	State	Status	Intervention area
28	Australia	Under design/negotiation	Aged care
29	Canada	Under design/negotiation	Long-term conditions
30	Canada	Under design/negotiation	Long-term mental health
31	Canada	Under design/negotiation	Cancer coaching
32	France	Under design/negotiation	Mental health and employment
33	Uganda	Under design/negotiation	Preventing sleeping sickness
34	Mexico	Under design/negotiation	Diabetes prevention
35	India	Under design/negotiation	Maternal and infant health
36	Mozambique	Under design/negotiation	Malaria reduction

Sources: Authors' elaboration based on Tan et al. (2015), National Governors Association (2015), New Zealand Ministry of Health (2015), Nippon Foundation (2015), Harchaoui et al. (2016), Dear et al. (2016)

5 Description of Case Studies

In this section, eight SIBs under implementation worldwide in the healthcare sector are described and analyzed based on the available public data.

5.1 The Nurse-Family Partnership SIB (USA)

The Nurse Family Partnership SIB is an evidence-based community health programme that connects low-income, first-time parents with maternal and child health nurses who provide support for a healthy pregnancy, knowledgeable and responsible parenting and a strong start in infancy for children born in the State of South Carolina (US) (Milner and Eldridge 2016). In February 2016, the South Carolina Department of Health and Human Services led a state-wide expansion to include an additional 3200 first-time low-income mothers over the following four years, beyond the 1200 who had already participated in the programme (Social Finance US 2016). The BlueCross BlueShield of South Carolina Foundation, The Boeing Foundation, The Duke Endowment, Greenville County SC First Steps, Laura and John Arnold Foundation, Medicaid and a consortium of private funders funded the expansion of the programme through a pay-for-success contract. The SIB aims to improve the wider health and wellbeing of communities. It includes a randomized controlled trial to measure (1) the reduction in preterm births; (2) the reduction in child hospitalization and emergency department usage due to injury; (3) the increase in healthy spacing between births; and (4) the increase in first-time moms served in ZIP codes with high concentrations of poverty (Nurse-Family Partnership 2016). Technical details of the SIB are summarized in Table 4.3.

Social Finance US provided the programme design and support in raising capital, and it negotiated the performance management services

Table 4.3 SIB Nurse-Family Partnership (South Carolina—US)

SIB name: South Carolina Nurse-Family Partnership			
State	South Carolina (US)	Date of launch	February 2016
Duration	4 years	Service provider	Nurse Family Partnership
Investment	17,500,000 USD (BlueCross BlueShield of South Carolina Foundation, 3.5 M; The Duke Endowment, 8 M; The Boeing Company, 0.8 M; Greenville County, SC First Steps, 0.7 M; Laura and John Arnold Foundation, 0.491 M; consortium of local investors, 4 M) Additional funding provided by Medicaid of 13 M USD via a 1915 (b) Medicaid Waiver, awarded to the South Carolina Department of Health and Human Services by the federal Centers for Medicare and Medicaid Services		
Target population	3200 first-time, low-income mothers over four years		
Outcome metrics	(1) reduction in preterm births; (2) reduction in child hospitalization and emergency department usage due to injury; (3) increase in healthy spacing between births; (4) increase in first-time moms served in ZIP codes with high concentration of poverty		
Evaluation method	Randomized Controlled Trial		
Outcome payments/ returns (maximum amount eligible)	South Carolina will make up to $7.5 M in success payments		
Public savings expected (in healthcare sector)	Reduction of 25% in the healthcare cost of services for mothers and children		

Sources: Authors elaboration based on Nurse Family Partnership (2016) and Social Finance US (2016)

provided, in part, by the Harvard Kennedy School Government Performance Lab (Social Finance US 2016). The SIB investors agreed to reinvest 100% of the SIB's success payments in the Nurse-Family Partnership programme beyond the duration of the SIB. For this reason, they are defined as *philanthropic funders* and not simply as *investors* (Nurse-Family Partnership 2016).

5.2 Social Impact Bond for Prevention of Type II Diabetes (Israel)

The Israeli health system decided to extend, through the SIB model, diabetes prevention measures to 2250 Israelis at risk of type 2 diabetes (Social Finance Israel 2016). The health impact bond intends to test a preventative (and scalable) diabetes model targeting lifestyle changes for the Israeli health system. The interventions will last for two years, and programme participants will receive support for an additional three years (Social Finance Israel 2016). The technical details are illustrated in Table 4.4.

Table 4.4 Prevention of type II diabetes SIB (Israel)

SIB name: Prevention of type II diabetes			
State	Israel	Date of launch	March 2016
Duration	3 years	Service provider	Bwell
Investment	5,500,000 USD (Group of investors coordinated by UBS banking corporation)		
Target population	2250 people at risk of developing type 2 diabetes		
Outcome metrics	Proportion of the cohort that are prevented from developing type 2 diabetes compared to a control group that continues to receive the existing standard of care		
Evaluation method	Control group		
Outcome payments/ returns (maximum amount eligible)	Outcomes payments information not yet available		
Public savings expected (in healthcare sector)	An effective intervention could lead to a reduction of (not exactly estimated) of both indirect and direct non-medical costs		

Source: Authors' elaboration based on Social Finance Israel (2016) and Cohen (2016)

The outcome metric used in this SIB is focused on the proportion of each cohort (three in total) that are prevented from developing type 2 diabetes, compared with a control group that continues to receive the existing standard of care offered by their healthcare providers. If successful, a reduction in type 2 diabetic cases will generate significant savings for the Israeli Health Maintenance Organizations and the social security system of Israel (Clalit and Leumit, National Insurance Institute), which will repay the investors a pre-agreed amount (still not publicly available) for each successful case (Social Finance Israel 2016).

5.3 The Reconnections SIB (UK)

Reconnections is a new health programme that aims to address loneliness among older people living in Worcestershire and reconnecting them with interests and activities in their local community through a network of volunteers and community-based organizations (Fulton and Jupp 2015; Jopling 2015). Worcestershire County Council and the three Clinical Commissioning Groups in Worcestershire commissioned the intervention, which is funded through a SIB contract. The investors in the Reconnections SIB are Nesta Impact Investments and the Care and Wellbeing Fund. The project will measure the change in participants' loneliness using a frequently used survey, the Revised University of California Loneliness Scale (R-UCLA) (Big Society Capital 2015). The technical details are summarized in Table 4.5.

One of the innovative elements of Reconnections is the fact that an explicit aim of the service is to fund new approaches to addressing loneliness. Moreover, the Reconnections project adds to the understanding of the cost of loneliness in the United Kingdom.

5.4 The Resolve Social Benefit Bond (Australia)

In late 2015, the Australian State of New South Wales (NSW) released a request for proposals that called for innovative social impact investment proposals targeting the areas of chronic health conditions and mental health hospitalizations. In 2017, the NSW government subsequently

Table 4.5 Reconnections SIB (Worcestershire—UK)

SIB name: Reconnections			
State	Worcestershire (UK)	Date of launch	May 2015
Duration	3 years	Service provider	Age UK
Investment	850,000 GBP (Care and Wellbeing Fund Nesta Impact Investments)		
Target population	3000 people aged 50 years and older classified on the UCLA loneliness scale as 8 to 12		
Outcome metrics	The targeted outcome is the reduction in participants' loneliness score, measured using the Revised UCLA scale of loneliness		
Evaluation method	Revised UCLA scale of loneliness		
Outcome payments/ returns (maximum amount eligible)	Outcomes payments are capped to 540,000 GBP from Worcestershire CCG, to 480,000 GBP from Clinical Commissioning Group of Wyre Forest, South Worcestershire and Redditch and Bromsgrove. Further payments are available from Social Outcomes Fund and are capped to 1,000,000 GBP. Globally there is an overall cap on returns of 12%		
Public savings expected (in healthcare sector)	An effective intervention could lead to a reduction in future welfare services use of 17% for a cohort of 5000 lonely individuals		

Sources: Authors' elaboration based on Big Society Capital (2015) and Tan et al. (2015)

announced that it would proceed to negotiate the first SIB targeting the complex issue of mental health, called the Resolve Program (NSW Gov 2017). The service provider is Flourish Australia, a national leader in the employment and support of mental health peer workers (NSW Gov 2017). The key technical information is summarized in Table 4.6.

As we can observe from the information in Table 4.6, in this SIB, financial returns are of two typologies: fixed and performance related. The outcome metric used to evaluate performance is the percentage of reduction in health-related service consumption represented by the *National Weighted Activity Units* (NWAU), an activity measure for determining total health-related service consumption, which also accounts for the severity and duration of services consumed, including hospital admissions (Social Venture Australia 2017).

Table 4.6 Resolve social benefit bond (New South Wales—AUS)

SIB name: Resolve social benefit bond			
State	Australia—New South Wales	Date of launch	June 2017
Duration	8 years	Service provider	Flourish Australia
Investment	7,000,000 ASD (The 50 investors range from high-net-worth individuals and foundations to institutional investors, such as NGS Super and Grosvenor Pirie Super)		
Target population	Approximately 530 mental health patients in the Western NSW and Nepean Blue Mountains local health districts		
Outcome metrics	Percentage reduction in National Weighted Activity Units (NWAU—An activity measure for determining total health-related service consumption, which also accounts for the severity and duration of services consumed, including hospital admissions) incurred by the individuals in the programme over their two-year measurement periods relative to those incurred by a control group		
Evaluation method	Live control group		
Outcome payments/returns (maximum amount eligible)	Returns are 2% pa fixed interest payments over 4.75 years. The performance coupons will occur if the NWAU reduction is more than 17.5%. In case of success, I.R.R. p.a. range from 4% to 11% (for a NWAU reduction over 40%)		
Public savings expected (in healthcare sector)	Savings are quantified in *National Weighted Activity Units* (NWAU) reduction. In case of programme success, a minimum of a 17.5% NWAU reduction is required		

Source: Authors' elaboration based on Social Venture Australia (2017)

5.5 The Heart and Stroke Social Impact Bond (Canada)

In October 2016, the Public Health Agency of Canada (PHAC), in partnership with the Heart and Stroke Foundation and the MaRS Centre for Impact Investing, launched the first SIB in Canada. The Heart and Stroke SIB aims to fund the Community Hypertension Prevention Initiative, an evidence-based programme designed to address hypertension (high blood pressure) among seniors by improving their ability to manage their modifiable risk factors (e.g., exercise, dietary changes, smoking cessation)

(Farthing-Nichol and Jagelewski 2016). With the SIB model, governments have the potential to achieve measurable change in health outcomes that has not yet been seen through traditional funding approaches (MaRS 2017). The players involved in the SIB are The Heart and Stroke Foundation, which is responsible for achieving the outcome targets, and the PHAC will pay investors if the programme meets its targets. The MaRS Centre for Impact Investing managed the raising of capital from 10 investors. The Social Research and Demonstration Corporation will independently validate the intervention's results (Farthing-Nichol and Jagelewski 2016). The full details of this SIB are summarized in Table 4.7.

As indicated in Table 4.7, the SIB includes two payment metrics. Notably, PHAC did not select an SIB model to generate public savings. It commissioned a PFS contract with the aim to better understand the degree to which its programmes help people and to demonstrate strategies that increase the adoption of healthy habits (Farthing-Nichol and Jagelewski 2016).

Table 4.7 Hearth and stroke social impact bond (Canada)

SIB name: Hearth and stroke			
State	Canada	Date of launch	October 2016
Duration	3.5 years	Service provider	Heart and Stroke Foundation
Investment	2,000,000 CAD of capital raised (10 investors—foundations, high-net-worth individuals and companies)		
Target population	7000 pre-hypertensive older adults (60+) in Toronto and Vancouver. The SIB will also count pre-hypertensive adults 40 years and older		
Outcome metrics	Performance will be measured for an Intake Volume Metric and a Blood Pressure Metric		
Evaluation method	Live but not counterfactual methodology		
Outcome payments/returns (maximum amount eligible)	In case of success, investors will receive a maximum internal rate of return of 8.8% on their investment. Investor commitments are partially protected by a CAD 1 M outcomes payment guarantee from the PHAC as outcomes funder		
Public savings expected (in healthcare sector)	As savings did not motivate the PHAC to pay for outcomes, PHAC did not rely on those savings to assign payments		

Source: Authors' elaboration based on Farthing-Nichol and Jagelewski (2016)

5.6 New Zealand Social Bond Pilot (New Zealand)

The first proposed New Zealand social bond aims to improve employment outcomes for individuals with mental health conditions, thereby reducing welfare dependence and improving mental health outcomes (NZ Gov 2017). The service delivery started in February 2017 and will continue for five years. The target population will receive services by an experienced for-profit service provider, APM Workcare Ltd. The target for the service is for 43% of participants to obtain work, compared with the 30% target of other government contracts (NZ Treasury 2017). In Table 4.8, the key elements of the New Zealand SIB are summarized.

As reported in Table 4.8, to improve potential interest in the bonds, NZD 1.5 million of private investments see two classes of investors: those with less and more risk. Based on the case assumptions, less risky capital

Table 4.8 New Zealand social bond pilot (New Zealand)

SIB name: New Zealand social bond pilot			
State	New Zealand	Date of launch	Feb-17
Duration	5 years	Service provider	APM Workcare
Investment	1,500,000 NZD of capital raised (APM Workcare Janssen—Prospect Investment Management Limited—Wilberforce Foundation)		
Target population	1700 people with diagnosed mental health conditions		
Outcome metrics	The two metrics by which success will be measured are the percentage of people that enter employment and the extent to which employment is sustained		
Evaluation method	Validated administrative data		
Outcome payments/returns (maximum amount eligible)	The contract caps maximum potential yields at 9% for less risky capital, and 17% for more risky capital		
Public savings expected (in healthcare sector)	A conservative approach has been used for the analysis of this SIB, where savings only include the direct benefits from benefit cessation and expected income tax gains from work. Savings are only attributed during the bond's life and capped after two years' employment for any participant, so they do not include gains from those who stay in even longer-term employment		

Source: Authors' elaboration based on New Zealand Treasury (2017)

will return 7%, and riskier capital will return 13%. The contract caps the maximum potential yields at 9% and 17%, respectively (NZ Treasury 2017). Finally, the expected performance occurs when 43% of referred clients obtain employment. This compares with a condition where 10% find employment without any interventions, and a 30% target for the main comparable MSD intervention, Work-to-Wellness contracts (NZ Treasury 2017).

5.7 Mental Health and Employment Partnership SIB (UK)

Individual Placement and Support (IPS) is an evidence-based UK programme that embeds employment specialists within mental health teams (CBO 2017). The SIB mental health and employment aims to expand IPS delivery to up to 2500 people who are unemployed and are in contact with secondary mental health services (MHEP 2015), and it expects to facilitate 500–800 job placements over three years (Social Finance 2015). More technical details of this SIB are provided in Table 4.9.

The expansion of IPS delivery involves a combination of two key elements: (a) combining funding from employment and health via co-commissioning arrangements between national commissioners, such as DWP, CCGs and local authorities in different areas, and (b) a PbR mechanism to enable high-quality IPS providers to manage the financial risk of outcomes-based funding models. The mental health and employment SIB aims, therefore, to test both of these elements. To do so, the Mental Health and Employment Partnership (MEHP), intermediary Special Purpose Vehicle, has partnered with local commissioners in Haringey, Tower Hamlets and Staffordshire to secure £1.3 million of outcomes-based IPS services. In each area, the local commissioner pays for 70% of the service cost, with MHEP paying for the remaining 30%. MHEP has raised the residual impact capital from Big Issue Invest. Big Issue Invest's initial £400,000 investment is partly in the form of equity (into MEHP) and partly a loan repayable at an interest rate of 8% (CBO 2017). Over time, MHEP's investors will be repaid by the Cabinet Office and Big Lottery Fund based on achieving the pre-defined outcomes, as reported in Table 4.9.

Table 4.9 Mental health and employment SIB (United Kingdom)

SIB name: Mental health and employment partnership SIB			
State	United Kingdom	Date of launch	January 2016
Duration	3 years	Service provider	Health and employment partnership
Investment	£400,000 from Big Issue Invest		
Target population	2500 people who are out of work and in contact with a secondary mental health service (typically with a diagnosis of psychosis, such as bipolar disorder or schizophrenia, or severe depression or anxiety)		
Outcome metrics	The three metrics by which success will be measured are user engagement, job entry and job sustainment		
Evaluation method	Validated administrative data		
Outcome payments/ returns (maximum amount eligible)	The total potential outcome payments for the three contracts let to date is estimated to be ±£2.9 m		
Public savings expected (in healthcare sector)	The long-term goal of the mental health and employment SIB is to demonstrate the viability of rolling out high-quality, high-fidelity IPS services nationally. Therefore, job outcomes are the primary goals. Indirectly, support from IPS services will also enable users to recover more rapidly and effectively, enabling them to live full and fulfilling lives and reduce their use of high-cost mental health services		

Source: Authors' elaboration based on MEHP (2015), CBO (2017)

5.8 Ways to Wellness SIB (UK)

The Ways to Wellness SIB aims to add to and complement medical support with social prescribing for patients suffering from long-term conditions. It provides access to community-based activities that help them, for example, become more active, learn to eat and cook more healthily or get back to work. Ways to Wellness will run for seven years starting in 2015, and it aims to improve the health of approximately 11,000 people who have one or more long-term conditions and live in the west of Newcastle. Over time, the services should improve the quality of life for patients in the programme while also reducing the demands on the NHS primary and secondary care (Tan et al. 2015). The full details of the SIB are reported in Table 4.10.

Table 4.10 Ways to wellness SIB (United Kingdom)

SIB name: Ways to wellness SIB			
State	United Kingdom	Date of launch	March 2015
Duration	3 years	Service provider	Ways to Wellness
Investment	£1,700,000 from Bridge Ventures		
Target population	11,000 people with long-term health conditions, such as lung disease, diabetes and asthma		
Outcome metrics	The two metrics by which success will be measured are improvement in wellbeing and reduction in secondary care costs		
Evaluation method	Wellbeing is measured every six months using a "Wellbeing Star" (standard tool of measuring wellbeing). Reduction in secondary care cost is calculated by comparison with a matched cohort of similar individuals without access to social prescribing		
Outcome payments/returns (maximum amount eligible)	The total expected outcomes payments made to Ways to Wellness in its first six years of operation are £8.2 m For the first outcome, payments are contingent upon the Wellbeing Star indicators, with payments increasing incrementally up to £500 per beneficiary. The remaining payments are contingent upon reduced secondary care costs, for which the Clinical Commissioning Group (CCG) will pay a maximum of £330 per annum In case success targets are achieved, the estimated money multiple over seven years will be c.1.38 times the initial investment of Bridges Ventures		
Public savings expected (in healthcare sector)	Anticipated secondary care cost savings for the CCG: £10.8 m Estimated broader public service savings: £13.6 m		

Source: Authors' elaboration based on Tan et al. (2015), CBO (2016)

As reported in Table 4.10, payments are made based on the achievement of two primary outcomes. In the long term, 30% of outcome payments are contingent upon the achievement of the "improvement of wellbeing" outcome (CBO 2016). The "reduction of secondary care costs" outcome concerns the reduced cost of secondary healthcare services as a result of improvement in the self-management of long-term conditions. In detail, this is defined as (1) the cost of use of hospital services (reductions in GP visits are not counted because these services fall to NHS England, not the CCG), (2) planned and unplanned admissions and (3) the use of out-patient and accident and emergency services. In the long term, 70% of outcome payments are contingent upon the achievement of this outcome (Bridge Ventures 2015). Ways to Wellness represents an unprecedented case of commissioning of large-scale social prescribing to improve long-term health outcomes through the commitment of all parties to a truly innovative approach, which would have been too risky without seed funding from social investment. Moreover, it introduces an innovative linking of outcome payments to unprecedented improvements in the self-management of long-term conditions.

6 Learning from Case Studies

The case study analysis provides evidence of multiple funding designs and of innovations introduced with the launch of health impact bonds. It is important to note the different typologies of funding adopted under the profile of returns, investors, investment and metrics. A summary of key issues is reported in Table 4.11.

The profiles of the investors engaged span from "pure philanthropy oriented" (such as in the case of the Nurse-Family Partnership, where investors agreed to totally reinvest future financial returns) to "pure for-profit oriented" (such as in the case of Resolve SBB, where the 50 investors involved will receive a fixed coupon, beyond the performance-based financial returns). Furthermore, in the case of the New Zealand SIB, we found two classes of investors (and returns): less (for the capital covered by warrant) and high risk (investment not covered by guarantee). At the same time, in the Heart and Stroke SIB, we observe diversified investors with a high level of (and guaranteed) returns. The presence of a financial intermediary (UBS) is a characteristic of the Israeli SIB, while Bridges Ventures, in the Ways to Wellness SIB, plays a primary and direct role as the *prime contractor*. Moreover, in two cases, investors are also the co-founders of the total capital commitment, sharing the risks with the public actors. Guarantees for capital loss are present in the case of the Canadian SIB and, partially, in the Resolve SBB. Finally, key innovations introduced by the SIBs analyzed in the case studies can be identified in terms of (a) expansion of an evidence-based programme (with a well-

Table 4.11 Case comparison

SIB name	Objective of SIB intervention	Outcome metrics adopted	Funding
Nurse-Family Partnership (South Carolina—US)	Extension to large scale of people of an *evidence-based* programme	(1) reduction in preterm births; (2) reduction in child hospitalization and emergency department usage due to injury; (3) increase in healthy spacing between births; (4) increase in first-time moms served in ZIP codes with high concentration of poverty	(1) Total financial returns will be re-invested in the programme extension; (2) Investors are co-funders (with public authorities) of the total capital commitment
Preventing Type II Diabetes (Israel)	The expansion through the SIB of a healthcare model more effective than other traditional forms of care, because it is focused expressly on prevention but is still not widespread	Proportion of the cohort that is prevented from developing type 2 diabetes compared with a control group that continues to receive the existing standard of care	(1) Presence of a financial institution (UBS) as a fundraiser
The Reconnections (UK)	The connection of the improvement of quality of life, especially in terms of reduction of risk factors for various diseases of the elderly, with the reduction of their degree of loneliness and social isolation	The targeted outcome is the reduction in participants' loneliness score, measured using the Revised UCLA scale of loneliness	(1) Investors accepted the adoption of innovative (and, consequently, risky) outcome metrics

(*continued*)

Table 4.11 (continued)

SIB name	Objective of SIB intervention	Outcome metrics adopted	Funding
Ways to Wellness	Longer-term support for an innovative service targeted at improving the quality of life for people living with long-term conditions. In detail, social prescribing had not been done on this scale before and measured so rigorously	Improvement in wellbeing and reduction in secondary care costs	(1) Investor (Bridges Ventures) acts as the *prime contractor*, working directly with the service provider as the performance manager; (2) The role of the prime contractor represents a mitigation risk factor directly related to the adoption of a highly innovative (and risky) outcome metric
Mental Health and Employment Partnership	The long-term goal of the mental health and employment SIB is to demonstrate the viability of rolling out high-quality, high-fidelity IPS services nationally	User engagement, job entry and job sustainment	(1) Investors are co-founders (with public authorities) of the total capital commitment
New Zealand Social Bond Pilot	Improvement of the employment outcomes for those with mental health conditions, delivering reduced welfare dependence and improved mental health outcomes	The percentage of people that enter employment, and the extent to which employment is sustained	(1) Presence of two classes of investors (and financial returns): less and more risk

(*continued*)

Table 4.11 (continued)

SIB name	Objective of SIB intervention	Outcome metrics adopted	Funding
Hearth and Stroke SIB	Through the Heart and Stroke contract, commissioner hopes to demonstrate strategies that increase the adoption of healthy habits	Intake Volume Metric and a Blood Pressure Metric	(1) Presence of full guarantee for the investment; (2) Even if investment receives total protection, there is an expected return over the medium market rate (8.8%)
Resolve SBB	The Resolve SBB is expected to improve the mental health and wellbeing of participants, while generating significant savings for the state through a reduction in participants' utilization of health and other services, in particular by reducing the number of days spent in the hospital	Percentage reduction in NWAU	(1) Diversified typology of financial returns (fixed coupon beyond performance-based returns); (2) Partial guarantee for capital loss

Source: Authors' elaboration

known positive impact evaluation) and (b) new approaches/policies to address health outcomes that present different levels of (social) risk accepted by SIB investors. Outcome metrics identified reflect this dichotomy. For example, the "increase in wellbeing" outcome in the case of Ways to Wellness, as measured through the Wellbeing Star, or the decrease in loneliness scores, as measured by the UCLA loneliness scale, represent highly innovative outcomes adapted to highly innovative (and riskier) interventions.

7 Reflection and Suggestions for Ways Forward

The analysis of SIBs in this study suggests further considerations beyond those related to the lessons learned, as described in Sect. 6. First, the relatively restricted number of SIBs (11 compared with 89 implemented) now running in the healthcare sector reveals some degree of complexity in designing the types of interventions in this sector that are able to be implemented under a PbR contract. On the other hand, their integration under a SIB contract permits the introduction of high-potential prevention policies, thanks to the intervention of impact investors that bear the risks of the non-achievement of the targeted social outcomes. Furthermore, as suggested by Edmiston and Nicholls (2017), an in-depth analysis of such instruments is still lacking; when such an analysis is conducted, it reveals technical differences from the standardized model proposed by the academic literature on SIBs. Such divergences can be connected to the national peculiarities of the financial and provider markets, the type of intervention funded and, finally, on the limitations provided by national laws.

An enabling legal and policy environment is important for SIB development. A government can create a conducive ecosystem for SIBs by introducing support for a particular service in a policy framework or a strategy document. For instance, the United Kingdom, which has issued the majority of SIBs, has one of the most developed ecosystems. The Centre for Social Impact Bonds has been established in the Prime

Minister's Cabinet Office as part of the Social Investment Finance Team, and it launched the Social Outcomes Fund in November 2012, with 20 million GBP available for SIBs. In 2014, it also introduced legislation providing tax relief that applies to SIBs. Additionally, in Australia, in the state of NSW, the Social Impact Investment Policy was implemented in 2015.

As stated previously, a good SIB ecosystem also requires an enabling regulatory framework, if we consider that regulation impacts the activities of all stakeholders engaged in an SIB mechanism: government authorities, investors, intermediaries, and service providers. In the United States, for example, a specific normative and budgeting innovation was tested before the implementation of the SIBs in the country. For these reasons, future investigations are needed to explore the existing best practices in regulatory and risk-sharing frameworks. This study contributes to enriching the empirical evidence on SIB experiences but is still too limited to conclusively confirm the main narrative evidenced by Fraser et al. (2016) and Edmiston and Nicholls (2017).

Empirical evidence could be enriched by studies using interviews and questionnaires with the stakeholders involved in SIB programmes. The analysis performed in this work gives preliminary insight regarding the viability of such instruments in Italy.

Regarding the Italian context, one the barriers evidenced by early studies exploring the application of SIBs found a common opinion regarding the legal barriers to SIB development. In particular, limitations due to the market, public budgeting and commissioning have been well evidenced, respectively, by Bengo and Calderini (2016), Del Giudice (2015) and Dal Maso et al. (2013). In SIBs, the presence of operational risk bearing from investors distinguishes them from the legal concept of the "provision of service." Therefore, SIBs under Italian law could be tested more efficiently, in accordance with public accounting and public contracts laws.

The commissioning of an SIB could be related to public cost savings as well as to the introduction of innovation in public welfare policies. To achieve this objective, the engagement of third-sector organizations remains crucial.

8 A Focus on an Italian Legislative Framework for the Development of PbR

Potentially applicable regulations could result from the New Italian Public Procurement Code, contained in the Legislative Decree n. 50/2016, implementing European Parliament and Council Directives 2014/23/EU, 2014/24/EU e 2014/25/EU.

In particular, article 20 of Legislative Decree n. 50/2016 could be applied; this provides, with regard to public works carried out at the expense of private works, that the code does not apply if a public authority concludes an agreement by which a public or a private entity is committed to achieve, in its total care and with all necessary permits, a public work or a part of this, as provided by urban planning tools or programmes (without prejudice to article 80).

Before the agreement is signed, the public authority evaluates whether the project to be performed (with details about the deadline by which they must be completed and the scheme of procurement contracts proposed by the counterparty) is respondent to the implementation of public works. The agreement should also regulate the consequences in case of a breach of contract, including contractual penalties and substitution powers.

Article 35 of Legislative Decree n. 50/2016 states that provisions of the code shall apply to public contracts whose amount, excluding VAT, is equal to or greater than € 750,000,00 for social services procurement (and other specific services listed in Annex IX).

Legislative Decree n. 50/2016 provides different arrangements for the publication of notices (article 142) and, furthermore, the possibility of awarding the contract exclusively to third-sector organizations (article 143).

More specifically, the procuring entities may be reserved for certain organizations that have certain requirements, which give them the right to participate in competitions organized for the award of public procurement in healthcare, social and cultural services, but these awards must meet all the following conditions:

1. the organizations have the statutory objective of pursuing a public service mission linked to the provision of the services covered by the award;
2. the organizations' profits are re-invested to achieve the statutory objective (if profits are distributed or redistributed, this should be based on participative considerations);
3. the management or ownership structures of the organization performing the contract are based on employee ownership or participatory principles or require the active participation of employees, users or stakeholders;
4. the organization has not been awarded a contract for the services concerned by the contracting authority concerned pursuant to this article within the past three years.
5. The contract shall not exceed three years.

In addition to the procedures governed by the code, the following additional methods may be useful:

- authorization/accreditation (ANAC Decision n. 966/2016);
- co-design (ANAC Decision n. 32/2016, law n. 328/2000; Prime Minister's Decree dated 30 March 2001) as a functional form to solve "specific social issues" with "innovative and experimental" measures;
- direct agreements with associations.

Therefore, following these regulations, the SIB's contractual terms may be defined according to each concrete social situation connected to a SIB. In this respect, the issue of controls is important and worthy of adequate analysis, also through the formulation of proposals for possible legal provisions. As this last point is important, slightly more detail is provided in the following subsection.[1]

[1] With regard to Sects. 8.1 and 9, the author would like to express gratitude for the discussions, inspiration, valuable contributions and participation of Dr. Valentina Pupo and Dr Andrea Lollo, Department of Legal, Historical, Economic and Social Science, University Magna Graecia of Catanzaro (Italy).

8.1 Control Activities

Controls should be considered both in terms of the Public Administration's (PA) vigilance to ensure the quality standards of services provided to users (Blasini 2015) and in terms of the wider monitoring of the entire public/private collaboration mechanism that would be implemented. The aim of this is twofold: on the one hand, it aims to constantly monitor the activity of providers identified on a case-by-case basis (Fiorentino 2013; Blasini 2015), since it is a PA's task to care for public interests, providing the indispensable sanctions and necessary substitution mechanisms useful to address possible cases of default. On the other hand, it aims to prevent and, where appropriate, adequately penalize possible forms of corruption and criminal infiltrations that might interest the collaborative formulas and public/private partnerships set up.

9 Conclusions

The application of PbR logics has been explored in the context of the innovative financial instruments represented in SIBs. The involvement of social investors constitutes a characteristic that distinguishes such instruments from classic PbR schemes. The focus on social outcomes represents a further element of distinctiveness. The peculiarities of SIBs emerged from the in-depth analysis conducted through an MCS analysis, and the study of single SIBs revealed a need for more empirical research in this direction. Differences in funding schemes, outcome metric designs and risk-sharing models outlined in the analysis reveal a series of research questions that could be useful to investigate in the future, not only to improve the academic debate on such contractual schemes but also to provide robust frameworks to public commissioners and specialized intermediaries for more adherent SIB designs.

With regard to applying such an instrument in Italy, the lesson learned through the analysis led us to hypothesize on the legal nature of SIBs within the Italian law system. Furthermore, it is important to highlight how the use of such innovative social finance instruments poses new research questions on the nexus between social finance and public finance. At the same time, it is conducive to more general considerations regarding the empowerment of the Italian non-profit sector to engage in more impactful and sustainable public partnership experiences.

Additionally, the Public Procurement Code, Legislative Decree n. 112/2017 (Discipline on Social Enterprise) and Legislative Decree n. 117/2017 (Third Sector Code) have been enforced, both implementing law n. 106/2016.

All these regulations, which aim to regulate social services in a context where economic and financial resources are lacking, could allow third-sector organizations to enhance their structures and realize their activities efficiently and effectively, thus playing an important role regulated by the SIB's contractual terms.

Finally, the role of local governments (such as administrative regions), given their proximity to local communities, could permit the identification of specific and more urgent social interventions, minimizing the dispersal of valuable resources and testing modern and innovative solutions, according to efficiency and effectiveness principles that inspire public action. As indicated by both constitutional and accounting jurisprudence, the matter of awarding public services to private individuals must be constantly inspired by the binding principles of legality and the good performance of administrative action. Moreover, that perspective would enable the concrete implementation of the subsidiarity principle set out in article 118 of the Italian Constitution, particularly in its horizontal connotation.

Acknowledgment The authors express their gratitude to the editors—Professor Mario La Torre and Professor Mario Calderini—for the opportunity to contribute to this book. They also wish to extend their gratitude to anonymous reviewers for their useful contributions and comments.

References

Abbott, T., White, S. M., & Pandit, J. J. (2011). Factors affecting the profitability of surgical procedures under 'payment by results'. *Anaesthesia, 66*(4), 283–292.

Appleby, J., Harrison, T., Hawkins, L., & Dixon, A. (2012). *Payment by results: How can payment systems help to deliver better care*. London: The Kings Fund.

Arena, M., Bengo, I., Calderini, M., & Chiodo, V. (2016). Social impact bonds: Blockbuster or flash in a pan? *International Journal of Public Administration*. https://doi.org/10.1080/01900692.2015.1057852.

Barby, G., & Gan, J. (2014). *Shifting the lens: A de-risking toolkit for impact investment*. Retrieved from http://www.trilincglobal.com/wp-content/uploads/2014/01/BV_BoA_de-risking_report_FINAL-2.pdf.

Baumol, W. J. (1975). Payment by performance in rail passenger transportation: An innovation in Amtrak's operations. *The Bell Journal of Economics, 6*(1), 281–298.

Baxter, P., & Jack, S. (2008). Qualitative case study methodology: Study design and implementation for novice researchers. *The Qualitative Report, 13*(4), 544–559.

Bengo, I., & Calderini, M. (2016). New development: Are social impact bonds (SIBs) viable in Italy? A new roadmap. *Public Money & Management, 36*(4), 303–306.

Big Society Capital. (2015). *Worcestershire awards UK's first innovative contract to tackle loneliness*. Press release. Retrieved from http://www.bigsocietycapital.com/sites/default/files/pdf/15.07.15%20Worcestershire%20awards%20UK's%20first%20innovative%20contract%20to%20tackle%20loneliness.pdf.

Blasini, A. (2015). *Nuove forme di amministrazione pubblica per negozio: I "social impact bonds"*, in Riv, Trim. di Diritto Pubblico, fasc.1, 2015, pag. 69.

Brandstetter, L., & Lehner, O. M. (2014). *Impact investment portfolios: Including social risks and returns*. Retrieved from https://papers.ssrn.com/sol3/papers.cfm?abstract_id=2519671.

Brandstetter, L., & Lehner, O. M. (2015). Opening the market for impact investments: The need for adapted portfolio tools. *Entrepreneurship Research Journal, 5*(2), 87–107.

Bridge Ventures. (2015). *Bridges commits £1.65m to first active social impact bond in the UK healthcare sector*. Press release. Retrieved from http://www.bridges-fundmanagement.com/bridges-commits-1-65m-first-active-social-impact-bond-uk-healthcare-sector/.

Burand, D. (2014). Globalizing social finance: How social impact bonds and social impact performance guarantees can scale development. *New York University Journal of Law and Business, 9*(2013), 447–502.

Carè, R. (2017). *Social impact bond: Beyond financial innovation*. Retrieved from https://papers.ssrn.com/sol3/papers.cfm?abstract_id=3030586.
Clifford, J., & Jung, T. (2016). Social impact bonds: Exploring and understanding an emerging funding approach. In O. M. Lehner (Ed.), *Routledge handbook of social and sustainable finance*. London: Routledge.
Clist, P., & Dercon, S. (2014). 12 principles for payment by results (PbR) in international development. *DFID Research for Development*. London: DFID.
Clist, P., & Verschoor, A. (2014). *The conceptual basis of payment by results*. Retrieved from https://www.gov.uk/dfid-research-outputs/the-conceptual-basis-of-payment-by-results#links.
Commissioning Better Outcomes (CBO). (2016). *Ways to wellness social impact bond: The UK's first health SIB*. Retrieved from http://vonne.us7.list-manage2.com/track/click?u=a106ebd5a965a1bdb55f8446e&id=6cff44fb88&e=e3cd771f75.
Commissioning Better Outcomes (CBO). (2017). *Mental health and employment partnership – In depth review*. Retrieved from https://www.biglotteryfund.org.uk/-/media/Files/Programme%20Documents/Commissioning%20Better%20Outcomes/comissioning_better_outcomes_in_depth_review.pdf.
Cooper, C., Graham, C., & Himick, D. (2016). Social impact bonds: The securitization of the homeless. *Accounting, Organizations and Society, 55*, 63–82.
Cohen, T. (2016). *RPT-Israel launches first social impact bond to prevent diabetes*. Retrieved from http://www.reuters.com/article/israel-diabetes-bonds-idUSL5N16M3NH.
Crowe, D., Gash, T., & Kippin, H. (2014). Beyond big contracts. *Institute for government*. http://www.instituteforgovernment.org.uk/sites/default/files/publications/Beyond% 20Big% 20Contra cts.pdf.
Daggers, J., & Nicholls, A. (2016). Academic research into social investment and impact investing: The status quo and future research. In O. M. Lehner (Ed.), *Routledge handbook of social and sustainable finance*. London: Routledge.
Dal Maso, D., Zanoni, D., & Boccia, M. (2013). *I social impact bond: La finanza al servizio dell'innovazione sociale?* "Quaderni dell'Osservatorio" n. 11.
Dear, A., Helbitz, A., Khare, R., Lotan, R., Newman, J., Sims, G. C., et al. (2016). Social impact bonds: The early years. *Social Finance*, July. Retrieved from http://socialfinance.org/content/uploads/2016/07/SIBs-Early-Years_Social-Finance_2016_Final.pdf.
Del Giudice, A. (2015). I social impact bond. *Franco Angeli*.

Di Raimo, R., & Mignone, P. (2017). Strumenti di finanziamento al terzo settore e politiche di intervento locale nella società inclusiva europea. Dalla filantropia alla finanza alternativa. Giustizia Civile 1/2017.

Edmiston, D., & Nicholls, A. (2017). Social impact bonds: The role of private capital in outcome-based commissioning. *Journal of Social Policy*, 1–20. https://doi.org/10.1017/S0047279417000125.

Eisenhardt, K. M. (1989). Building theories from case study research. *Academy of Management Review, 14*(4), 532–550.

Eisenhardt, K. M., & Graebner, M. E. (2007). Theory building from cases: Opportunities and challenges. *Academy of Management Journal, 50*(1), 25–32.

Emerson, J. (2012). *Risk, return and impact: Understanding diversification and performance within an impact investing portfolio*. Retrieved from http://www.impactassets.org/files/downloads/ImpactAssets_IssueBriefs_2.pdf.

Evans, M. (2013). Meeting the challenge of impact investing: How can contracting practices secure social impact without sacrificing performance? *Journal of Sustainable Finance & Investment, 3*(2), 138–154.

Farr, M. (2016). Co-production and value co-creation in outcome-based contracting in public services. *Public Management Review, 18*(5), 654–672.

Farrar, S., Yi, D., Sutton, M., Chalkley, M., Sussex, J., & Scott, A. (2009). Has payment by results affected the way that English hospitals provide care? Difference-in-differences analysis. *BMJ, 339*, b3047.

Farthing-Nichol, D., & Jagelewski, A. (2016). *Pioneering pay-for-success in Canada: A new way to pay for social progress*. Retrieved from https://www.marsdd.com/wp-content/uploads/2016/10/MaRS-Pioneering-Pay-For-Success-In-Canada-Oct2016.pdf.

Fiorentino, L. (2013). I corpi tecnici nelle amministrazioni: Problemi attuali. *Rivista Trimestrale di Diritto Pubblico, 2*, 479–487.

Fulton, L., & Jupp, B. (2015). *Investing to tackle loneliness: A discussion paper*. London: Social Finance.

Fox, C., & Albertson, K. (2011). Payment by results and social impact bonds in the criminal justice sector: New challenges for the concept of evidence-based policy? *Criminology and Criminal Justice, 11*(5), 395–413.

Fraser, A., Tan, S., Lagarde, M., & Mays, N. (2016). Narratives of promise, narratives of caution: A review of the literature on social impact bonds. *Social Policy & Administration*. https://doi.org/10.1111/spol.12260.

Giantris, K., & Pinakiewicz, B. (2013). Pay for success-understanding risk trade-offs. *Community Development Investment Review, 9*(1), 35–39.

Godeke, S., & Resner, L. (2012). *Building a healthy & sustainable social impact bond market: The investor landscape*. New York: Godeke Consulting. Retrieved from https://thegiin.org/knowledge/publication/building-a-healthy-sustainable-social-impact-bond-market-the-investor-landscap.

Griffiths, A., & Meinicke, C. (2014). *Introduction to social impact bonds and early intervention*. London: Early Intervention Foundation. Retrieved from http://cdn.basw.co.uk/upload/basw_42717-3.pdf.

Gustafsson-Wright, E., Gardiner, S., & Putcha, V. (2015). *The potential and limitations of impact bonds: Lessons from the first five years of experience worldwide*. Global Economy and Development at Brookings. Retrieved from https://www.brookings.edu/wp-content/uploads/2016/07/Impact-Bondsweb.pdf.

Harchaoui, S., van der Meer, D., & Zafar, S. (2016). *Health impact bond*. Amsterdam: Society Impact. Retrieved from http://www.societyimpact.nl/wp-content/uploads/2016/02/Society-Impact-Health-Impact-Bond.pdf.

Heywood, J. S., Siebert, W. S., & Wei, X. (1997). Payment by results systems: British evidence. *British Journal of Industrial Relations, 35*(1), 1–22.

Jackson, E. T. (2013). Evaluating social impact bonds: Questions, challenges, innovations, and possibilities in measuring outcomes in impact investing. *Community Development, 44*(5), 608–616.

Jopling, K. (2015). *Promising approaches to reducing loneliness and isolafion in later life*. London: Age UK. Retrieved from https://www.campaigntoendloneliness.org/wp-content/uploads/Promising-approaches-to-reducing-loneliness-and-isolation-in-later-life.pdf.

Karanikolos, M., Mladovsky, P., Cylus, J., Thomson, S., Basu, S., Stuckler, D., et al. (2013). Financial crisis, austerity, and health in Europe. *The Lancet, 381*(9874), 1323–1331.

Kim, J., & Kang, S. (2012). CSO-state partnerships and social finance: Smart social capital and shared incentives towards public-private partnership efficiency using social impact bonds. *International Studies Review, 13*(2), 53–86.

Klein, R. (2006). The troubled transformation of Britain's national health service. *The New England Journal of Medicine, 355*(4), 409–415.

Lancefield, D., & Gagliardi, C. (2016, September). What to know before you sign a payment -by-results contract. *Harvard Business Review*, Retrieved from https://hbr.org/2016/09/what-to-know-before-you-sign-a-payment-by-results-contract

Leibenstein, H. (1966). Allocative efficiency vs. "X-efficiency". *The American Economic Review, 56*, 392–415.

Liebman, J. (2011). *Social impact bonds: A promising new financial model to accelerate social innovation and improve government performance*. Washington, DC: Center for American Progress. Retrieved from https://cdn.americanprogress.org/wp-content/uploads/issues/2011/02/pdf/social_impact_bonds.pdf.

Loxley, J. (2013, January). *Social impact bonds*. Canadian Centre for Policy Analysis Review: Economic and Social Trends. Retrieved from https://www.policyalternatives.ca/sites/default/files/uploads/publications/Manitoba%20Office/2013/01/CCPA%20Review%20Social%20Impact%20Bonds_0.pdf.

Lucas, W. A. (1974). *The case survey method: Aggregating case experience*. Santa Monica, CA: Rand.

Maier, F., & Meyer, M. (2017). Social impact bonds and the perils of aligned interests. *Administrative Sciences, 7*(3), 24.

MaRS Centre for Impact Investing (MaRS). (2017). *Canada's first social impact bond in healthcare*. Retrieved from https://impactinvesting.marsdd.com/chpi/.

Martin, M. (2015). Building impact businesses through hybrid financing. *Entrepreneurship Research Journal, 5*(2), 109–126.

Mason, P., Fullwood, Y., Singh, K., & Battye, F. (2015). *Payment by results: Learning from the literature*. Birmingham: ICF International.

McHugh, N., Sinclair, S., Roy, M., Huckfield, L., & Donaldson, C. (2013). Social impact bonds: A wolf in sheep's clothing? *Journal of Poverty and Social Justice, 21*(3), 247–257.

MHEP, Mental Health and Employment Partnership. (2015). Mental health and employment social impact bond. Retrieved from http://www.socialfinance.org.uk/wp-content/uploads/2016/04/MHEP-SIB-Summary-vfinal.pdf .

Milner, J., & Eldridge, M. (2016). *From evidence to outcomes: Using evidence to inform pay for success project design*. Retrieved from https://www.urban.org/research/publication/evidence-outcomes-using-evidence-inform-pay-success-project-design.

Mulgan, G., Reeder, N., Aylott, M., & Bo'sher, L. (2011). *Social impact investment: The challenge and opportunity of social impact bonds*. London: The Young Foundation.

National Governors Association. (2015). *Social impact bonds for public health programs: An overview*. Retrieved from http://www.nga.org/files/live/sites/NGA/files/pdf/2015/1508SocialImpactBondsPublicHealthPrograms.pdf.

New South Wales Governement (NSW Gov). (2017). *Resolve social benefit bond: Australian first social impact investment to improve mental health outcomes*. Press release. Retrieved from http://osii.nsw.gov.au/news/2017/05/05/resolve-social-benefit-bond-australian-first-social-impact-investment-to-improve-mental-health-outcomes/.

New Zealand Governement (NZ Gov). (2017, February 21). *First social bond to focus on mental health*.

New Zealand Ministry of Health. (2015). *Potential social impact bond – Improving mental health through supported employment*. Retrieved from http://www.health.govt.nz/our-work/preventative-health-wellness/social-bonds-new-zealand-pilot/potential-social-bond-improving-mental-health-through-supported-employment.

New Zealand Treasury (NZ Treasury). (2017). *Social bonds information release*. Retrieved from www.treasury.govt.nz/publications/informationreleases/socialbonds.

Ng, A., Mirakhor, A., & Ibrahim, M. H. (2015). Risk sharing and social impact partnerships. In *Social capital and risk sharing* (pp. 133–156). Palgrave Macmillan US.

Nicholls, A., & Tomkinson, E. (2013). *The Peterborough pilot social impact bond*. University of Oxford: Saïd Business School.

Nicholls, A., & Tomkinson, E. (2015). Risk and return in social finance: 'I am the market'. In A. Nicholls, R. Paton, & J. Emerson (Eds.), *Social finance*. Oxford: Oxford University Press.

Nippon Foundation. (2015 April, 14). *Exploring "Social Impact Bond" structure in Japan*. Press Release.

Nurse-Family Partnership. (2016). *Gov. Nikki Haley launches landmark "pay for success" project to improve maternal and child health, increase government accountability*. Press release. Retrieved from http://www.nursefamilypartnership.org/getattachment/home/SC-Pay-for-Success-Press-Release-final-for-NFP-website.pdf.aspx.

Olsen, I. T. (2011). *Result-based financing in the health sector: Experiences from Norway and from low-income Countries*. Internal Norad Document.

Palandijan, T., & Hughes, J. (2014). *A strong field framework for SIBs*. Stanford Social Innovation Review. Retrieved from http://www.ssireview.org/blog/entry/a_strong_field_frame work_for_sibs.

Pasi, G. (2015). Challenges for European welfare systems: A research agenda on social impact bonds. *Review of Applied Socio-Economic Research, 8*(2), 141–151.

Patton, E., & Appelbaum, S. H. (2003). The case for case studies in management research. *Management Research News, 26*(5), 60–71.

Perrin, B. (2013, January). *Evaluation of payment by results: Current approaches, future need.* Working Paper, DFID. Retrieved from https://www.gov.uk/government/uploads/system/uploads/attachment_data/file/213938/payment-results-current-approaches-future-needs.pdf.

Rizzello, A., & Carè, R. (2016). Insight into the social impact bond market: An analysis of investors. *ACRN Oxford Journal of Finance and Risk Perspective, 5*(3), 145–171.

Rizzello, A., Migliazza, M. C., Carè, R., & Trotta, A. (2016). Social impact investing: A model and research agenda. In O. M. Lehner (Ed.), *Routledge handbook of social and sustainable finance.* London: Routledge.

Ronicle, J., Fox, T., & Stanworth, N. (2016). Commissioning better outcomes fund evaluation: Update report. N.d.: Big Lottery Fund, ATQ Consultants, Ecorys.

Rotheroe, A. (2014). *Lessons and opportunities: Perspectives from providers of social impact bonds.* London: New Philanthropy Capital.

Rowe, R., & Stephenson, N. (2016). Speculating on health: Public health meets finance in 'health impact bonds'. *Sociology of Health & Illness, 38*(8), 1203–1216.

Roy, M. J., McHugh, N., & Sinclair, S. (2017). Social impact bonds: Evidence based policy or ideology? In B. Greve (Ed.), *Handbook of social policy evaluation* (pp. 263–278). Cheltenham: Edward Elgar.

Salamon, L. M. (2014). *New frontiers of philanthropy.* Jossey Bass Wiley.

Saltuk, Y. (2012). *A portfolio approach to impact investment: A practical guide to building, analyzing and managing a portfolio of impact investments.* JP Morgan. Retrieved from https://www.jpmorganchase.com/corporate/socialfinance/document/121001_A_Portfolio_Approach_to_Impact_Investment.pdf.

Schinckus, C. (2017). The valuation of social impact bonds: An introductory perspective with the Peterborough SIB. *Research in International Business and Finance.* Retrieved July 13, 2017, from https://doi.org/10.1016/j.ribaf.2017.07.126.

Sheil, F., & Breidenbach-Roe, R. (2014, April). *Payment by results and the voluntary sector.* London: NCVO.

Sinclair, S., McHugh, N., Huckfield, L., Roy, M., & Donaldson, C. (2014). Social impact bonds: Shifting the boundaries of citizenship. In K. Farnsworth, Z. Irving, & M. Fenger (Eds.), *Social policy review 26: Analysis and debate in social policy* (p. 119). Bristol: Policy Press.

Social Finance. (2015). *Social Finance launches 2 new social impact bonds for vulnerable young people and people with mental health issues*. Press release. Retrieved from http://www.socialfinance.org.uk/wp-content/uploads/2015/03/Teens-and-Toddlers-and-HEP-release2.pdf.

Social Finance Israel. (2016). *Israel leads the way in introducing a social impact bond for prevention of type II diabetes*. Press release.

Social Finance US. (2016). *Pay for success in South Carolina and Connecticut*. Press release.

Social Impact Investment Taskforce. (2014). *Measuring impact: Subject paper of the Impact Measurement Working Group*. London: Social Impact Investment Taskforce.

Social Venture Australia. (2017). *Resolve social benefit bond, information memorandum*. Retrieved from http://www.socialventures.com.au/assets/Resolve-SBB-IM-web.pdf.

Tan, S., Fraser, A., Giacomantonio, C., Kruithof, K., Sim, M., Lagarde, M., et al. (2015). An evaluation of social impact bonds in health and social care: Interim report. *Policy Innovation Research Unit (PIRU)*. Retrieved from http://www.piru.ac.uk/assets/files/Trailblazer%20SIBs%20interim%20report%20March%202015,%20for%20publication%20on%20PIRU%20siteapril%20amendedpdf11may.pdf.

Thierry, H. (1987). Payment by results systems: A review of research 1945–1985. *Applied Psychology, 36*(1), 91–108.

Tomkinson, E. (2015). *Social impact bonds*. Retrieved June 30, 2015, from http://emmatomkinson.com/category/social-impact-bonds/.

Tomlinson, H. (2000). Payment by results? *Management in Education, 14*(2), 11–14.

Trotta, A., Carè, R., Severino, R., Migliazza, M. C., & Rizzello, A. (2015). Mobilizing private finance for public good: Challenges and opportunities of social impact bonds. *European Scientific Journal – ISSN* (print) 1857–7881 ISSN (online) 1857–7431.

Udal, J. P. (1924). Payment by results. *Proceedings of the Institution of Mechanical Engineers, 106*(1), 437–452.

Warner, M. (2012, September). Profiting from public value? The case of social impact bonds. In *Conference creating public value in a multi-sector, shared-power world* (pp. 20–22). Minneapolis: University of Minnesota.

Warner, M. E. (2013). Private finance for public goods: Social impact bonds. *Journal of Economic Policy Reform, 16*(4), 303–319.

Webster, R. (2016). *Payment by results: Lessons from the literature*. Retrieved from http://russellwebster.com/Lessons%20from%20the%20Payment%20by%20Results%20literature%20Russell%20Webster%202016.pdf.

Whitfield, D., (2015). *Alternative to private finance of the welfare state: A global analysis of social impact bond, pay-for-success & development impact bond projects*. Adelaide: University of Adelaine, Australian Workplace Innovation and Social Research Centre and European Services Strategy Unit. Retrieved from https://www.european-services-strategy.org.uk/wp-content/uploads/2015/09/alternative-to-private-finance-of-the-welfare-state.pdf.

Wong, J., Ortmann, A., Motta, A., & Zhang, L. (2016). Understanding social impact bonds and their alternatives: An experimental investigation. In *Experiments in organizational economics* (pp. 39–83). Emerald Group Publishing Limited.

Yin, R. (1994). *Case study research: Design and methods*. Beverly Hills, CA: Sage Publications.

Yin, R. K. (2013). *Case study research: Design and methods*. Thousand Oaks: Sage Publications.

5

Impact Investing Innovation: Bringing Together Public, Private and Third Sectors to Create Greater Value: The Case of the Public Private Partnership Initiative for the New Public Hospital of Treviso

Filippo Addarii, Fiorenza Lipparini, and Francesca Medda

1 The Case: Impact Investing Strategy in the PPP for the New Hospital of Treviso

The Public Private Partnership (PPP) for the new hospital of Treviso (Italy) is the first case in Europe of a large infrastructural project in which social impact investing principles have been applied to the design of the project financing, construction and operation phases of the

Our most sincere thanks for the support of our research to Lendlease Italy, the European-funded project Dolfins, and Regione Veneto's ULSS2 Marca Trevigiana.

F. Addarii (✉) • F. Lipparini
PlusValue, London, UK

F. Medda
QASER Laboratory, University College London, London, UK

M. La Torre, M. Calderini (eds.), *Social Impact Investing Beyond the SIB*, Palgrave Studies in Impact Finance, https://doi.org/10.1007/978-3-319-78322-2_5

development (Santarelli and EIB 2017). The chapter starts presenting the PPP structure and the impact investing strategy giving the reader the essential background information. Then the 'Shared Value' theory (Porter and Kramer 2011) is employed to analyse the achievements of this project against an international trend fostering a transformation of capitalism towards a new relationship with society and value creation beyond a restrictive interpretation as shareholders' interests. The 'Shared Value' theory captures a trend within the private sector and paves the way for a better alignment between public and private interests and, therefore, it helps to assess the value of the Treviso project and the original contribution of its analysis. On the other hand, this case provides evidence that 'Shared Value', despite having a fruitful intuition at its core, is still a work in progress and requires deeper research as well as innovation in the practice. The theory has been rightly criticised for its reductionist interpretation of the relationship between business and society (Crane et al. 2014).

The authors of the chapter have been directly involved in assisting the private sector partner of the PPP in devising the impact investing strategy of the project and its implementation. This gives a unique vantage point in the analysis of the case that brings together research and practice, and contributes to the advancement of the impact investing field both in practice and policy.

1.1 PPP for the New Hospital in Treviso

In December 2015, the concession contract for the new hospital of Treviso was awarded to Ospedal Grando S.p.A. (OG), the Special Purpose Vehicle (SPV) established by Lendlease (through its subsidiary Finanza e Progetti) together with other financial and industrial partners (for a more in-depth overview, see Fig. 5.1). Lendlease is an Australian multinational corporation specialised in urban regeneration and infrastructural projects. It is a developer and investor that designs, finances and manages its projects in partnership with public institutions.

Treviso is a prosperous town in Veneto (northeast of Italy) and an industrial hub hosting international brands like Benetton and Geox,

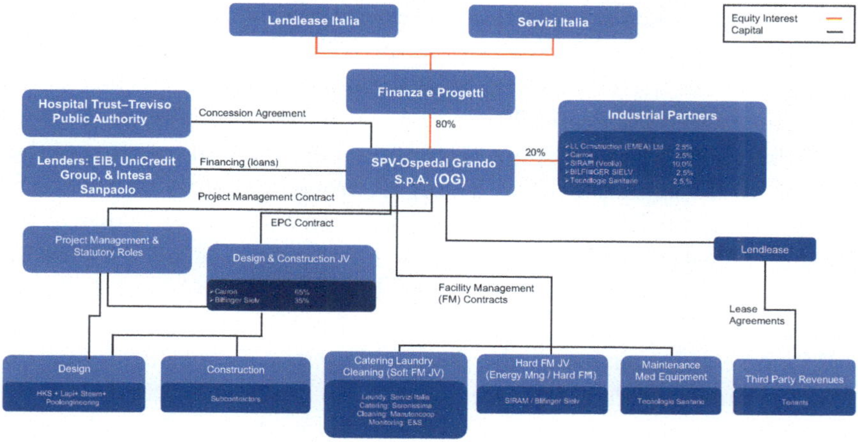

Fig. 5.1 Corporate, economic and financial structure of the PPP for the new hospital of Treviso. Source: Author's elaboration based on Lendlease's internal documentation

which makes investing for the renewal and upgrade of its social infrastructures strategic in order to maintain its competitive advantage internationally. The Treviso hospital, the main one in the province offering specialist services, serves the community in the province of Treviso, which has a population of up to one million people. The upgrade of the hospital follows the recent restructuring of the regional Sistema Sanitario Nazionale–National Health Service (SSN).

The concession contract for the new hospital demands an extensive renewal and the partial refurbishment of the hospital, and the provision of asset management and facility management services for 21 years from the signature of the concession. The construction part aims at rebuilding a large portion of the hospital maintaining the overall surface of 160,000 sqm (with 1000 beds) with an upgrade of core and intensive health care services including day surgery, and a general technological enhancement. The new and refurbished buildings will comply with the latest safety and anti-seismic structural regulations (Italian Ministerial Decree 14th January 2008 and subsequent modifications) as well as higher energy standards allowing for savings and CO_2 emissions reduction (Interministerial Decree 26th June 2015 and subsequent modifications).

The goal is to make the hospital of Treviso a regional hub that will serve as a model for the enitre health service in the region, as stated by Luca Zaia, the president of the Veneto Region, at the ceremony to lay the first stone on 17 June 2017 (Wolanski 2017).

We briefly review the corporate, economic and financial structure of the PPP to put the development of the impact investing strategy into context. OG is a company limited by shares registered in Italy and 80% owned by Finanza e Progetti of which Lendlease holds a 50% share. Originally, Finanza e Progetti shareholders were Lendlease (49%) and Palladio Finanziaria (51%), the latter being an Italian investment company. In 2015, there was a change in the shareholding structure. Palladio sold its shares in Finanza e Progetti to Lendlease, who then sold 50% of them to Servizi Italia, a new industrial partner, which provides laundry and sterilisation services for hospitals. Several industrial partners hold the other 20% ownership of OG: SIRAM (10%), Carron Italy (2.5%), Bilfinger SE (2.5%) and Tecnologie Sanitarie (2.5%). The construction subsidiary of Lendlease Construction also owns 2.5% of shares. According to the italian regulation, it is mandatory for the economic operator in charge of PPP contracts to include industrial partners that deliver works and services as shareholders of the SPV. The PPP for Treviso hospital is the first case in the country in which the leader and majority shareholder is a pure developer and investor, not a constructor—an element that explains the attention for innovative financial instruments, such as impact investing.

Figure 5.1 summarises the complexity of the PPP structure and the tight collaboration between public and private partners. The upper part illustrates the corporate structure of the PPP, which includes the flow of equity and capital. The bottom part of the figure summarises the services that OG provides to the public authority (identified as the Hospital Trust) and contractual relationship with all industrial partners. Lendlease acts as Project Manager whilst construction is delivered by Bilfinger SE and Carron Italy via an Engineering, Procurement, and Construction (EPC) contract. The other services are design and facility management. They include energy supply, laundry, cleaning, catering, building maintenance, purchasing and maintenance of medical equipment, and management of tenants (i.e., all commercial activities within the hospital premises such as bar, restaurant, shopping, units and car park). All these services are essential for an effective functioning of the hospital, to serve staff and users, and as source of revenues to repay investors. However, health services, which are the core mission of a hospital, are excluded from the PPP, as the public authority is in charge of them.

The finalisation of the concession contract was a long journey started in 2012 when OG won the public tender and was awarded the preferred bidder status. Nevertheless, the bureaucratic itinerary and start of the final negotiation were not finalised until 2015. Public authorisations, further administrative checks, and a lawsuit led by competitors delayed the process for three more years. In this project, more than 50% of the equity invested by the private partners was absorbed in the pre-construction phase at full risk of the private party. The ability of OG to minimise the additional costs generated by the delays in the approval process has been essential for the positive outcome of the project, though the inefficiencies in such a process increased costs and wasted public resources. The ultimate results are a reduction in international competitiveness, market efficiency and innovation.[1] Paradoxically, such a challenging environment forces both the public and private partners to devise new solutions as this case demonstrates.[2]

When, in December 2015, OG finally confirmed the concession contract, the financial terms were the following: 250 million euros total value of the investment, 124 of which came from the public sector and 126 from the private sector. European accounting rules require more than 50% of the capital investment to be borne by the private sector for the project to be considered a PPP. This is a condition for the public sector to account the investment off balance sheet and avoid the limits imposed by the European Growth and Stability Pact on public indebtment—one of the main reasons for the local authorities to opt for a PPP instead of the ordinary public procurement process (Vecchi and Leone 2016). OG has invested 20 million euros in equity and sourced 80 million euros from the debt market.[3] The other financial resources are generated by the

[1] Elaboration of the author based on interviews with Andrea Ruckstuhl (President of OG and CEO of Lendlease Italy) and Francesco Mandruzzato (CEO of OG and Head of PFI at Lendlease Italy).

[2] Those new solutions are not always within the legal boundaries and the reputation of PPP sector has been undermined by misdeed and financial scandals.

[3] Both figures are approximations due to the complexity of project finance but reflect the order of magnitude (source: Francesco Mandruzzato).

project itself by the provision of services. Several options were considered and a bank loan was deemed to be the most efficient, mainly because the interest rates at that time were close to zero, and because of the flexibility that loans offer, compared to other financial instruments such as project bonds. Banks provided the loan and the financial closing was reached in July 2017: 27 million euros by UniCredit Bank Group (the Lead Arranging Bank), 24 million euros by Intesa Sanpaolo (of which six million were provided by Banca Prossima, Intesa's subsidiary bank specialised in credit to the third sector), and 29 million euros by European Investment Bank (EIB). EIB has also financed 36 million euros to the ULSS Treviso (the Public Health Agency of Treviso Province) leading on the public sector side of the PPP.

1.2 Impact Investing Strategy of the PPP for Treviso Hospital

In February 2016, OG contracted PlusValue (PV), a London-based research and consultancy company specialised in social impact strategies, to provide assistance in devising a strategy for social impact investing. Lendlease, leader of OG shareholders, was interested in testing the possibility of developing a social impact bond or a similar financial instrument to source 80 million euros of debt finance. The inspiration came from the United Kingdom, although it had never been applied to infrastructural projects.

The rationale underpinning the choice was to create and sell a saving product to households and stakeholders in Treviso to finance the 80 million euro debt for the hospital. Families and institutions of the local community would make a good investment and, at the same time, finance the upgrade of the infrastructure that they would use in the future: it would therefore be a mutually advantageous situation. Obviously, OG expected investors to accept a lower financial return compared to the market rate—the difference being a trade-off for the public value: the upgraded hospital complemented by the commitment from OG to invest 100% of generated savings in initiatives with a clear and measurable positive impact on the community. This was an original proposal that would apply the principle of impact investing to project bonds, which in countries like the United States, are usually used to finance infrastructural projects.

However, these are just speculations because this proposal could not be implemented. Figure 5.2 illustrates the structure of the impact investing strategy as it was devised at the beginning. The initial structure was simple—reflecting the same simplicity of the Shared Value theory that we review later—but did not take into consideration the complexity that emerged as it had to be finalised and approved by all parties involved. OG was required by contract to have certainty on the full amount of debt capital and precise price—something that a project bond could not guarantee and that no bank was ready to write off capital and price in case the sale of bond hadn't reached the targets. The bank Natixis would have done it, but it would have applied market rates, thereby defeating the purpose of the impact investing strategy.

The solution came instead from the EIB when, in 2016, it offered to join the financing of the project in a club deal with the other banks. EIB took a leading role in relaunching investment in infrastructural projects following the global financial crisis started in 2008, especially through the Juncker Plan for strategic infrastructural investments. The EIB was

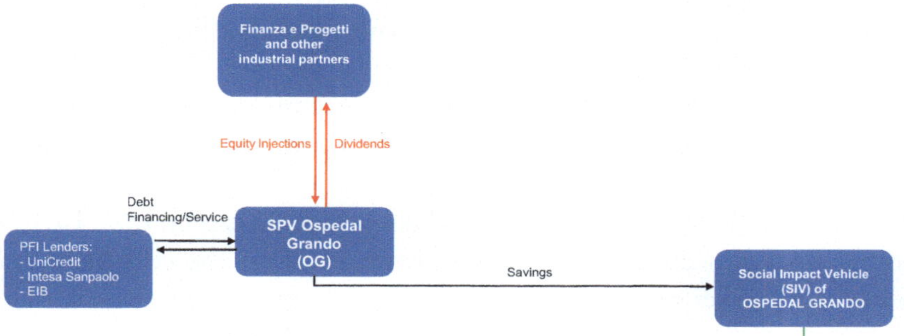

PFI Lenders	Commitment (€m)	Margins (bps)	Value generated for SIV OGII
UniCredit	27	230	0
Intesa Sanpaolo	24	230	0
EIB	29	140	C. €1.8m
	80	90	C. €1.8m

Fig. 5.2 The structure of the impact investing strategy as it was originally devised. Source: Author's elaboration based on Lendlease's internal documentation

willing to invest directly in a social infrastructure project in Italy. In the past, the bank did not invest in social infrastructures like hospitals, especially in a direct manner, instead lending capital to national banks.[4] The combination of the financial crisis that triggered a dramatic drop in public investment in social infrastructures and the launch of the Juncker Plan changed EIB's lending strategy.

The collaboration with EIB made the social impact investing strategy possible because it lends at the lowest rate in the market, thereby significantly reducing the cost of lending compared to any other commercial bank. OG was therefore able to save 90 basis points (−0.9%) on the interest cost of the debt—compared to the market price made by UniCredit, the leading arranging bank, and shared by Intesa Sanpaolo and Banca Prossima, the other commercial banks in the club deal. Moreover, further savings were made on the upfront and commitment fees. At the financial signing in July 2017, OG realised 1.8 million euros in total savings thanks to the EIB loan.[5] At the same time, the partnership with EIB has become a validation of the social impact investing strategy vis-à-vis the other banks and public sector partners. The Juncker Plan, for the first time, included 'societal impact assessment' in the investment policy criteria of the EIB (Lipparini et al. 2015) and the bank has acknowledged that the project in Treviso is the first funded by the bank with an explicit commitment to use derived benefits for social impact investing (Santarelli and EIB 2017).

The portion of the debt leveraged for the impact investing strategy could have been greater if all banks had taken part. Instead, the commercial banks were not able to offer a discount below the market price, which they could have done it if they also had borrowed the capital from EIB. In doing so, they would have benefited from price on the cost of capital below the market rate and could have transferred the savings—partially

[4] Interview with Lendlease's senior management.

[5] The financial costs of the debt are upfront fee, commitment fee and interest fee. The upfront fee charged by EIB is sensibly lower than the one of commercial banks, but the benefits were absorbed by extra transaction costs for the negotiation with EIB. The commitment fee of EIB is half of the one of commercial banks—approximately 50 basis points—making OG to realise savings from the financial closing and diminishing over time until the end of construction phase. The interest fee is 90 basis points lower than the commercial one, and realised on the actual borrowed capital over 16 years—duration of the debt repayment.

or entirely—to the impact investing vehicle. However, this option was not implemented due to the risks attached. OG did not want to increase risks that might have jeopardised the main project financing.

Changes in the credit rate of intermediary banks is a significant risk, especially in countries like Italy where the banking sector is under strains. If the credit rate deteriorates, the EIB can withdraw the capital and have a veto power on the choice of other financial institutions that could step in. It is evident what risk the financial equilibrium of the project financing would have faced in a similar situation.

2 Shared Value' Theory as Interpretative Framework

To analyse the impact investing strategy of the Treviso case study we apply the 'Shared Value' framework developed by Michael Porter and Mark Kramer (Porter and Kramer 2011) as a blueprint for the redefinition of the role of capitalism in society—an interpretation that has had much traction in international corporate circles.

Porter and Kramer developed the framework to address the legitimacy crisis that the private sector has undergone following the global financial crisis started in 2008. Such a loss of legitimacy is harmful for both business and society because it triggers governments' action against business and hinders economic growth. As the authors stated (Porter and Kramer 2011), the crisis has proved that the neoliberal thinking that the main and only purpose of the company is to maximise short-term profits and shareholders' value as posited by Milton Friedman (Porter and Kramer 2011) is outdated and inadequate to address the challenges of the twenty-first century. On the contrary, companies should pay attention to social values and their impact on society. Social and environmental impact should not be understood as costs to be minimised, but as opportunities to create new markets. Therefore, companies should include social and environmental value creation in their business strategy as a source of efficiency, innovation and competitiveness. This is not a simple reconfiguration of Corporate Social Responsibility (CSR) or a form of philanthropy as wealth redistribution, but rather an opportunity to transform current business models, and expand markets and profits. This, ultimately, will change capitalism and enhance its power to generate both economic and social value.

Companies can do so by means of three different approaches that the authors identify as 'reconceiving products and markets', 'redefining productivity in the value chain' and 'enabling local cluster development'. In the first case companies can adapt or develop new products to meet society's unmet needs, whereas the second and third approaches target the network of suppliers and the community in which business operates.

We do not need to review the approaches in detail, but it suffices to highlight the main points of the third approach—the one that fits the Treviso hospital case. Porter and Kramer argue that companies must invest within the communities in which they operate: address their structural weaknesses, develop their public assets, infrastructures and institutions, and work in partnership with local stakeholders including the public sector and civil society. Their investment is repaid by having access to a greater pool of talents and bigger markets, and preventing future costs such as environmental degradation and unhealthy workforce.

On the other hand, Shared Value theory as formulated by Porter and Kramer presents interpretative limitations defining the public sector's role, and identifying the challenges that any company would face building and managing multi-stakeholder governance, devising an appropriate investment strategy and measuring social value. These are the four aspects that the case of the Treviso hospital helps us to consider, providing suggestions to address them.

2.1 The Public Sector's Role in Impact Investing and Multistakeholders' Governance

Porter and Kramer assign to the public sector the role of setting the standards for social value creation, establishing incentives for business and monitoring compliance with standards. These are certainly tasks for the public sector but do not exhaust its role. The case of Treviso hospital, on the contrary, supports the interpretation of the 'Entrepreneurial State' as devised by Mariana Mazzucato (Mazzucato 2013). The public sector is not just a fixer of market failures as often portrayed in the neoliberal thinking that underpins Porter and Kramer, but shapes markets, builds market infrastructures and invests to grow new markets often stepping in first, taking the highest risks and attracting private sector partners. Mazzucato's perspective is more effective in interpreting the role of the public sector in the Treviso hospital case. Figure 5.3 illustrates the role of EIB (public sector) in financing the impact strategy and devising its governance structure.

Firstly, the role of the EIB as investor has made the social impact investing strategy possible. Neither the companies nor the commercial banks were able to provide the capital to start the initiative. Secondly, the EIB helped designing the governance structure between the project finance and impact investing. Initially, the social impact vehicle was supposed to be a subsidiary of OG that would have collected the savings generated from the loan as equity capital, and invested on behalf of OG. This solution was problematic since the dependency of one company on the other would have connected the risks of the project finance to the impact investments with possible recourse claims on both sides. The EIB proposed, instead, to create a sister company called Ospedal

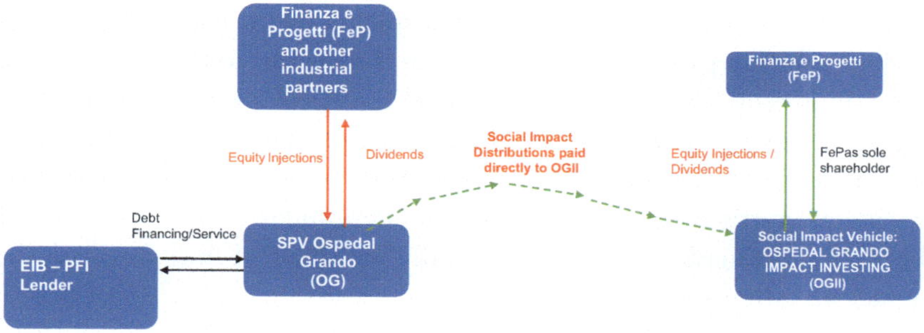

PFI Lenders	Commitment (€m)	Bps (margin)	Value generated for SIV OGII
EIB	29	140 (90)	C. €1.8m

- The discount on margin provided by EIB will generate savings for OG which must be distributed as "Social Impact Distributions" to OGII
- Social Impact Distributions will be equity paid in OGII to be invested in social impact initiatives

Fig. 5.3 Role of EIB (public sector) in financing the impact strategy and devising its governance structure. Source: Author's elaboration based on Lendlease's internal documentation

Grando Impact Investing (OGII) that would be capitalised by the shareholders of OG with the savings generated by the European loan. Doing so, the impact investment stream was ring-fenced from the risk of project finance and vice versa. The EIB also provided the solution for the transfer of the savings generated by the European loan to the impact investing vehicle. Such savings are returned to OG shareholders as a special type of dividends—the so-called 'social impact dividends' in the contract of financing. Shareholders give mandate to OG to transfer the dividends to the impact vehicle as these are generated in the form of 'social impact distributions'. So, de facto, it is an equity investment that OG shareholders make in a new company.

Finally—as a counterproof—the lack of government initiative in defining the boundaries of a new social impact investing market in Italy has been a source of misunderstanding and delays between the parties involved. Contrary to the United Kingdom, Italy does not have a clear policy and legal framework for impact investing, and lacks experts and intermediaries. So, the default position for companies willing to share value with the community is the traditional philanthropy or support to not-for-profit sector: for instance, financing the hospital's kindergarten. Initially, the plan to set up an investment vehicle generating both financial and social returns was viewed with suspicion by the partners. Actually, the first solution proposed was to transfer the savings to the public sector and cut its costs. However, that would have defeated the purpose of impact investing by implicitly stifling the entrepreneurship displayed by the private sector, and it would have certainly been a missed opportunity to generate further value for both shareholders and the community. Only the moral persuasion of EIB changed the situation and justified the impact investing strategy.

Hence, the case of Treviso provides evidence against reductionist theories on the role of the public sector, showing not only the active role that it can have but also the necessity for its initiative and different shapes that it can take. In this project, a European institution took the lead, rather than regional or national public authorities. The Treviso project vindicates Mazzucato's theory of government, and reminds the proponents of Shared Value theory and any other theory of public private partnership about the pivotal role of the public sector and the diversity of its manifestations.

In this context, coalitions play important roles in the effective implementation of the agreement and project, as observed: 'Companies should try to enlist partners to share the cost, win support, and assemble the right skills. The most successful cluster development programs are the ones that involve collaboration within the private sector, as well as trade associations, government agencies, and NGOs' (Porter and Kramer 2011). Nonetheless, the authors underestimate or ignore the challenges implied in multi-stakeholder action. Instead, according to Olson (1965), building a coalition of several and diverse partners is a public good—in the economic definition of the term. A cost-benefit analysis usually cannot justify such an effort. Furthermore, the costs are increased by the number and diversity of members in the coalition as the expected benefits are not the same. Certainly, they do not all respond to economic rationality alone, and it is naïve to posit that different stakeholders are due to join in a coalition because of an apparent opportunity to create public value. The politics of collective action is beyond what economic rationality can explain.

The project in Treviso clearly illustrated these challenges. Commercial banks were not able or willing to join for commercial reasons although they were attracted by the branding opportunities—especially in a wealthy province such as Treviso, where the reputation of the banking sector is plummeting due to the collapse of the two main local banks.[6] The philanthropic foundations were called to be part of such an initiative, but they had their own agendas and binding rules on how to use their resources. Most Italian foundations struggle to endorse impact investing for both cultural and legal reasons—not to mention vested interests. The same case applies for potential co-investors approached in the process. The various stakeholders in the community did not have a unique and shared view, but identified different priorities for the impact investing strategy: projects and initiatives to invest.

Even in this case, the interpretative framework of Porter and Kramer is not of great help due to its limited analysis of social dynamics. However, Pasi (2017) argues that impact investing is a new field that brings together actors from all sectors forcing every player to reposition goals and patterns

[6] Banca Popolare di Vicenza and Veneto Banca are bankrupt and have been sold to Intesa Sanpaolo for 1 euro each one (June 2017) with great financial loss of account holders and small investors.

of behaviour. A natural alignment of professional cultures and values cannot be expected or taken for granted. The development of the field requires forms of brokerage and intermediation. Pasi's interpretation is validated by the choice of British government that since 2000 has made impressive investments in new intermediaries to foster the impact investing market.[7]

In the case of the Treviso project, OG tasked PV, as an external and knowledgeable broker, to map the local stakeholders, identifying needs and opportunities, and devise an impact assessment methodology customised for the project. Contrary to the simplistic interpretation of Porter and Kramer, local stakeholders and civil society do not simply respond to leadership and opportunities offered by the private sector. Actually, the consultation of the community revealed that the initial assumptions for the impact strategy were wrong. While OG assumed that the main need in the community was the improvement of services for children and the elderly, it turned out that the priority was young people, including talent retention and new job opportunities. This simple observation explains the expectation of local stakeholders and civil society to be part of the strategic phase. For this purpose, Fondazione FITS! (a corporate foundation belonging to the Intesa Sanpaolo Bank Group) proposed to establish a Community Foundation to institutionalise the community's participation in the decision-making process. The proposal was not brought forward, but the investment policy of OGII acknowledges the inputs of the community and commits to the transparency of process and accountability on the final investment choices. It also foresees to bring in an external certifier to assess the realised impact. Transparency and accountability are key for community engagement, as testified by the wide consensus in the scientific literature (Putnam et al. 1994; Fukuyama 2015).

Eventually the governance for the impact investing strategy in Treviso found a solution at the financial closing (July 2017): Finanza e Progetti (the majority shareholder of OG controlled by Lendlease) is in full control, leaving the financing banks veto power on investment decisions,

[7] In Italy, the only financial intermediaries for impact investing with a track record and significant size are Banca Prossima (subsidiary of Intesa Sanpaolo) UBI Banca and OltreVenture (impact equity fund) with little or no support from government.

room for consultation to the community, opportunity to co-invest together with other investors, and relying on external experts for validation and impact assessment. As confirmed by both the experience of the authors, and the Treviso project, that designing a multi-stakeholder governance system gathering a highly diverse membership of partners is the most challenging aspect of projects of this kind—more than raising capital. Moreover, it is a dynamic process that cannot be reduced to the simplicity and predictability of corporate governance rules.

2.2 Impact Investment Mission and Assessment

The Treviso hospital project proves how difficult it is to devise an effective investment policy. Figure 5.4 summarises the agents and flows of the impact investment policy. The first challenge was to choose the legal form for the impact investing vehicle given the fact that the Italian legislation does not contemplate anything as such. Within Italian law, a company is for profit, not for profit or a cooperative.[8] OGII was set up as a company limited by shares and the impact mission was written in its Memorandum and Articles of Association. This makes impact considerations mandatory in every investment decision made by the OGII Board of Directors. The localisation of the social mission is another important element: the investment decisions must be in line with the PPP main project, and therefore they have to be related to the fields relevant to the hospital such as health, education and social services, or the local community in Treviso or the Veneto region.[9] The legal rationale behind this choice is the comparison of OGII's social mission to compensatory works often included in a PPP although not directly related to the core project.[10] More broadly, such a convergence generates a multiplier of value creation for the overall

[8] New legislation on the reform of the third sector and social enterprise has just been approved by Parliament, but the effective outcomes are far from being definitive.

[9] In Italian, article 4 of OGII's Memorandum of Understanding: 'Partecipazione ad iniziative economiche in Italia nel settore sociale o che abbiano finalità di impatto sociale, ivi incluso a titolo meramente esemplificativo iniziative riguardanti la fornitura di servizi socio-sanitari, assistenziali, welfare, culturali o didattici ovvero di sostegno all'ambiente e al turismo eco-sostenibile'.

[10] Interpretation of Bonelli Erede, the law firm assisting EIB.

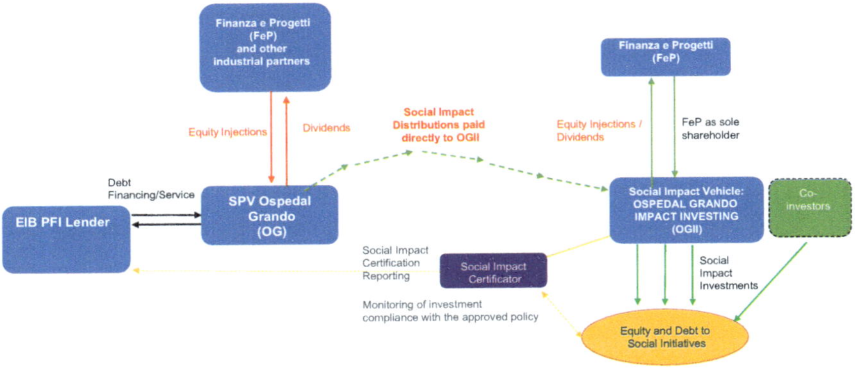

Fig. 5.4 Agents and flows of the impact investment policy. Source: Author's elaboration based on Lendlease's internal documentation

investment and local community, and justifies the discount on the loan of the EIB.

In respect to the market standards as defined by the international impact investing community and summarised in the final report of the Taskforce on social impact investing of G7: 'The Invisible Heart of the Markets' (Social Impact Investing Taskforce 2014), OGII's mission and governance is only partially aligned. OGII has a mission-lock—in other words, the board of directors must take into consideration the impact dimension in every strategic decision and share it with the banks.[11] The financing contract with the banks bars the board of directors from modifying the mission of OGII and the provisions on impact. On the other hand, OGII has a partial cap on both profit distribution and asset transfer. The cap lasts for the entire duration of the repayment of the project finance loan (i.e., 16 years). Until that time expires, profits generated by successful investment must be reinvested in OGII. The company could be liquated on the sixteenth year at the end of the repayment of the project finance loan. Before that date, shareholders can sell their shares in OG to third parties with no obligation to take part in the impact strategy for the latter. However, they are due to compensate OGII in case of loss of

[11] Only EIB finances the impact investing vehicle, but all the banks involved in the project financing of the main project are included in the impact investing decisions.

expected capital generated by savings on the loan providing the equivalent capital. All these elements make OGII a straightforward for-profit enterprise with impact.

OGII is almost unique in Italy for its governance as well. In Italy, the governance of social enterprises is usually democratic, as a consequence of the cooperative movement tradition. On the contrary, OGII has adopted an outright corporate governance, leaving the full control to its only shareholder, i.e. Finanza e Progetti (Lendlease, majority shareholders). The other shareholders of OG (holding 20%) have forfeited their shares in favour of the former. In this model of governance, OGII is a vehicle for venture capital investments with impact embedded in the core mission.[12] OG shareholders' commitments to the impact investing strategy are ironclad as the savings from the financing are generated. This is formalised in a financing contract between OG and the banks. At the same time, this model justifies the direct investment of EIB as its benefits are not privatised, but reinvested by the shareholders in the community to generate further value for all parties involved.

All these elements make OGII a real novelty in the national and international scenario assimilating it to a form of corporate venture capital with positive social impact embedded in its mission (Growth Capital Ventures 2017). It should not be considered a mature model for impact investing and entrepreneurship but an experimental hybrid (Venturi and Zandonai 2014). In any case, its success would prove that impact investing can be a component of a new business strategy that aligns private and public interests, and is suitable for mainstream and sizeable companies and investors.

In the Treviso project, PV has been contracted by OG to put in place a framework for impact assessment following the mapping of stakeholders and their needs. The investment policy of OGII requires an impact assessment based on the mapping, consultation with the local community and stakeholders, and coherence with the international standards applied by Lendlease to every project in the world

[12] It is the view of Sir Ronald Cohen (Chairman of the G8 Taskforce on social impact investing) reiterated in numerous occasions by other early impact investors such as Luciano Balbo (OltreVenture) that impact investing is a declination of venture capital applied to the social sector (Vecchi et al. 2015).

(Lendlease 2016). All the investors have demanded in written form in the financial contracts that the assessment is taken regularly to evaluate achievements against targets, the perception of the local community and stakeholders, and possible improvement and adaptations to increase value generation. As of the time of writing this chapter, the evaluation has not started yet.

Porter and Kramer recognise the importance of measuring impact—they call it social value—and collecting data to build a baseline for market growth. This is certainly reasonable, but the researchers underestimate the difficulty of doing so. The measurement of impact or social value is not as straightforward as measuring financial value: it is based on decisions that are affected by the different stakeholders involved, and is sector specific—measuring results in health is quite different from measuring results in education. Impact measurement in the United Kingdom exemplifies the challenge. Government has been fostering impact measurement for almost 20 years and, in 2013, it has put it into law with the Social Value Act requiring social impact measurement in public procurement for all public services. Despite these efforts, the potential and some success, social impact measurement is still far from becoming an exact science, as public assessment for the British government has recognised (Young 2014).

The impact assessment is based on the Social Return on Investment (SROI) approach, the international standard method to account for both monetisable and non-monetisable impact (Social Value UK 2012). It is the basis for a comprehensive assessment framework system to collect, monitor and analyse socio-economic impact data, both from available databases and crowdsourced data. It includes a set of socio-economic goals (e.g., increased well-being of the local population, jobs and enterprises created, increased social capital for defined social groups, etc.); a set of impact indicators (e.g., number of new jobs and enterprises, increase in salaries, investment in local area, reported satisfaction of local citizens, number of people using public spaces, etc.); and methods and tools to collect, store and share data (e.g., subjective/self-reported indicators vs. objective indicators, existing data vs. new data, desk research vs. interviews, surveys, crowd-sourcing, social media analysis). The SROI is to be matched with an experimental online open data platform to track and analyse social media activities related to the project. Social media data are processed through a mix of natural language analysis, network analysis, geo-referencing and machine learning developed by Human Ecosystems, to provide a thorough assessment of the impact of the project. A similar approach has already been successfully tested and implemented in Bologna (HUB – Human Ecosystems Bologna 2015).[13]

The second observation concerning the comparison between the Shared Value theory and the actual development of the impact project in Treviso is the non-linearity of the process of impact assessment. Porter and Kramer present social value recording as a mere accounting job, but in reality the complexity of interactions, time lapses, unforeseen causes and consequences make the impact assessment often impossible, at least in terms of causal attribution and monetary equivalent. Looking at it from a mere corporate prospective, how can an investment be deemed successful or not if its contribution to the bottom-line cannot be defined? Usually the only certain attribution is the expenses, which makes it like a charitable initiative. A concrete example related to Treviso can illustrate the point. One of the initiatives that could be the target of OGII action is the plan to create a new international Faculty of Medicine in the premises of the hospital, bringing together higher education and practice to attract students from all over the world.[14] This project would increase the value of the overall investment in the hospital, but measuring the return on investment for the developer is not evident and might not be carried out exhaustively.

3 Conclusions

The analysis of the case of the project in Treviso has been a unique opportunity to test the potential of impact investing to lead a corporation to move beyond the current mind-set in which the business model is reduced to short-term profit maximisation, erasing any awareness of interdependencies between the company and all the other stakeholders

[13] For further information on the methodology, see https://www.he-r.it/.

[14] Interview with Francesco Benazzi, CEO of ULSS Treviso (Provincial NHS authority).

that populate the environment in which it operates. Instead, the Treviso case study embraces a non-zero-sum approach that, not only recognises, but also capitalises on such interdependencies to increase value creation, thereby aligning public and private interests.

In practical terms, the results generated by the project are multiple and it is useful to recapitulate them to provide the full picture, as illustrated in Fig. 5.5. Firstly, the case study has tested and proved that the impact investing strategy has a transformative power in infrastructural projects generating new resources to increase the overall value of the investment. By including impact investing in the plan of the PPP for the new hospital in Treviso, OG, the SPV created by Lendlease and its industrial partners to carry out the concession contract to design, finance, build and manage the hospital, was able to secure a loan of 29 million euros from the EIB at a discount price compared to the market rate. The optimisation of the project financing has generated an extra 1.8 million euros that OG shareholders used in its entirety to capitalise a new vehicle—OGII—established to invest in entrepreneurial and financial initiatives that combine both financial and social value creation. The latter will support initiatives that expand the services of the hospital and opportunities in the local community.

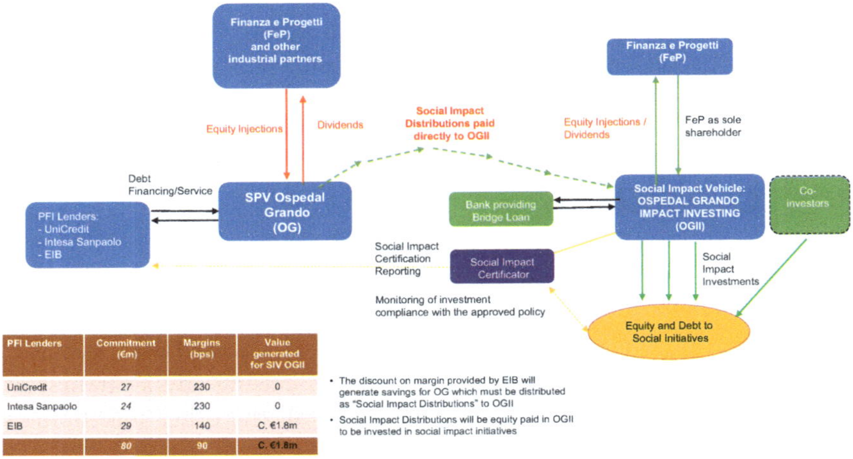

PFI Lenders	Commitment (€m)	Margins (bps)	Value generated for SIV OGII
UniCredit	27	230	0
Intesa Sanpaolo	24	230	0
EIB	29	140	C. €1.8m
	80	90	C. €1.8m

Fig. 5.5 Summary of the finalised impact investing model. Source: Author's elaboration based on Lendlease's internal documentation

If the investment phase will work as well, it will generate a sustained positive feedback that will induce further investments in OGII, more capital for enterprises, more jobs, better services for the community and a greater commitment of the community stakeholders in sustaining the positive cycle. This would be a new frontier for sustainability and resilience.[15]

Secondly, the project in Treviso has offered the EIB a framework to realise the ambition of the Junker Plan to relaunch investments in strategic infrastructures across Europe, proving how to address societal impact in the investment policy of the European bank. This result has been acknowledged in the official communication of EIB and could be replicated across Europe with an impact on up to 0.5 trillion euros, which is the investment target of the reviewed Juncker Plan (European Commission 2016). The project has also identified areas of improvement in the investment policy of the European bank to increase its impact and power to leverage private capital. Actually, the EIB leadership can induce private banks and investors to follow the example. In the case of Treviso, we have seen the influence that EIB had on UniCredit Group and Intesa Sanpaolo, the two main Italian banks, in getting them to move beyond their comfort zone—although the concrete results in terms of extra capital for the impact strategy did not materialise due to bank policies. Those policies can be improved in the future to mobilise more commercial partners, which currently represents a priority. The British government established a working group to engage insurance groups and pensions funds (Independent Dormant Asset Commission 2017), and was followed by the European Commission (European Commission and High-Level Expert Group 2017). The market is mature for the main investors to step in and embed impact investing principles in their mainstream operations.

The project has also revealed a flaw in the funding system, which could be addressed by EIB leadership. In Treviso, we were not able to mobilise the traditional public and philanthropic resources—for example, bank foundations, corporate foundations and structural funds. The funding

[15] In October 2017, Lendlease won the public tender to regenerate the site where EXPO Milan took place in 2015, and was awarded the concession contract to design, finance, build and manage the site for 99 years. This is a €2 billion investment project and includes a social impact investing strategy that replicates the model piloted for Treviso hospital but eight times larger.

environment for entrepreneurship and innovation is still very fragmented, and the impact investing and entrepreneurship ones are even more scattered in multiple, small initiatives that do not represent a critical mass. Funders pursue individual agendas and there are no incentives to join forces. Moreover, the hybridisation of commercial practices and philanthropic resources faces cultural and legal barriers that represent a real obstacle for impact investing. Projects like OGII in Treviso exemplify the emergence of alternatives, but cannot scale without the intervention of policy-makers to address structural shortfalls.

Thirdly, the project in Treviso has become an opportunity to devise new legal solutions to embed impact investing principles in current business practices, even in a country like Italy where government action has been deficient in developing the market infrastructure. The law firms that assisted OG and the banks were creative in devising legal arrangements that ring-fenced the risks of the project finance from the ones of impact investing, creating two separate companies but aligning their mission. OG and OGII are sister companies with almost the same shareholding structure (Finanza e Progetti holds 80% of OG shares and 100% of OGII shares) and the commitment to invest in projects related to the hospital and the local community is spelled out in the Memorandum and Articles of Association of OGII. Moreover, an ingenious solution has been devised for the transfer of the savings due to the loan to the impact investing vehicle: the savings are in principles dividends for OG shareholders, which have mandated OG to transfer to OGII as 'Social Impact Distributions' the savings generated during the course of the project (16 years). This is an elegant solution that avoids any risk of recourse, and turns the operation into a form of corporate venture capital with impact.

However, the model designed still has a problem: EIB releases the capital step by step and savings on the financing of the project are realised over 16 years. This means that OGII, in principle, would be capitalised in full not before 2033 and only then it would be able to invest. To implement the impact investing strategy from the beginning of the construction phase there is a need to anticipate the capital against the future savings. OG shareholders could advance the capital[16] and get repaid as

[16] Italian legislation allows for 'prestito soci', a loan between shareholders or partners in business.

the savings are realised. In this scenario, the challenge for the industrial partners would be to price the risk and define the expected return. In any case, the remuneration would be high and arbitrary. Therefore, Lendlease has opted for a bridge loan by the banks as professional lenders. The proposal is under discussion with the commercial banks,[17] and the solution of this point will be particularly relevant for the evolution of the market. The discount on the pricing of the loan would be a proxy to measure the banks' commitments to impact[18]—a method developed and piloted by Engaged Investment Ltd. (Evenett and Richter 2011). There is a further point that is also not solved yet: delays or missed payments due to issues with main project finance will have a negative impact on the release of savings. Who will bear the risk and pays for the extra costs? Lendlease's proposal is that the lent capital would be swapped for shares of OGII in proportion of the loss, thus turning the lender into a shareholder. For the time being, the agreement on the bridge loan has not yet been finalised. In any case, this is an *ad hoc* solution. So even this situation requires greater attention to develop structural solutions for the market.

Finally, the hospital of Treviso is, to our knowledge, the first project of this scale and complexity in which the private sector partners—with no request from the public counterpart—have not only committed to an impact investing strategy, but have also included an independent assessment of the outcomes and the inclusion of the main community stakeholders in the whole cycle, and even considered the use of experimental methods based on online tools. Such a commitment is formalised in the investment policy of OGII and financial contracts between the banks and OG.

The 'Shared Value' theory as an interpretative framework for private sector's initiative in aligning its values to the ones of society has been helpful to analyse the structure of value generated by the project in Treviso. At the same time, we pointed out the limits of the theory compared to developments in the field. As argued earlier, Porter and Kramer's framework shows severe limitations on multiple points: in identifying the role of the public sector as co-leader in building the market infrastructure

[17] Interview with Francesco Mandruzzato, CEO of OG and head of PFI at Lendlease Italy.

[18] An approximate estimate of the interest fee is around 6% (source: Francesco Mandruzzato).

of impact investing and early investor; the complexity of building multi-stakeholder coalitions that bring together stakeholders from different sectors in a joint action to pursue both their individual interests and public good; and the challenges in devising an investment policy that meets the profit-making mission of a company with the aspiration to generate positive impact in the community. Such a balance is far from evident. Finally, the 'Shared Value' theory underestimates the different methodology for assessing social values compared to monetary value. The former is far from financial accounting and quantifiable measurements.

These remarks question the validity of the 'Shared Value' theory—although we acknowledge the contribution of the intuition underpinning the theory and its ability to influence the course of theory and practice of capitalism—and should be taken as new starting points for future research in the field. Our conclusion is the need to move beyond a corporate perspective, since companies are just one type of agents in a highly diverse environment. The company is not a closed system but rather an element of a complex and dynamic system. Hence, impact investing theory requires a system perspective that embraces a multi-stakeholder approach and aims at redefining the terms and practice for long term socio-economic sustainability and resilience (Directorate-General for Research and Innovation et al. 2017).

References

Crane, A., Palazzo, G., Spence, L. J., & Matten, D. (2014). Contesting the value of "creating shared value". *California Management Review, 56*(2), 130–153.

Directorate-General for Research and Innovation, Directorate-General for Employment, Social Affairs and Inclusion, Innovation, D. F., A., Directorate-General for Regional and Urban Policy, & Europa, I. (2017, October 23). *Vision and trends of social innovation for Europe*. Retrieved from https://publications.europa.eu/en/publication-detail/-/publication/a97a2fbd-b7da-11e7-837e-01aa75ed71a1/language-en.

European Commission. (2016, September 14). *State of the union 2016: Strengthening European investments for jobs and growth. Towards a second phase of the European Fund for Strategic Investments and a new European External*

Investment Plan. COM(2016) 581. Retrieved from http://eur-lex.europa.eu/legal-content/EN/TXT/?uri=CELEX%3A52016DC0581.

European Commission, & High-Level Expert Group on Sustainable Finance Secretariat Provided by the European Commission. (2017, July). *Financing a sustainable European economy*. Retrieved from https://ec.europa.eu/info/sites/info/files/170713-sustainable-finance-report_en.pdf.

Evenett, R., & Richter, K. H. (2011, October). *Making good in social impact investment*. Retrieved from http://www.bing.com/cr?IG=64999745FECA4E669D367D2AAA2A5B6B&CID=229A7C96E5FC671E283B77CFE45366EA&rd=1&h=l8-0467nDeS5B7KR2OQMy1nJOD7xnAIFo_030KUKgzA&v=1&r=http%3a%2f%2fwww.engagedx.com%2fdownloads%2fMaking_Good_In_Social_Impact_Investment.pdf&p=DevEx,5065.1.

Fukuyama, F. (2015). *Political order and political decay: From the industrial revolution to the globalisation of democracy*. London: Profile Books.

Growth Capital Ventures. (2017). *Investing in breakthrough corporate venture capital*. Retrieved from https://info.growthfunders.com/investing-in-breakthrough-corporate-venture-capital-volans.

HUB – Human Ecosystems Bologna. (2015). *Human ecosystem bologna report*. Retrieved from http://dati.comune.bologna.it/file/hub-report_eng.pdf.

Independent Dormant Asset Commission, Department for Digital, Culture, Media & Sport, HMRC. (2017, March). *Dormant assets commission: Final report to government tackling dormant assets recommendations to benefit investors and society*. Retrieved from https://www.gov.uk/government/publications/dormant-assets-commission-final-report-to-government.

Lendlease. (2016, February). GRMRs global minimum requirements – Environment, health & safety. *Lendlease*. Retrieved from https://www.lendlease.com/-/media/llcom/investor-relations/governance/2015-global-minimum-requirements-framework.ashx.

Lipparini, F., Phillips, S., Addarii, F., & Johar, I. (2015, March). *From good to growth: Promoting social investment and public good to stimulate the European economy*. Retrieved from https://youngfoundation.org/wp-content/uploads/2015/10/From-good-to-growth.pdf.

Mazzucato, M. (2013). *The entrepreneurial state: Debunking public vs. private sector myths*. London: Anthem Press.

Olson, M. (1965). *The logic of collective action: Public goods and the theory of groups*. Cambridge, MA: Harvard University Press.

Pasi, G. (2017, June). *Modelli di Risposta ai Nuovi Bisogni Sociali e Possibili Scenari di Riforma*. Retrieved from http://www.socialimpactagenda.it/wp-content/uploads/2017/06/Modelli-di-risposta-ai-nuovi-bisogni-sociali-e-possibili-scenari-di-riforma_def.pdf.

Porter, M. E., & Kramer, M. R. (2011). The big idea: Creating shared value – How to reinvent capitalism and unleash a wave of innovation and growth. *Harvard Business Review, 89*(1–2), 62–77.

Putnam, R. D., Leonardi, R., & Nanetti, R. Y. (1994). *Making democracy work: Civic traditions in modern Italy*. Princeton, NJ: Princeton University Press.

Santarelli, M., & European Investment Bank (EIB). (2017, July 25). *Italy: Juncker plan – EIB finances better healthcare in the Veneto Region*. Retrieved from http://www.eib.org/infocentre/press/releases/all/2017/2017-215-juncker-plan-eib-finances-better-healthcare-in-the-veneto-region.htm.

Social Impact Investment Taskforce. (2014, September 15). *Impact investment: The invisible heart of markets. Harnessing the power of entrepreneurship, innovation and capital for public good*. Retrieved from http://www.socialimpactinvestment.org/reports/Impact%20Investment%20Report%20FINAL%5B3%5D.pdf.

Social Value UK. (2012). *A guide to social return on investment*. Retrieved from http://www.socialvalueuk.org/resources/sroi-guide/.

Vecchi, V., & Leone, V. (2016). *Partnership pubblico privato: Una guida manageriale, finanziaria e giuridica*. Milano: Egea.

Vecchi, V., Balbo, L., Brusoni, M., & Caselli, S. (2015). *Principles and practice of impact investing* (1st ed.pp. 275–293). Palgrave Macmillan US.

Venturi, P., & Zandonai, F. (2014). *Ibridi organizzativi: L'innovazione sociale generata dal Gruppo cooperativo Cgm*. Bologna: Il Mulino.

Wolanski, F. D. (2017, June 17). *Nuovo ospedale di Treviso: Zaia posa la prima pietra – Cronaca*. Retrieved from http://tribunatreviso.gelocal.it/treviso/cronaca/2017/06/16/news/apre-il-cantiere-300-park-gia-per-aprile-1.15499561.

Young, L. (2014). *Social value act review report to government*. Retrieved from https://www.gov.uk/government/uploads/system/uploads/attachment_data/file/403748/Social_Value_Act_review_report_150212.pdf.

6

The Evolution of a Social Service Crowdfunding Platform Towards an Investing Logic: The Meridonare Case Study

Carmen Gallucci, Michele Modina, and Antonio Minguzzi

1 Introduction

The creation of economic value by means of the generation of shared value, which is the only form of value that can sustain communities' equity conditions, has become the new challenge of modern society. The last decade, characterized by the financial crisis, has highlighted the important role of social entrepreneurs in the promotion of community-friendly initiatives in three ways: the offering of innovative solutions to unsolved social problems, the centering of their corporate mission on the concept of shared social value, and their intention of contributing to the progress and sustainability of the global economy (Nel and McQuaid 2002).

C. Gallucci (✉)
University of Salerno, Fisciano, Italy
e-mail: cgallucci@unisa.it

M. Modina • A. Minguzzi
University of Molise, Campobasso, Italy

M. La Torre, M. Calderini (eds.), *Social Impact Investing Beyond the SIB*, Palgrave Studies in Impact Finance, https://doi.org/10.1007/978-3-319-78322-2_6

Public funds allocated to welfare policies have been progressively reduced, particularly in highly developed economies and countries. This situation has led scholars, practitioners and policy makers to address the necessity of identifying innovative funding models capable of attracting private financial resources to be channeled towards the improvement of the sustainability of welfare systems (Azemati et al. 2013; Social Impact Investment Task Force 2014; Del Giudice 2015).

The issue under investigation has been worsened by the occurrence of two macro phenomena: the financial crisis, which has reduced the financial resources available to many European countries, even in those where the welfare state system was more developed, and the demographic transition, which has produced a progressive aging of the population, a consequent increase in elderly care services and a reduction in the young working population, which can contribute to the reduction of social spending. Such a situation raises the need to channel new key players, whether public or private, into the market of social activities and to offer them administrative support and financial benefits when community-friendly social conditions are met. Citizens play a key role since they are called upon to contribute to both the planning and production of services and to shape the highly democratic model of a welfare society (Venturi and Zandonai 2014), the alternative to the traditional model of a welfare state, in which the administration of social issues is a prerogative of the state, which collects the financial resources from the citizens through taxation and then redistributes those resources back to them through the welfare system.

The reconfiguration of public expenditures on welfare policy is one of the main drivers for the development of new forms of financing useful for social innovation (Azemati et al. 2013). The construct of Social Finance, defined as the set of processes directed towards the collection of financial resources implemented by all organizations or individuals whose aim is to satisfy a social need, can be useful for studying these issues because it attempts to achieve a positive impact, in both social and environmental terms, by offering a wide range of financial products and services (Weber 2012; Geobey and Weber 2013). In the broader context of Social Finance, impact investing is one of the emerging asset classes (Martin 2013; Trotta et al. 2015). The term "impact investing" refers to the specific branch of finance whose aim is to sustain investments directed towards reaching measurable social goals that can, at the same time, generate an economic return for investors. The specificity of this new business model can be retraced in the coexistence of social goals and economic returns and in the qualification of the specific trade-off.

A strong impulse towards the framing of social finance in an international context was provided with the British G8 presidency, in June 2013, during which Prime Minister David Cameron set up a task force whose job was to promote the development of social impact investments and to balance the growth of countries. Moving in the same direction, Italy, during the G8, established the Social Impact Investment Task Force. This group, with the contribution of the national advisory boards, provided a first definition of the term "social impact investing": "(all those) investments which intentionally aim to the reaching of measurable social goals and to the generation of measurable economic returns" (Social Impact Investment Task Force 2014).

The aforementioned theoretical framework includes all approaches whose aim is to provide financial means and services to all organizations that pursue social goals based on the co-participation and collaboration of the actors involved. However, the offering of social impact investments, perfected by using a variety of financial instruments, both traditional and innovative, must still be defined. If, from the point of view of supply, it is clear who the key players are, whether they are profit organizations or non-profit organizations offering these kinds of services in the marketplace, that is, all actors whose actions are "impact-oriented," the overall framework of those instruments, usually divided into equity and debt instruments, has still not been defined. If some of those instruments appear to be mature and offered by established financial intermediaries, the marketplace also includes financial instruments in their embryonal phase or, in some cases, as yet non-existing financial instruments offered by pioneering intermediaries (Fig. 6.1).

It appears to be evident that finance scholars are being called upon to spot new methods of provision of financial resources and to identify new modes of interaction with beneficiaries to make the social finance market as effective and efficient as possible while preserving the central role of the community (Nicholls et al. 2015). The search for new and more articulated operational responses to relevant social issues has found its expression in emerging academic approaches that place their attention on a

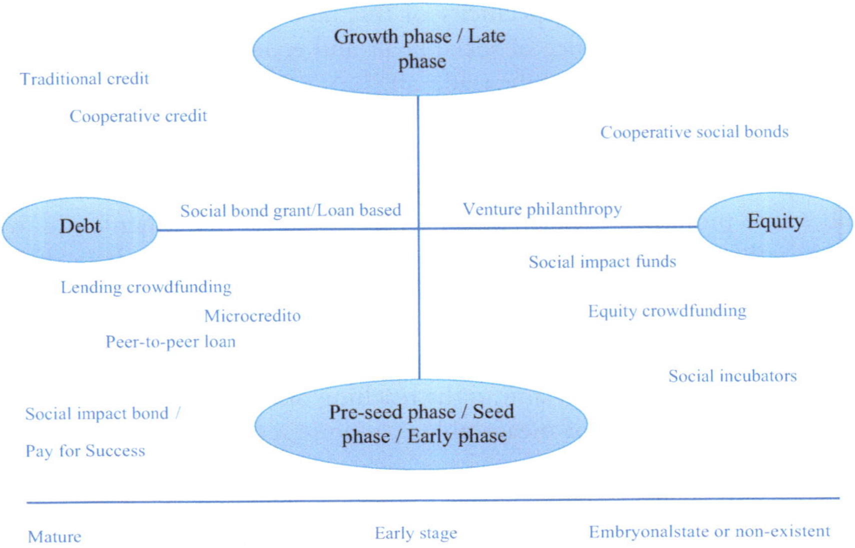

Fig. 6.1 The instruments of Social Impact in Italy. Source: Authors elaboration based on Social Impact Investment Italian Task Force (2014, p. 41)

financial innovation ever more functional to the communities' social needs and which constitute the "alternative voices" (Rappaport 2012; Shiller 2012) when compared to the traditional financial approaches, which showed their limits and inadequacies during the recent financial and economic crisis (Krugman 2014).

In this scenario, the Meridonare social crowdfunding platform constitutes a best practice because it has permitted the Banco di Napoli Foundation to generate a social multiplicator of 400% compared with traditional philanthropic activities. Through a descriptive and exploratory analysis of the resource allocation procedures based on a "pay-for-performance" rewarding mechanism, the authors aim to identify an innovative financial structure. This emerges through conjunct financial and relational efforts, which make the funded organizations financially sustainable and are capable of creating a shared social impact in the economic and social context. The new financial architecture can be legitimately included in the framework of social impact investing instruments, thereby contributing to the ongoing academic debate. The present work contributes to the current literature on the effective use of financial instruments in welfare policies and has implications for both entrepreneurs and crowdfunding platform owners whose aim is to set up an effective and successful crowdfunding industry for social finances.

2 Literature Review

The theory of social capital (Coleman 1990; Putnam 2000) suggests that a network of social relationships can constitute a strategic resource for undertaking and conducting social business initiatives, since the social context in which an entrepreneur is embedded is an additional and important contributor to entrepreneurship (Know and Arenius 2010). The strong interdependence between business and community (Porter and Kramer 2011), where the social capital community produces its benefits on the business (Roxas and Azmat 2014), has produced the emergence of even more business initiatives oriented towards the promotion of social changes and a sense of greater cohesion within communities. Recent literature has dedicated particular attention to the definition of new business models capable of promoting innovative yet sustainable social initiatives, since many of them present high levels of risk associated with medium-long-term sustainability (Bammi and Verma 2014; Letts et al. 1995).

In response to this need, in recent decades, new forms of Social and Sustainable Finance have been born, particularly financial platforms whose aim is to support social entrepreneurship initiatives. Financial and non-financial support to the social entrepreneurship is becoming fundamental in terms of contribution to the progress of the global economy. In the broad range of the Social and Sustainable Finance landscape (Harji and Hebb 2010; Weber 2012; Geobey and Weber 2013; Hochstadter and Scheck 2015), an important role is played by the "Social Impact Investment," a branch of study that aims to favor the intervention of private financial resources in the financing of social programs (Martin 2013). It promotes innovative financial structures capable of attracting different types of investors aware of the fact that their financial resources are directed to activities that produce both measurable financial and social returns (Viviers et al. 2011; Jackson 2013; Wood et al. 2013; Evans 2013). In the current literature, a distinction between Impact Investing, an expression coined by two international financial institutions, J.P. Morgan and The Rockefeller Foundation, and Social Impact Investing is not yet clear. The current literature (Freireich and Fulton 2009; Nicholls 2010; Harji and Jackson 2012; Louche et al. 2012; Martin 2013; Clarkin and Cangioni 2016) has included in the definition of "Impact Investing" different financial manifestations, such as blended value investing and all financial instruments meant to create both social and financial returns. This has led some scholars to suggest that the two terms are synonyms (Imbert and Knoepfel 2011) or that "Social Impact Investing" is a subcategory of "Impact Investing" (Hill et al. 2011).

According to the definition of the Global Impact Investing Network (GIIN), impact investing includes all investments in social enterprises, organizations and financial funds made by companies, organizations and funds with the intent of generating measurable social and environmental impacts jointly with an economic return. Compared to socially responsible and ethical investments, which are built on the will to respect environmental, moral and social values, impact investing is characterized by the explicit intention to generate a measurable, positive social impact without refusing, at the same time, to create an acceptable yield for investors. Together with the intent to produce socially relevant and measurable improvements, the yield can be seen as one of the qualifying elements of this form of investing. Social Impact Investments, in contrast, are investments primarily directed to the generation of a positive social impact, as they consider the social impact itself as the main driver of the investment. The financial architecture is implemented with the sole scope of making the investment procedure both sustainable and lucrative: financial capital is no longer the goal but rather a means by which the social finality can be achieved (Crescentini and Zaccardi 2016).

It appears to be evident that the characterizing element of both categories is the joint achievement of a social impact and a financial return on the investment (Hochstadter and Scheck 2015). Nicholls and Daggers (2016) affirm, however, that Social Impact Investment refers to organizations that deliberately aim to create measurable social and environmental value and, if possible, to obtain a financial return on the investment.

From this perspective, Social Impact Investments are investments capable of sustaining social enterprises in the creation of a social impact where the attention is concentrated more on the organization in which the investment is made (investee) rather than on the investors (Cantino et al. 2016). However, the current banking and financial literature (O'Donohoe et al. 2010) labels both categories of emerging assets as characterized by atypical risk-return relations. Thus, social impact configures a third essential dimension in the evaluation of investments: if traditional finance suggests considering only the trade-off between risk and return, in social impact investing, it is necessary to introduce the dimension of the social impact that the investment is able to create. This will induce investors to consider as worthy even those investments with returns in line with or below those of the market that permit the generation of measurable social impacts (outcome).

The cultural revolution that financial instruments for social impact can generate finds its origin in the collaborative approach adopted to reach community goals. Overcoming a perspective based exclusively on the achievement of single outputs in the short term makes it possible to create an action model based on financial blending, which consists of the fusion of public and private funds finalized to the financing of social development projects (Geobey and Weber 2013; Jackson 2013). In this way, a short-term vision, based on the mere production of outputs, leaves room for an outcome-oriented approach finalized at the attainment of behavioral, institutional and social effects observable in the medium and the long terms.

Creating social value thus means determining a tangible and durable change in a specific context (Crutchfield and Grant 2008; Perrini 2007) by significantly modifying the life conditions of the recipients of the social mission (Roche 1999). In other words, creating social value also means producing behavioral, institutional and social changes observable in the medium and the long terms (between 3 and 10 years) made possible by means of the firms' short-term results (outputs). The outcome, however, is sustainable long-term change that influences the population and the environment that has been determined by the intervention of the organization, intervention that is also influenced by exogenous variables and that is verifiable with a counterfactual analysis, a type of evaluation that allows us to verify what would have occurred in the absence of the intervention of the organization itself. An impact value chain is a tool that allows us to identify the steps that constitute the so-called Theory of Change (ToC), a theory based on a logic setting that begins with the identification of the specific need that must be satisfied and then leads to the desired change by performing the processes of setting goals, identifying causal nodes and acting consistently with the decisions made (Zamagni et al. 2015). In this way, the Theory of Change constitutes a reliable framework: this strategic tool, more and more widespread and adopted in international philanthropy initiatives, starting from the identification of the social impact goal, explicates the causal process "outcome-output-activities," defines evidence-based modes to produce the desired change and sets measurable indicators adopted to both monitor the whole process and to verify if the financed project is running smoothly (Castello and Lévêque 2016). It is then important to evaluate the importance of each activity and the corresponding resources to invest in the realization of change (Kail and Lumley 2012).

Hence, performance measurement becomes a relevant issue for the community, which benefits both from the improved transparency and reliability of the results (Solari 1997) and from the actions performed by the investor himself, who needs to improve resource allocation efficiency (Nel and McQuaid 2002; Nicholls 2009; Zamagni et al. 2015) through the selection of high-impact projects, portfolio management activities, reporting processes and an effective communication of the chosen investment models (Perrini and Vurro 2013). Focusing philanthropic interventions on those organizations that have centered their mission around the creation of shared social value and are able to replicate in a virtuous manner the achievable results is becoming a fundamental step in the selection of community-friendly initiatives.

The modification made regarding the so-called Third Sector has been particularly cautious in giving an answer to the European guidelines on the subject of the evaluation of social impact through the adoption of evaluation methods capable of finding the correct balance between qualitative and quantitative data (CESE 2013). Although the entire social impact investing sector is working on social impact evaluation practices, a reliable set of evaluation tools has not yet been identified: the Impact

Reporting and Investment Standards (IRIS) and the Global Impact Investment Rating System (GIIRS) can be qualified as attempts to standardize the procedures through which organizations can communicate their performance by favoring the comparison between the investment made and the corresponding benchmarks and by providing measurable indicators. Thus, this new emerging industry has started to create a network and metrics to measure the value of its social impact, which is usually seen as a qualitative variable (Jackson 2013; Clarkin and Cangioni 2016).

Social enterprises are then called upon to report the produced social impact, the latter intended as the significant change of communities' welfare conditions determined by the allocation of social investment capital in order to become recipients of social impact financial instruments.

The first academic studies on social investment and impact investing date back to 2011 (Viviers et al. 2011). Since then, several other studies (Nicholls et al. 2015; Schinckus 2015; Brandsetter and Lehner 2015; Daggers and Nicholls 2016; Lehner 2016; Weber 2016) have featured the observations of practitioners (Saltuk et al. 2011) and institutions (Social Impact Investment Task Force 2014; OECD 2015; Sodalitas Foundation 2015; Gonnella and Cerlenco 2016). A recent work (Rizzello et al. 2016) provides a picture of the existing state of the Social Impact Investments academic landscape. The authors note three "domains" of research: sustainable finance, impact entrepreneurship and public policy in the social sector. The need has emerged to define a map of innovative models of financial investment, such as Social Impact Bonds, Social Bonds, venture philanthropy and lending and equity crowdfunding, which could transform the supply of social services.

Among others, we focus on crowdfunding, arisen as one of the innovative financing and fundraising tools. From the analysis of the current literature, a lack of attention emerges regarding the role of crowdfunding in the impact investing field.

The crowdsourcing revolution (Howe 2006) has made possible the beginning of a process based on the co-creation of value through digital technologies: the disintermediation of web-based platforms and online communities, which has given easy access to widespread financial resources, allowing firms to fundraise their activity (Landstrom 1992; Schwienbacher and Larralde 2010; Ordanini et al. 2011; Freund 2012; Wheat et al. 2013; Belleflamme et al. 2014; Marlett 2015).

Crowdsourcing is influencing innovation processes through a mechanism of interaction between the providers and the seekers of strategic resources. If, initially, the strategic resources were mainly knowledge based, currently the financial-based resources are becoming a relevant aspect of crowdsourcing thanks to crowdfunding, which in recent years has been considered capable of turning a large audience of customers into investors (Schwienbacher and Larralde 2010; Ordanini et al. 2011; Belleflamme et al. 2014; Feola et al. 2017). Crowdfunding literally connects entrepreneurs with potential funders or individuals who can supply financial capital (Wheat et al. 2013; Marlett 2015). This is possible thanks to intermediation Internet-based platforms, which act as an alternative finance marketplace where it is possible to collect and channel the private capitals to sustain business ideas (Agrawal et al. 2011).

It is possible to distinguish different typologies of crowdfunding (Schwienbacher and Larralde 2010). On the one hand, we find token crowdfunding, dealing with the donation-based model, which entails online charity fundraising campaigns; on the other hand, literature identifies investing crowdfunding, encompassing in this category the lending-based, the reward-based and the equity-based models, differing from each other on the basis of the returns (interests, rewards and dividends).

Crowdfunding, as a bottom-up financing approach, might be able to collect and to redirect all the financial resources that are usually overlooked by the traditional banking intermediaries. Those resources are potentially ready to be transformed into investments directed towards high-impact social and environmental initiatives (La Torre 2013). Thus, crowdfunding seems to be capable of producing a social impact, especially considering its vocation to fund social enterprises, very close to the phenomenon of impact investing (Shaw and Carter 2007; Bull 2007; Nicholls 2009; Arvidson et al. 2010; Slootweg et al. 2011; Lane and Casile 2011; Barraket and Yousefpour 2013; Estévez et al. 2013). Starting from these premises, the authors study the role of crowdfunding campaigns and impact investing.

3 Aim and Methodology

In the current ever-changing scenario, one of the main challenges consists of encouraging the process of promotion of social finance initiatives oriented towards impact investing. From the analysis of a successful case of a crowdfunding donation—reward-based platform, the present work aims to understand how a platform that integrates fund gathering with the assignment based on a "pay-for-success" mechanism might evolve in an impact investing logic.

The current nature of the topic, the paucity of data, the early stages of the analyzed phenomenon and the explorative nature of the research led the authors to apply a case study approach (Yin 2014). Specifically, our research uses a qualitative approach to perform an exploratory analysis compiled with primary data sources: official documents integrated with published reports, online databases and interviews with key informants (top management of foundations and the head of Meridonare). Therefore, the research is designed as a qualitative and epistemological investigation with a holistic approach.

In particular, we adopted a single case study. This choice is motivated by the fact that we are examining an unusual case. A case is unusual when it presents some peculiarities that justify an in-depth study, which could also reveal insights into the normal processes/procedures/techniques and thus have repercussions useful for everyday practice (Yin 2014). The research methodology adopted and the study of a specific case have made it possible to capture the dynamics of the specific phenomenon, relatively new in the literature (Eisenhardt 1989).

This chapter outlines the decision-making process followed by a banking foundation in selecting projects of investment with a high social impact, gathering and allocating capital efficiently with the aim of creating a Social Impact Investing model capable of increasing the value added of the foundation. The strategic management of philanthropic initiatives must necessarily be oriented to the careful research of solutions of the optimizing processes. Therefore, the decision to associate traditional fundraising with a crowdfunding platform is definitely a more effective way to gather resources. In this context, the "Meridonare" case study, the first social crowd-fundraising platform in Southern Italy, can be considered a best practice. In 2016, the Banco di Napoli Foundation, thanks to a wide range of online and offline services (planning and development of the crowd-fundraising plan, social communication, social networking and social reporting of the project), increased the capital gathered in the territory by 400%. Diversifying the raising of capital by leveraging on the crowd and investing in social impact projects were aimed at creating added value exponentially.

The present chapter aims primarily at a twofold goal: first, describing a Social Finance best practice (Meridonare social crowdfunding platform—Banco di Napoli Foundation) that collects capital and provides services to social organizations with the intent of giving an impulse to the creation of relational and social capital, and second, configuring an innovative financial architecture to gather capital to be invested in social activities to create both social and economic value. Accordingly, the new financial structure identifies a new role for the Banco di Napoli Foundation, which from "impact facilitator" elevates itself to "impact generator" as a key player of Social Impact Investment.

4 The Meridonare Case Study: An Innovative Social Service Platform

The "Meridonare" crowdfunding platform operates as a limited liability company (Meridonare Ltd.) characterized by the "Startup Innovativa a Vocazione Sociale (SIAV)" legal form. This legal form makes it possible to preserve both its innovative setup and its social and philanthropic vocation. In Italy, SIAVs were created with the clear intention of facing the difficulties encountered by many social organizations when the collection of capital, both from donations and equity/debt capital, is needed. Today, this particular legal form represents the most important means for encouraging the use of additional financial resources besides philanthropic funds. However, an appropriate financial literacy is not yet present in the Third Sector. For this reason, banks and foundations have implemented in recent years several financial experiments aimed at collecting capital and promoting local communities.

Meridonare was established in November 2015 and is led by Banco di Napoli Foundation (an Italian banking foundation), which considers it as an instrument for enhancing its social interventions. Italian banking foundations are defined by the Italian law as "Enti privati con finalità sociali" (i.e., "Private Entities with Social Purposes") and use their assets to promote philanthropic activities in the territory to which they belong. Meridonare's mission is "to plan and develop its activity of capital collection by means of innovative financial instruments, which are intended to promote the culture of giving and its reciprocity, the social well-being and the development of local communities through the creation of social infrastructures and of social capital enhancement mechanisms." The purpose of Meridonare is to become the reference point for all who aim at planning social, cultural or civic interventions targeted to promote a new way of intending active citizenship in local urban areas by using the crowdfunding platform to improve, from both qualitative and proactive standpoints, the welfare of Southern Italy. Meridonare's goal is to support all worthy and innovative social, cultural and civic ideas and projects directed at promoting the culture of philanthropic giving, the sense of community and the creation of strong and cohesive social bonds by having as its main reference the South of Italy, its resources, its talents and its unlimited potential.

The platform is strongly service oriented towards those who propose ideas rooted in reliable empirical evidence. Those proposing institutions, especially in the Third Sector, usually lack the ability to collect funds by using crowdfunding platforms and to utilize effectively all marketing tools aimed at promoting the initiative to be funded. Meridonare offers several online and offline services to assist the promoter from the presentation phase all the way through the realization phase. The assistance services given in the phase of definition of the fundraising campaign have been improved, and today Meridonare offers many services to the promoters of the idea, which cover the entire life cycle of a project (Fig. 6.2).

A fundamental theme in the development of the crowdfunding platform has been the instrumental relationship with the Banco di Napoli Foundation, which in addition to funding the startup phase of the project, has been, since the early phase, the main funder of Meridonare's

Fig. 6.2 Main services offered by Meridonare. Source: Authors' elaboration

campaigns, which has always been considered a platform targeted at promoting the social interventions of the Foundation.

Over time, the applicant's evaluation process, which initially was performed preventively by the board of directors of the Banco di Napoli Foundation based on an inquiry conducted on the documental archives, has been modified. In fact, the greater variety and richness of the information produced during the interviews with the applicants has created the need for a measurement of the social value of a project. Despite the common difficulties encountered in the evaluation of social initiatives because of the adoption of objective criteria, a more well-structured process of evaluation oriented to the creation of social evaluation reports of the campaigns has been adopted. The reports are then presented to the board of directors of the Foundation, which eventually grants an incentive program targeted to the involvement of the applicant organization in the funding phase and in the realization phase of the project.

Figure 6.3 illustrates the process of evaluation currently adopted and highlights object, goal, measurable indicators and performances of each evaluation phase.

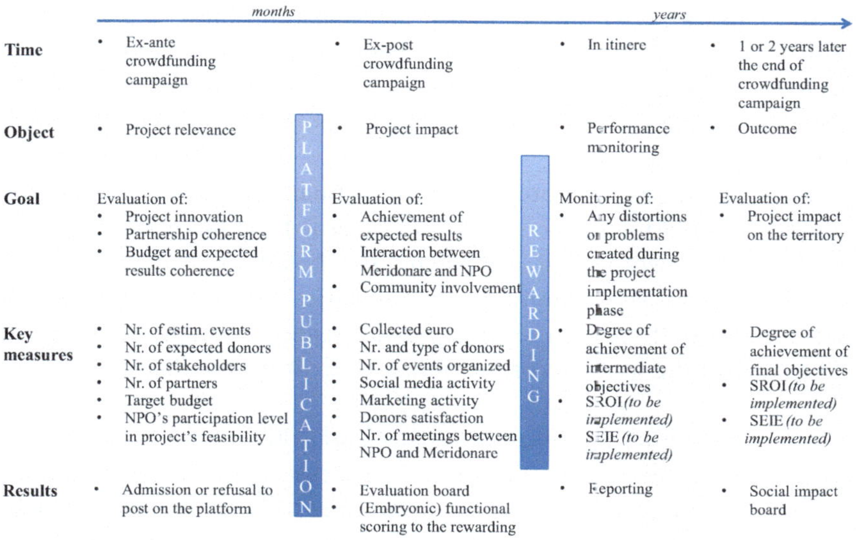

Fig. 6.3 The evaluation process of Meridonare

The evaluation process is not a "black-box" but is shared with the applicants right from the planning phase of the proposal. The sharing of the ex-ante, ex-post, in itinere and final evaluation mechanisms helps to implement effective and efficient behaviors and actions for the following:

- the financial target of the crowdfunding campaign (funding);
- the implementation of the intervention (output) controlled by Meridonare, then publicized on the platform;
- the evaluation of the social impact (outcome) made by the Foundation, published annually in the social balance sheet.

The evaluation process of the Banco di Napoli Foundation, in accordance with the fundamentals outlined by the Theory of Change, represents a first step in supporting the industry's various players by means of an impact model that permits the allocation of resources in a rational and strategic manner on efficient projects that conform to the Foundation's vision and mission.

The Banco di Napoli Foundation has identified in the evaluation of the social impact not only a tool to attract donations but also a means to monitor and evaluate the efficacy of its own social intervention. Such a mechanism actually makes it possible to establish specific priorities with reference to those projects that can be proposed for additional funds (Table 6.1).

The incentive program provides eventual financial intervention by the Foundation only for projects that have exceeded the financial target set out for the crowdfunding campaign. The board of directors of the Foundation evaluates monthly the analytical reports prepared by Meridonare's staff for each campaign and decides to assign an incentive and to deliver the funds according to the procedure described here:

- If the crowdfunding project collects at least 100% of the funds (funding target achieved), it receives an incentive from the Foundation, which determines the amount of resources to be transferred (which range from 7% up to 15%) in accordance with the score obtained.

Table 6.1 The mechanism of rewarding

Key measure (% of collected funds)	Rewarding applicability and conditions for availability of funds	Percentage of the rewarding
<15%	NO NPO will not receive the funds	0%
15% < X < 50%	NO NPO must remodel the project and the availability depends on the degree of conviction generated by the project	0%
50% < X < 100%	NO NPO will receive immediately the funds	0%
100%	YES	Class scoring E: 0% Class scoring A, B, C, D: from 7% to 15% of the collected funds

- If the crowdfunding project collects more than 50% of the funds, then resources are available for the NPO.
- If the crowdfunding project collects between 15% and 50% of the funds, the applicant organization ought to modify its proposal to persuade both Meridonare and the Foundation that the additional funds will contribute significantly to the finalization of the project (e.g., the NPO wants to buy a nine-seater bus, but, alternatively, chooses to buy a six-seater bus or to acquire a bus by recurring to debt capital and then using the funds collected and the incentives to extinguish the payments).
- If the crowdfunding project collects less than 15% of the funds, the NPO will not receive the funds, and the funds will be devolved to another project on the platform.

In conclusion, in the authors' opinion, the monitoring and evaluation mechanism outlined above includes all the elements needed to generate a social scoring/rating system instrumental to the development and improvement of the entire evaluation chain. According to the present view, it is necessary to both refine the measurable indicators adopted throughout the whole process and to validate such a mechanism through a statistical-quantitative analysis conducted on the projects funded to date. Furthermore, the incentive mechanism is functional to the introduction of the pay-for-success mechanism, which characterizes the funding structure proposed in the following paragraph.

5 Future Directions: A New Financial Structure for Social Impact Investments

The current operating model of Meridonare follows a traditional scheme. Meridonare is a crowdfunding platform where private individuals provide resources in the form of endowment in favor of social projects conveyed on the platform. So defined, the scheme falls into the category of donation/reward crowdfunding. As such, it does not currently feature characteristics that could determine its inclusion into the category of Social Impact Investment financial instruments.

However, for the purposes of the present chapter, two important characteristics of Meridonare are taken into account.

The first is the holistic approach that accompanies the entire fundraising process. Not a mere online platform, Meridonare offers a number of online and offline solutions ranging from the project submission phase to the end of the crowdfunding campaign.

The second element concerns the project evaluation activity that occurs at the stage either before or after the crowdfunding campaign. In the pre-campaign phase, Meridonare analyzes the project in terms of completeness, potentiality and social impact by assigning its own evaluation judgment. The preliminary assessment of the project aims to decide whether to place the request on the platform without the assignment of a score to be communicated to the donors. In the final phase, namely, at the end of the campaign, Meridonare assesses the social impact of the campaign on the community and evaluates the social report of the funded project.

The evaluation process adopted by Meridonare is a first step towards the development of a social rating system, which, as we will see later in the work, is a prerequisite for the qualitative-quantitative evaluation of projects with a social impact. By referring to the formal system developed by Meridonare, it is possible to map the evolution towards a social score/rating system that can guide the project's financial viability. For the internal rating systems adopted in the banking sector, obtaining a favorable score enhances the financeability of the social impact project in terms of the speed of the fund collection, the size of the funds collected and the conditions applied (for example, in the case of lending crowdfunding and social bonds).

As described in the previous paragraph, the rewards assigned by Meridonare are already based on a reward (greater contribution) appointment mechanism (pay for success) in the presence of a virtuous fundraising campaign in terms of funds raised over the target (output) and a set of qualitative parameters (including social activism, which demonstrates good mobilization of stakeholders). In this context, Meridonare and, consequently, the Foundation, act as "facilitators of impact," and the NPO, endangering its reputation with the risk of failure in implementing the project, is encouraged to act successfully through the mechanism of reward.

Based on these assumptions, it is possible to hypothesize an evolution of Meridonare's financing structure in accordance with the paradigm of performance/risk/social impact. The new potential financial structure helps guide the shift of Meridonare's (and the Foundation's) role from "impact facilitator" to "impact generator." The evolution drives the transition from donation/reward crowdfunding to a more systematic scheme (social impact logic) that, thanks to the presence of new actors, can virtuously combine the peculiarities of some of the funding instruments used in Social Finance: social bond grant/loan based, lending crowdfunding, social impact bond/pay for success and venture philanthropy.

Table 6.2 presents the characteristics of the financing instruments and the peculiarities of each of them as found in the case under examination.

More specifically, the hypothesized scheme provides the translation from a two-dimensional structure of impact-investing tools to a three-dimensional structure. From this perspective, Meridonare, while continuing to act as a crowdfunding platform, might propose a new financial structure (Social Bond Crowdfunding based—SBCb). In line with the social impact investment logic, the SBCb groups the peculiarities of the aforementioned typologies of social financing and obtains the right to be fully inserted into the SII tools landscape.

Table 6.2 The peculiarities of the social financing instruments present in the examined case (Social Impact Investment Italian Task Force 2014; The Cariplo Foundation 2013)

Type	Description	The peculiarities of the social financing instruments present in the case examined
Social bond grant/loan based	Bonds with lower market yields; the sums collected are intended to finance social projects by way of donation and/or financing on competitive terms	It is expected to issue bonds with features of social bond loan based
Lending crowdfunding	Loan form that, through an online platform, allows private investors to give as interest or zero rate funds for social value projects	Meridonare is the online crowdfunding platform through which social fundraising projects are presented in form of both donation/reward (as is) and lending (to be)
Social impact bond/pay for success	Configurable as a partnership between various actors to raise private capital to promote innovative public policies by contractual forms of "payment for results"	The financing structure takes on typical characteristics of the social impact bond with particular reference to both the payment for success and the mechanism for evaluating and monitoring the results
Venture philanthropy	A series of both financial and non-financial initiatives with a long-term horizon aiming to increase the social impact of projects promoted by ILOs	Banco di Napoli Foundation supports the activity of Meridonare and the nascent intermediary (SPV) to increase the extent and depth of its philanthropic mission

To better understand the extent of the change, a description of the financing scheme is provided below: (a) presentation of the actors involved; (b) illustration of the operating mechanism; (c) description of the peculiarities of the various funding instruments present in the proposed model; and (d) description of the risk/performance/social impact paradigm for each of the actors (Fig. 6.4).

By referring to the SIB structure, the proposed scheme consists of five stakeholders who are linked to each other by bilateral long-term contracts:

- Non-Profit Organization (NPO);
- Crowdfunding platform (Meridonare);
- Banking foundation (Banco di Napoli Foundation);
- Specialized intermediary (SPV-Special Purpose Vehicle);
- Private and institutional investors with social and impact investor purposes (social and impact investor).

The specialized intermediary (SPV) issues social bonds that are subscribed to by private and institutional investors (social impact investors). The bonds issued provide a more competitive (i.e., lower) remuneration

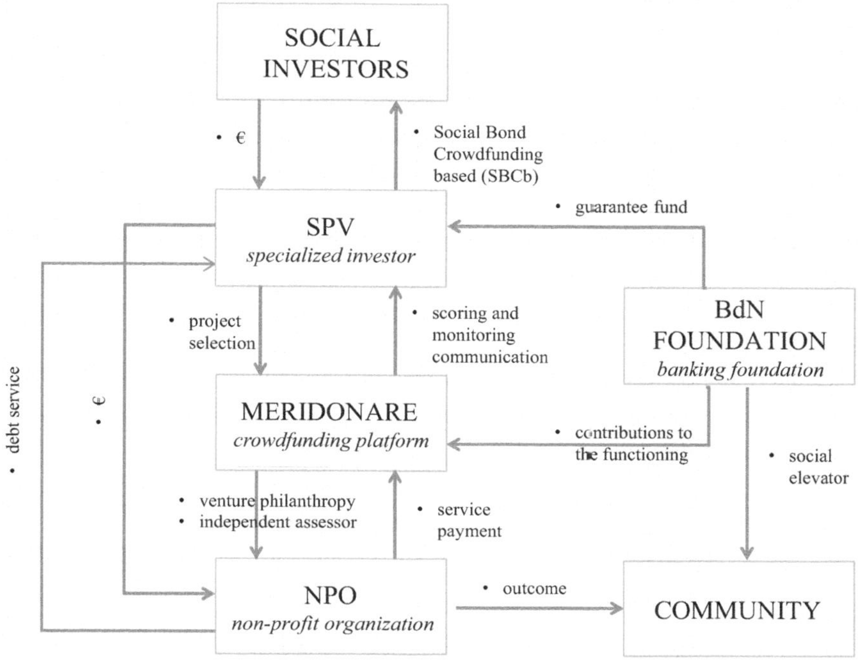

Fig. 6.4 The operating diagram of SBCb

than market securities with similar characteristics and durations. In the first stage, the remuneration is fixed, and the repayment of the capital occurs in a single solution (bullet bond).[1] The money collected by SPV is devoted in the form of lending to high social impact projects run on the crowdfunding platform managed by Meridonare. A part of the funds raised (assumed at 1%) is used to cover SPV's management costs and transaction costs. To mitigate the emerging opportunistic behavior of the NPO, fund distribution occurs not in a single solution but in a gradual manner according to the need for funds to cover implementation costs.

SPV acts as a specialized intermediary and, as an asset manager, administers the resources collected in compliance with the risk/performance/social impact criteria. The selection of projects and, therefore, the allocation of the funds gathered benefit from Meridonare's evaluation activity. By acting as an independent assessor as well as the platform manager, Meridonare defines the scoring system and the monitoring and measuring system of the final performance. Specifically, the allocation of resources is influenced by the score assigned by the evaluator to each project. Assigning a good score favors campaign closing speed and mitigates funding conditions. In addition to the assignment of a score, Meridonare continuously monitors the project funded, measures the performance and certifies the achievement of the goal by communicating its outcomes to the SPV. If delays to the achievement of the social objective arise, SPV has the contractual power to request revisions and adjustments in the funded project.

The ex-ante, on-going and ex-post evaluation process plays a key role in ensuring the proper functioning of the mechanism as a whole. It follows that the role of Meridonare, and its coordination with SPV, are critical factors of success based on the professionalism, independence and experience of the two players.

With the funds raised through the placement of bonds, the SPV can grant medium- and long-term funding to non-profit organizations (NPOs) at a reduced rate compared to the conditions normally applied

---

[1] Fixed remuneration is an element of diversity compared to the standard scheme of a Social Impact Bond (SIB). However, as will be seen later, the proposed scheme retains the peculiarities of the "pay for success" mechanism.

to similar funding. The lower yield offered to bond subscribers is transferred entirely, in terms of the rate of interest rate reduction applied, to these funds. The scoring system contributes to the application of cheaper rates according to a reverse pay-for-success scheme. As mentioned, the assignment of a more favorable score improves the financing conditions. In the case of a high-standing project, the actual cost of financing may be lower than that accorded to investors by the rewarding mechanism: in this case, the Foundation provides contributions to the NPO based on the merit awarded by Meridonare to the project.

In addition to supporting a specialized brokerage (SPV) and crowdfunding platform (Meridonare), the Foundation also guarantees default in the repayment of the loan by acting as a last-resort lender. In this context, the Foundation allocates a sum of non-repayable resources that serve as a guarantee to cover the investment. Although this element differs from the financial structure proposed by the classic SIB scheme (i.e., the concentration of financial risk on the part of investors), we believe that such correction is necessary to mitigate the financial damage at the expense of the social investor and, therefore, to help remove one of the critical obstacles that restrain, for now, the spread of financing in the sector of social innovation services.

An example clarifies the operation of the proposed financial structure.

Let us assume that the SPV issues a bond of 1 million euros. The bond expires in five years and grants a 3% yield rate of less than approximately 200 basis points on securities with similar characteristics without any social purpose.

The SPV invests in two high-impact projects run by Meridonare: the first project presents an excellent score, whereas the second receives a score that is positioned in the mid-range. To both projects, €500,000 is assigned at a rate of 3% (you can assume, for ease of calculation, that the SPV management costs are null).

Consequently, instead of an amount of 30-thousand-euro annuity interest, the SPV receives 30 thousand, of which 15 thousand is from project A and 15 thousand is from project B. However, the actual cost for the most virtuous social project (or project A, to which Meridonare has awarded a better score) will be lower because it will benefit from the Foundation's contribution in the form of a reward. If the reward recognized by the Foundation amounts to €10,000, the financial cost for Project A will fall from 3% to 1%, thereby encouraging the adoption of virtuous behavior by the NPO. Seeing as, for the reasons stated below, it is expected that social bonds will produce a fixed remuneration (3%) in the first stage, the higher the expected target of the funded project, the higher the contribution of the foundation.

Thus, the pay-for-success mechanism would still have its own application, though in a way different to the classic one. In the traditional pay-for-success mode, when the achievement of the minimum social objective is certified (or when the project is successful), the lent capital is given back and, based on the results, the return on capital may vary up to the prefixed maximum value. In the model presented, the remuneration of the capital is fixed and guaranteed to overcome the uncertainties of the investors and to promote the development of social bonds. The pay-for-success mechanism nevertheless finds its application: the achievement of the result is reflected not in the higher remuneration for the investor but in the lower cost sustained by the virtuous NPO thanks to the Foundation's free contribution. In our view, this circumstance finds its logical justification in the fact that the most virtuous project (or the one that has received a more favorable score) will produce a greater social impact (higher outcome). The higher social benefits generated in favor of the community justify the greater contribution to a non-profit that operates in the Foundation's area and encourages the adoption of virtuous behavior by the NPO.

The model proposed aims towards reconciliation, by means of the enhancement of the peculiarities of the financing instruments represented in Table 6.3.

The combination of the characteristic elements of the financing instruments serves as an amplifier for social impact initiatives and, if properly implemented, can make the new SBCb funding structure propagate as a replicable and scalable reference model through the involvement of other actors (e.g., banking foundation, public administration).

At the end of the description of the new funding structure, for each of the actors involved, the risk/performance/social impact paradigm is illustrated in Table 6.4.

Table 6.3 The peculiarities of funding instruments in the proposed scheme

Element	Instrument	Peculiarities of the case	Impact/ Presence
Activities in the social field	SILb, SIB, LC, VP	• Projects funded through Meridonare are only those that generate social and economic value	
Pay for success	SIB	• Although in a different mode, pay for success drives the award of the award from the Foundation to the NPO	
Presence of an independent evaluator	SIB	• Meridonare operates from an independent assessor by assigning a score to social projects according to a scoring system	
Knowledge and social experience	SILb, SIB, LC, VP	• Meridonare has developed social skills and provides online and offline integrated services to support crowdfunding campaigns	
Identifying target population	SILb, SIB, LC, VP	• Selection of beneficiary projects by SPV benefits from Meridonare's evaluation activity	
Long-term orientation	SILb, SIB, LC	• The Foundation addresses social issues with innovative tools and medium–long-term horizons	
Risk allocation	SIB	• Compared with SIB, the risk is not entirely allocated to investors by virtue of the role of guarantor exercised by the Foundation	

SILb social bond loan, *SIB* social impact bond, *LC* lending crowdfunding, *VP* venture philanthropy

6 Conclusion

The Social Finance research field, and in particular the Impact Investing field, has not yet been explored by finance scholars; therefore, it is worth identifying new social finance initiatives oriented towards impact investing. By describing and exploring the success of the crowdfunding donation-reward Meridonare platform, the present work aims to define an innovative financial structure: Social Bond Crowdfunding based

Table 6.4 The risk/performance/social impact paradigm in the SBCb

Actor	Yield	Risk	Social impact
NPO	The greater the score of the project, the greater the chances of successfully closing the crowdfunding campaign and obtaining better financing conditions thanks to the reward	The worse the score, the lesser the chances of success of the campaign, and the less favorable the financing conditions	Social value is the main determinant driving the score assignment
Meridonare	The success of the campaigns driven by the platform raises the reputation of Meridonare	Failure of the driven campaigns worsens the *standing reputation* of Meridonare	The platform raises the breadth and depth of social impact investments by measuring ex-ante and ex-post results through a score and monitoring process
Banco Napoli Foundation	The success of funded projects (outcome) maximizes the effectiveness of the Foundation's social activity	The inefficiency/ ineffectiveness of the proposed model worsens the social performance of the Foundation	As a facilitator and guarantor, the Foundation amplifies the scope of social impact contributions
Investors	The goodness of the funded projects raises the social dividend	The social bond yield is lower than the market value	The spread of new funding instruments raises the ability to raise funds for social finance interventions

(continued)

Table 6.4 (continued)

Actor	Yield	Risk	Social impact
SPV	The ability to build trust relationships between the various actors involved makes the SPV's role determinative	Failure of the financing scheme increases transaction costs until they become more sustainable	By acting as a specialized broker, SPV favors the introduction of new tools and reduces the adverse selection of the social impact projects

(SBCb). Through the gathering and usage of resources, it can preserve the central role of the community, the beneficiary of social interventions, and ensure an adequate return on the capital invested. In the authors' view, SBCb can be legitimately included in the framework of social impact investing instruments, contributing to the ongoing academic debate on the sustainability of social initiatives.

The analysis carried out is based on the in-depth reading of a case study that highlights a precise evolution in the process of the assignment of financial resources to the requesting social organizations.

Whereas in a first phase, the Banco di Napoli Foundation assigned the resources according to the traditional scheme based on a request for contributions, the creation of the Meridonare crowdfunding platform changed the resource assignment procedures by applying an "impact model" evaluation process. This model, according to the postulates of the Theory of Change, represents a first step in the allocation of financial resources in a rational and strategic way to efficient projects in line with the Foundation's vision and mission. However, in its current state, the Meridonare crowdfunding platform represents only a collection mechanism for social initiatives, and it lacks the investing perspective. Moving from the strength of the crowdfunding platform and the procedures based on a "pay-for-performance" rewarding mechanism, we have identified an innovative financial structure: SBCb. It may represent the subsequent evolution of the aforementioned transition since, as a financial instrument, it is able to support social enterprises in the creation of social impact and to refund and reward the investors (Fig. 6.5). SBCb identifies the Foundation among the key players of Social Impact Investing.

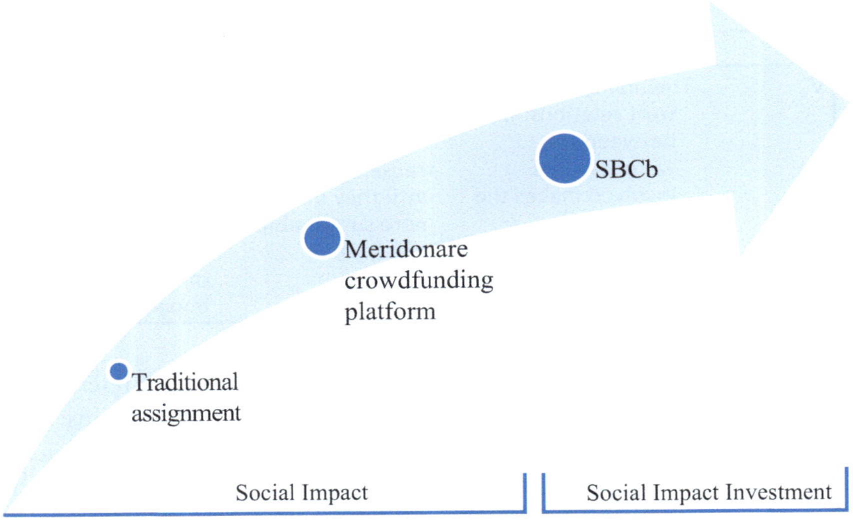

Fig. 6.5 The evolution process of the assignment of the financial resources

One of the aspects differentiating this new financial architecture from the preceding ones is the strategic role of the Foundation, which now is configured as a last-resort lender and as a guarantor for the repayment of the loan.

According to Social Impact Investment logic, the SBCb model focuses its attention on the beneficiary NPO (namely, the investee) rather than on the investors. The latter participate in the realization of a social project, accepting a yield that is below the average return that the market has to offer. In contrast, the beneficiary NPO benefits from the scoring system, which contributes to the application of cheaper rates according to a reverse pay-for-success scheme: the assignment of a more favorable score improves the financing conditions for the NPO. Therefore, the rewarding mechanism for resource allocation, already implemented by the Foundation through the services offered by the Meridonare crowdfunding platform, finds its higher expression in the new SBCb financial model.

This evolution drives the transition from donation/reward crowdfunding to a more systematic scheme (social impact logic) that, thanks to the presence of new actors, virtuously combines the peculiarities of some of the Social Impact Investment instruments: social bond grant/loan based, lending crowdfunding, social impact bond/pay for success and venture philanthropy.

Although a financial culture is not widespread among the foundations, a deep change has been observed in the international context. The role of foundations in the development of Social Impact Investing is becoming strategic. According to the Global Impact Investing Network (GIIN) and J.P. Morgan, 18% of the impact investments worldwide have in effect been made by foundations. Similarly, a *Financial Times'* recent survey noticed a convergence between the intervention models: 36% of the foundations in the sample are active in terms of both philanthropic interventions and Social Impact Investing (Financial Times 2016). With the new financial structure, the Banco di Napoli Foundation plays an important role in the challenge that Social Impact Investing represents for the key players. In fact, the Foundation may elevate itself to the role of "social impact generator" since it is directly capable of creating social change and of generating, at the same time, sustainable economic yields for the investors. In this way, the Foundation contributes to overcoming one of the major obstacles to the development and diffusion of social finance, namely, the skepticism of investors towards risk.

Despite the interesting results, the present work suffers from a series of limitations and offers several other suggestions for future research. First, the analysis of a single case, despite the fact that it may be justified by the newness of the topic and by the lack of empirical data, does not allow the validation of the proposed model, which has been analyzed without considering the inevitable obstacles deriving from the application of the current laws. Furthermore, it might be interesting to further study ex post the effectiveness of the social rating system and its possible development seeing that the Meridonare mechanism is still in an embryonal stage. The advancement in research could be carried out on the more than 100 projects supported by the Foundation to date. Lastly, we intend to evaluate the feasibility of an evolution of the present model, which considers a variable remuneration for investors that is closely linked to the social results of the project, with evident implications regarding the risk/return/social impact paradigm.

References

Agrawal, A. K., Catalini, C., & Goldfarb, A. (2011). *The geography of crowdfunding* (NBER Working Paper 16820). Cambridge, MA: National Bureau of Economic Research. Retrieved from http://www.nber.org/papers/w16820.

Arvidson, M., Lyon, F., McKay, S., & Moro, D. (2010). *The ambitions and challenges of SROI* (TSRC Working Paper 49). Birmingham: Third Sector Research Centre. Retrieved from http://www.tsrc.ac.uk/LinkClick.aspx?fileticket=QwHhaC%2br88Y%3d&tabid=500.

Azemati, H., Belinsky, M., Gillette, R., Liebman, J., Selman, A., & Wyse, A. (2013). Social impact bonds: Lessons learned so far. *Community Investment Review, 9*(1), 23–33.

Bammi, R., & Verma, A. (2014). Venture philantropy: An emerging paradigm of venture capital. *The XIMB Journal of Management, 11*(2), 127–140.

Barraket, J., & Yousefpour, N. (2013). Evaluation and social impact measurement amongst small to medium social enterprises: Process, purpose and value. *Australian Journal of Public Administration, 72*(4), 447–458. https://doi.org/10.1111/1467-8500.12042.

Belleflamme, P., Lambert, T., & Schwienbacher, A. (2014). Crowdfunding: Tapping the right crowd. *Journal of Business Venturing, 29*(5), 585–609. https://doi.org/10.2139/ssrn.1836873.

Brandsetter, L., & Lehner, O. M. (2015). *Impact investment portfolios: Including social risks and returns*. Oxford: ACRN Oxford Publishing House.

Bull, M. (2007). Balance: The development of a social enterprise business performance analysis tool. *Social Enterprise Journal, 3*(1), 49–66. https://doi.org/10.1108/17508610780000721.

Cantino, V., Coni, S., & Fiandrino, S. (2016). Venture philantropy: il supporto non finanziario a sostegno dell'imprenditorialità sociale. Il caso di Fondazione CRT. *Rivista impresa sociale, 8*. Retrieved from http://www.rivistaimpresasociale.it/rivista/item/160-venture-philanthropy-supporto-non-finanziario-imprenditorialita-sociale-fondazione-crt.html.

Castello, S., & Lévêque, C. (2016). La Theory of change come impact-model: diffusione e utilizzo a livello nazionale e internazionale. *Philanthropy Insights, 4*. Fondazione Lang Italia. Retrieved from http://en.fondazionelangitalia.it/wp-content/uploads/2016/03/Philanthropy-Insights-n_4.pdf.

CESE. (2013). *Parere sul tema "La misurazione dell'impatto sociale"*. Retrieved from http://www.socialelazio.it/binary/prtl_socialelazio/tbl_buonepratiche/misurazione_impatto_sociale.pdf.

Clarkin, J. E., & Cangioni, C. (2016). Impact investing: A primer and review of the literature. *Entrepreneurship Research Journal, 6*(2), 135–173. https://doi.org/10.1515/erj-2014-0011.
Coleman, J. (1990). *Foundations of social theory*. Cambridge: Harvard University Press.
Crescentini, L., & Zaccardi, E. (cur.). (2016). *Investimento ad impatto sociale: analisi ed opportunità*. Quaderno di approfondimento Assoprevidenza. Retrieved from https://assoprevidenza.it/quaderni/investimenti-a-impatto-sociale-analisi-e-opportunita-2/.
Crutchfield, L. R., & Grant, H. M. (2008). *Forces for good: The six practices of high impact nonprofits*. San Francisco, CA: Jossey Bass.
Daggers, J., & Nicholls, A. (2016). Academic research into social investment and impact investing: The status quo and future research. In O. M. Lehner (Ed.), *Routledge handbook of social and sustainable finance* (pp. 68–82). London: Routledge.
Del Giudice, A. (2015). *I social impact bond*. Milano: Franco Angeli.
Eisenhardt, K. M. (1989). Building theories from case study research. *Academy of Management Review, 14*(4), 532–550. https://doi.org/10.5465/AMR.1989.4308385.
Estévez, R. A., Walshe, T., & Burgman, M. A. (2013). Capturing social impacts for decision-making: A multicriteria decision analysis perspective. *Diversity and Distributions, 19*(5–6), 608–616.
Evans, M. (2013). Metting the challenge of impact investing: how can contracting practing secure social impact without sacrificing performance? *Journal of Sustainable Finance & Investment, 3*(2), 138–154.
Feola, M., Parente, R., D'Onofrio, T., & Marinato, E. (2017). The evolution of crowdfunding towards an impact investing logic: The case of Paulownia Social Project. *Journal of Modern Accounting and Auditing, 13*(1), 19–34.
Financial Times. (2016). Investing for global impact 2016.
Fondazione Cariplo. (2013). I social impact bond – La finanza al servizio dell'innovazione sociale. *Quaderni dell'Osservatorio, 11*.
Fondazione Sodalitas. (2015). *Introduzione alla finanza sociale*. Retrieved from http://www.sodalitas.it/public/allegati/Quaderno-Sodalitas-DEF_2015324184115309.pdf.
Freireich, J., & Fulton, K. (2009). *Investing for social & environmental impact: A design for catalyzing an emerging industry*. Cambridge, MA: Monitor Institute.
Freund, R. (2012). How to overcome the barriers between economy and sociology with open innovation, open evaluation and crowdfunding? *International Journal of Industrial Engineering and Management, 1*(3), 107–109.

Geobey, S., & Weber, O. (2013). Lessons in operationalizing social finance: The case of Vancouver City Savings Credit Union. *Journal of Sustainable Finance & Investment, 3*(2), 124–137. https://doi.org/10.1080/20430795.2013.776259.

Gonnella, C., & Cerlenco, S. (2016). *La finanza ad impatto sociale*. Fondazione Tertio Millennio-Onlus. Roma: Ecra.

Harji, K., & Hebb, T. (2010). *Investing for impact: Issues and opportunities for social finance in Canada*. Ottawa: Carleton Centre for Community Innovation.

Harji, K., & Jackson, E. T. (2012). *Accelerating impact: Achievements, challenges and what's next in building the impact investing industry*. New York, NY: The Rockefeller Foundation.

Hill, K. R., Walter, R. S., Bozicevic, M., Eder, J., Headland, T., Hewlett, B., et al. (2011). Co-residence patterns in hunter-gatherer societies show unique human social structure. *Science, 331*(6022), 1286–1289. https://doi.org/10.1126/science.1199071.

Hochstadter, A. K., & Scheck, B. (2015). What's in a name: An analysis of impact investing understandings by academics and practitioners. *Journal of Business Ethics, 13*(2), 449–475.

Howe, J. (2006). The rise of crowdsourcing. *Wired Magazine, 14*(6), 1–4.

Imbert, D., & Knoepfel, I. (2011). *360-degrees for mission – How lending European foundations use their investment to support their mission and the greater good*. Stocholm: Mistra.

Jackson, E. T. (2013). Evaluating social impact bonds: Questions, challenges, innovations, and possibilities in measuring outcomes in impact investing. *Community Development, 44*(5), 608–616. https://doi.org/10.1080/15575330.2013.854258.

Kail, A., & Lumley, T. (2012). *Theory of change. The beginning of making a difference*. London: New Philantropy Capital.

Know, S., & Arenius, P. (2010). Nations of entrepreneurs: A social capital perspective. *Journal of Business Venturing, 25*(3), 315–330.

Krugman, P. (2014, September 14). How to get it wrong. *The New York Times*. Retrieved from https://www.nytimes.com/2014/09/15/opinion/paul-krugman-how-to-get-economic-policy-wrong.html.

La Torre, M. (2013). Banche e welfare: Microcredito, crowdfunding e social impact investments. *MK, 5*, 28–34.

Landstrom, H. (1992). The relationship between private investors and small firms: An agency theory approach. *Entrepreneurship & Regional Development, 4*(3), 199–223. https://doi.org/10.1080/08985629200000012.

Lane, M. D., & Casile, M. (2011). Angels on the head of a pin: The SAC framework for performance measurement in social entrepreneurship ventures. *Social Enterprise Journal, 7*(3), 238–258. https://doi.org/10.1108/17508611111182395.

Lehner, O. M. (2016). *Routledge handbook of social and sustainable finance*. London: Routledge.

Letts, C. W., Ryan, W. P., & Grossman, A. S. (1995). Virtuous capital: What foundations can learn from the venture capitalists. *Harvard Business Review, March–April*.

Louche, C., Arenas, D., & van Cranenburgh, K. (2012). From preaching to investing: Attitudes of religious organizations towards responsible investment. *Journal of Business Ethics, 110*(3), 301–320. https://doi.org/10.1007/s10551-011-1155-8.

Marlett, D. (2015). Crowdfunding art, science and technology: A quick survey of the burgeoning new landscape. *Leonardo, 48*(1), 104–105. https://doi.org/10.1162/LEON_a_00813.

Martin, M. (2013). *Making impact investible* (Impact Economy Working Papers 4). Lausanne: Impact Economy. Retrieved from http://www.impacteconomy.com/download/Impact%20Economy%20-%202013%20-%20Making%20Impact%20Investible.pdf.

Nel, E. L., & McQuaid, R. W. (2002). The evolution of local economic development in South Africa: The case of Stutterhein and social capital. *Economic Development Quarterly, 16*(1), 60–74. https://doi.org/10.1177/0891242402016001007.

Nicholls, A. (2009). We do good things, don't we? Blended value accounting in social entrepreneurship. *Accounting, Organizations and Society, 34*(6–7), 755–769.

Nicholls, A. (2010). The legitimacy of social entrepreneurship: Reflexive isomorphism in a pre-paradigmatic field. *Entrepreneurship Theory and Practice, 34*(4), 611–633. https://doi.org/10.1111/j.1540-6520.2010.00397.x.

Nicholls, A., & Daggers, J. (2016). *The landscape of social impact investment research: Trends and opportunities*. Oxford: University of Oxford.

Nicholls, A., Nicholls, J., & Paton, R. (2015). Measuring social impact. In A. Nicholls, J. Emerson, & R. Paton (Eds.), *Social finance* (pp. 253–281). Oxford: Oxford University Press.

O'Donohoe, N., Leijonhufvud, C., Saltuk, Y., Bugg-Levine, A., & Brandeburg, M. (2010). *Impact investments: An emerging asset class*. New York: JP Morgan Social Finance-GIIN.

OECD. (2015). *Social impact investment: Building the evidence base*. Retrieved from http://www.oecd.org/sti/ind/social-impact-investment.pdf.

Ordanini, A., Miceli, L., Pizzetti, M., & Parasuraman, A. (2011). Crowd-funding: Transforming customers into investors through innovative service platforms. *Journal of Service Management, 22*(4), 443–470. https://doi.org/10.1108/09564231111155079.

Perrini, F. (2007). *Social entrepreneurship. imprese innovative per il cambiamento sociale*. Milano: Egea.

Perrini, F., & Vurro, C. (2013). *La valutazione degli impatti sociali. Approcci e strumenti applicativi*. Milano: Egea.

Porter, M. E., & Kramer, M. R. (2011). The big idea: Creating shared value. *Harvard Business Review, 89*(1), 2.

Putnam, R. D. (2000). *Capitale sociale e individualismo. Crisi e crescita della cultura civica in America*. Bologna: Il Mulino Saggi.

Rappaport, A. (2012). *Salvare il capitalismo. Come riprendere il controllo della finanza e tornare a creare valore a lungo termine*. Milano: Franco Angeli.

Rizzello, A., Migliazza, M., Carè, R., & Trotta, A. (2016). Social impact investing: A model and research agenda. In O. M. Lehner (Ed.), *Routledge handbook of social and sustainable finance* (pp. 102–124). London: Routledge.

Roche, C. (1999). *Impact assessment for development agencies: Learning to value change*. Oxford: Oxfam GB.

Roxas, H. B., & Azmat, F. (2014). Community social capital and entrepreneurship: Analyzing the links. *Community Development, 45*(2), 134–149. https://doi.org/10.1080/15575330.2014.880495.

Saltuk, Y., Bouri, A., & Leung, G. (2011). *Insight to the impact investing market: An in-depth analysisof investor perspectives*. New York: JP Morgan Social Finance-GIIN.

Schinckus, C. (2015). The valuation of social impact bonds: An introductory perspective with the Peterborough SIB. *Research International Business and Finance, 35*(C), 104–110. https://doi.org/10.1016/j.ribaf.2017.07.126.

Schwienbacher, A., & Larralde, B. (2010). Crowdfunding of small entrepreneurial ventures. In D. Cumming (Ed.), *Handbook of entrepreneurial finance* (pp. 3–19). Oxford: Oxford University Press.

Shaw, E., & Carter, S. (2007). Social entrepreneurship: Theoretical antecedents and empirical analysis of entrepreneurial processes and outcomes. *Journal of Small Business and Enterprise Development, 14*(3), 418–434. https://doi.org/10.1108/14626000710773529.

Shiller, R. J. (2012). *Finanza e società giusta*. Milano: Il Mulino.

Slootweg, R., Vanclay, F., & van Schooten, M. (2011). Function evaluation as a framework for the integration of social and environmental impact assessment. *Impact Assessment and Project Appraisal, 19*(1), 19–28. https://doi.org/10.3152/147154601781767186.

Social Impact Investment Task Force. (2014). *La finanza che include: gli investimenti ad impatto sociale per una nuova economia*. Retrieved from http://www.socialimpactagenda.it/wp-content/uploads/2016/04/La-finanza-che-include.pdf.

Solari, L. (1997). Implicazioni organizzative di un approccio multistakeholder. *Impresa Sociale, 31*, 43–47.

Trotta, A., Carè, R., Severino, R., Migliazza, M. C., & Rizzello, A. (2015). Mobilizing private finance for public good: Challenges and opportunities of social impact bonds. *European Scientific Journal, 1*, 259–279.

Venturi, P., & Zandonai, F. (2014). *Ibridi organizzativi. L'innovazione sociale generata dal gruppo cooperativo Cgm*. Bologna: Il Mulino.

Viviers, S., Ratcliffe, T., & Hand, D. (2011). From philanthropy to impact investing: Shifting mindsets in South Africa. *Corporate Ownership and Control, 8*(3–1), 25–43. https://doi.org/10.22495/cocv8i3c1p5.

Weber, O. (2012). *Social finance and impact investing*. Retrieved from http://ssrn.com/abstract=2160403.

Weber, O. (2016). Impact investing. In O. M. Lehner (Ed.), *Routledge handbook of social and sustainable finance* (pp. 85–101). London: Routledge.

Wheat, R. E., Wang, Y., Byrnes, J. E., & Ranganathan, J. (2013). Raising money for scientific research through crowdfunding. *Trend in Ecology & Evolution, 28*(2), 71–72. https://doi.org/10.1016/j.tree.2012.11.001.

Wood, D., Thornley, B., & Grace, K. (2013). Institutional impact investing: Practice and policy. *Journal of Sustainable Finance & Investment, 3*(2), 75–94. https://doi.org/10.1080/20430795.2013.776256.

Yin, R. K. (2014). *Case study research: Design and methods*. Thousand Oaks: Sage.

Zamagni, S., Venturi, P., & Rago, S. (2015). Valutare l'impatto sociale. La questione della misurazione nelle imprese sociali. *Impresa Sociale, 6*, 77–97.

7

Benefit-Cost Evaluation of Prevention and Early Intervention Measures for Children and Youth in Sweden

Lars Hultkrantz

1 Introduction

In a series of studies, Heckman and collaborators (e.g., Heckman 2006; Cunha and Heckman 2010) have observed that there is a high social rate of return on investments in young people. Heckman's work brought attention to how it is possible to estimate the economic yield to efforts invested in children, such as early interventions. Remarkably, while a substantial effort has been put in for decades in the United States and to some extent in the United Kingdom (Edovald et al. 2013) into such analysis, there is not much corresponding work in continental Europe. For instance, a recent "Frankfurt declaration" issued by the German Congress on Crime Prevention (2016) observes that this country offers next to nothing in terms of cost-effectiveness and benefit-cost analysis (BCA) for assessing such interventions. Here, I report on an on-going effort by several researchers to create a BCA model with Swedish data for evaluation

L. Hultkrantz (✉)
Örebro University School of Business, Örebro, Sweden
e-mail: Lars.Hultkrantz@oru.se

M. La Torre, M. Calderini (eds.), *Social Impact Investing Beyond the SIB*, Palgrave Studies in Impact Finance, https://doi.org/10.1007/978-3-319-78322-2_7

of causal effects of interventions that can be used by public and private bodies that design, select and finance social impact investments[1] targeting children and young people.

A role model for the Anglo-Saxon work in conducting evidence-based assessment of public policy measures is the Washington State Institute of Public Policy (WSIPP). WSIPP's appraisals are based on a meta-analytic approach for assessing the effectiveness of various programmes combined with BCA calculations for assessing their societal efficiency (WSIPP 2016). The BCA is based on normalised intervention effects that are, in a second step, linked to projected medium- and long-term economic effects. This procedure is, however, naturally set within a specific social, institutional and economic context, which means that results are not obviously transferable over the Atlantic Ocean or even across various countries in Europe. This is therefore a main motivation for the pursuit to build a model that reflects the characteristics of the Swedish context. However, the different national setting also opens up possibilities to make a range of improvements to the basic model design, for instance, by exploiting access to comparatively rich longitudinal data in Sweden from administrative registers and other sources.

Further, a specific driver for this work is the expressed needs for economic evaluation tools expressed by a variety of "social investment funds" (SIFs) that have been set up in recent years by local and regional governments in Sweden, including the three largest cities, Stockholm, Göteborg and Malmö. These funds aim to foster, finance and learn from innovative projects for implementing and testing new practices for supporting children with different needs by services provided by the municipalities through pre-schools, schools, health care and social work. These funds are based on the impact investment concept, which means that they are (1) intended to make (social) impact, (2) have return expectations, in particular by expected reduction of future public spending needs and (3) require measurement and reporting of the performance and progress of the investments made (see OECD 2015, p. 58). However, as these funds

[1] Impact Investments are defined by the Global Impact Investing Network (www.thegiin.org) as "investments made into companies, organisations, and fund with the intention to generate social and environmental impact alongside a financial return" (OECD 2015, p. 58).

have come into operation, the absence of valid tools for assessing both the overall impact on social welfare, or the net present value of societal benefits, and the financial returns, that is, the expected reductions of future public expenditure, from such projects has become immanent.

For this reason, a feature of the framework for economic evaluation of interventions for children and youth at some developmental risk that is being developed in Sweden is that the level of analysis is local. This means that programme evaluations are as far as possible adapted to the size and other characteristics of the local population or treatment group as well as to the local cost level and other specific economic circumstances. The aim of this chapter is to give an overview of the current state of these efforts, including both published studies and on-going work.

The plan of the chapter is as follows. The next section gives a brief background on the local social investment funds. Then, an overview of the BCA model with a description of empirical components of the model in various stages of completion follows. After that comes a summary of methods and results of two case studies; one on a supported employment programme for pupils in the final year of special secondary school, and the other on training programmes for parents to children with indicated externalising behavior.

2 Social Investment Funds[2]

The city of Norrköping established in 2010 a SIF for financing "social investments" that can be expected to yield future returns both from direct cost offsets to the municipality and more generally as "human benefits" (Norrköping 2010). The initiative got nation-wide attention and ignited a series of similar decisions by other municipalities. As shown by a survey in May 2014 (Balkfors 2015; Hultkrantz 2014), more than a fifth of the 290 Swedish municipalities had allocated resources to a SIF at that time. While several of these SIFs were small and loosely organised, some were rigorously controlled with elaborated procedures. Also, a couple of regional (county-level) governments and the three

[2] This section draws on Hultkrantz and Vimefall (2017) and Hultkrantz (2014).

largest cities (Stockholm, Göteborg and Malmö) have followed successively, which has enhanced the scale and sophistication of operations. Further, in 2015, a private philanthropist (Leksell Social Ventures) launched a social impact contract programme with the Norrköping SIF, which may set a standard for public-private partnerships.

In a case study based on experiences from SIFs in two medium-sized municipalities (Norrköping and Örebro), Hultkrantz and Vimefall (2017) observe that most projects that had received funding so far target youth and children with a high risk for social exclusion (foster children, individuals with some disability, etc.) or those already having problems (being absent from school, having a drug problem or engaging in criminal behavior). The main goal is to support these individuals to improve their long-term wellbeing and avoid future costs for the municipality. Funding is granted to innovative interventions that are not part of regular operations and that have a measurable impact that can be predicted and followed up, including estimates of predicted and achieved cost reductions.

A crucial feature of the first SIF in Norrköping was that sustained funding for new projects should be held by yields from previous projects. Paybacks were to be made by adjustments of the future internal budget frames of those administrative divisions that were expected to benefit from lower expenditure needs. For instance, if a school programme targeting potential high school dropouts is expected to reduce the expenditure needs for the social services in the coming years, then the budget frame of the social services unit will be adjusted accordingly when that happens and an equal amount will be allocated back to the SIF. While the original decision in 2010 stated that returns shall be based on expected cost reductions, it was later decided that paybacks are conditional on project evaluations showing that these reductions actually were realised.

In Örebro, re-payments are supposed to start three years after the project start while in Norrköping, the full amount is required to be returned within ten years. This therefore implies that the magnitudes of actual cost reductions need to be assessed and, since the outcome of the impact evaluations in this way may have direct economic consequences, their quality is likely to become an important issue in the project planning. The guidelines for the Örebro SIF state that priorities shall be based on, among others, efficiency, measured by socioeconomic effects and municipality cost reductions, and the credibility of the predicted size and timing of effects.

Thus, the SIFs by construction builds on an idea that proposed projects can be selected based on appraisals of the expected socioeconomic and financial returns and that the actual outcomes of implemented projects can be followed up economically and financially in ex-post evaluations. Decision makers have obviously presumed that tools for such socioeconomic and financial assessment exist and are readily available to be applied for this kind of investment analysis. Although societal BCA is indeed a well-developed and regularly used method in several other policy fields in Sweden (Svensson and Hultkrantz 2017), applications to the kind of interventions that are the focus of the SIFs have been rare or non-existent.

3 Overview of the BCA Approach

This section gives a brief overview of the general approach used for economic appraisal of measures investments targeting children or their families.

3.1 General Structure

The comprehensive economic performance measure that is used for BCA is the societal net present value (NPV). This is calculated as:

$$NPV = \Sigma_{(i=a)}^{65} \frac{1}{(1+r)^{(i-a)}} [\Delta B_i^m + \Delta B_i^n + \Delta C_i^{offset}] - (1+\theta) C_a^{treatment} \qquad (7.1)$$

with the following denotations:

r social rate of discount

a age of the child when treated

i	age of the child until retirement age ($i \geq 65$)
ΔB_i^m	expected monetary benefits at age i
ΔB_i^n	expected non-monetary (intangibles) benefits at age i
ΔC_i^{offset}	expected cost offsets (avoided costs) at age i
$C_a^{treatment}$	treatment cost
$1 + \theta$	marginal cost of public funds (for tax funded treatment)

Interventions are assumed to target children or their families. Treatment cost is the direct cost of a specific intervention. Expected cost offsets are the expected reduction of tax-funded costs (real use of resources, i.e., excl. welfare payments and other transfers). We use two sets of standard assumptions for the discount rate and the marginal cost of public funds: the Swedish standard $r = 0.035$ and $\theta = 0.3$ and the health economics standard $r = 0.03$ and $\theta = 0$.

As a scale invariant measure of societal profitability we use the Benefit-Cost Ratio (BCR). This is defined as:

$$BCR = \frac{NPV + (1+\theta)C_a^{treatment}}{(1+\theta)C_a^{treatment}} \tag{7.2}$$

As a supplementary *financial* measure, we use the cost Municipality Payback Period (MPP), defined as:

$$MPP = \frac{\Delta M_i^{offset}}{C_a^{treatment}} \tag{7.3}$$

where ΔM_i^{offset} represents expected expenditure offsets within the municipality economy. This includes all expenditure, for instance, transfers, irrespective of whether it corresponds to real use of resources; and excludes cost offsets by other public bodies (regional and state level) than the local government. This measure therefore can be used to evaluate the short-term ability of a social investment proposal to meet the payback requirements of a SIF.

3.2 Modelling of Effects

The economic analysis is based on measures of effects on a set of outcome variables from a specific intervention ("do something") in comparison to some reference treatment ("business-as-usual," "do something else" or "do nothing"). The preferred starting point for the analysis is results from one or several high-quality trials with controls that provide evidence of the effect of a specific intervention. These measures of effect size of outcome variables have then to be scaled to the target population of the analysis. The WSIPP approach builds on scaling of treatment effects on outcome variable means (WSIPP 2016). However, for economic evaluation of interventions targeting children at some kind of developmental risk, it is often more relevant to focus on the effect on the fraction of the target population that will pass a critical threshold, for instance, the share of individuals that will require clinical treatment or be eligible to pass on to a higher education level. An important technical contribution that is exploited in some of the Swedish work is therefore a method for doing this based on the whole distributions of the trial samples, demonstrated by Sarkadi et al. (2014) in an evaluation of a parenting programme for preschoolers with behavioral problems.

Another issue in measuring effects is that most trials do not follow subjects for a very long time, whereas early intervention and prevention measures frequently have a focus on medium-term returns within 5–10 years (payback requirements) or long-run returns spanning over the remaining lifetime of the treated individuals. Such effects therefore have to be modelled by short- or medium-term models, such as tree models or Markov models, by short- to long-term linkages over intermediate variables, or by combination of these approaches. Examples of both types of approaches are described below.

3.3 Cost Offsets

Cost offsets are future tax-funded costs that can be avoided if an intervention is successful. These costs can be borne by the local, regional or state government levels. In a BCA, only expenditure that represents real use of resources is included, but in a municipality, financial analysis of all expenditure is relevant.

Cost offset analysis is based on unit cost data, representing the average avoidable cost per individual. For instance, Hultkrantz et al. (2017), in a study that will be further described later in the chapter, use the average cost per year of occupation in a day-service programme, organised and paid for by the municipality for adults with intellectual disabilities that have not got (state-subsidised) employment at a regular workplace, in a cost-offset analysis of a programme supporting transition to work for special school pupils. Likewise, Wellander et al. (2016) calculate the monthly average cost for potentially avoidable additional support to compulsory school pupils with ADHD, psychosocial problems or anxiety/depression, respectively, in a school district in a Swedish city.

When the activity of interest is performed by a separate unit, like the day-service programmes in the first previous example, unit cost can be derived directly from accounting data for this unit, but when the cost offset relates to work by staff that also is performing other duties, as in the second example, it is necessary to collect additional time-use information. The total cost can then be calculated by multiplication with the direct, and possibly indirect, labour cost per unit of time.

3.4 Education-Earnings Linkage

Educational achievements provide a potential link between short-terms effects of interventions supporting children and long-term, life-course outcomes. Although statistical associations between schooling and later lifetime events may be due to selection on common unobserved individual characteristics, there exists evidence on causal relationships in some cases; one of them being average earnings. A model for this linkage is developed in Hultkrantz et al. (2017) based on a two-step procedure.

In the first step, the effect of high school (upper secondary school) graduation on life-course, labour-market earnings is estimated. This is made by estimation of age profiles based on a data-set containing data on earnings and educational status from administrative registers for the whole population 2009–2013. Separate such age profiles (second-order polynomials) are estimated for both gender and two educational status levels: compulsory school (nine years) and upper-secondary school (twelve years). These are then used to calculate the average earnings difference for each gender at all ages (20–65 years) and then the present value of these differences up until the age of 65. These values are based on gross earnings, including payroll taxes. According to basic economic theory, they can be used to calculate the real loss of marginal productivity to society.

These present values show the maximum average education premium. To take into account that only a portion of this maximum effect is causal, it is multiplied by a causal-correction factor. There exist several studies with Swedish population-wide register data that can be used to estimate such a factor. Meghir and Palme (2005) studied earnings differences of pupils living in municipalities where the extension of compulsory school from seven to nine years in school were made different years. Isacsson (2004) estimated earnings differences between twins. More recently, Lång and Nystedt (2016) report similar findings from estimations for a large set of dizygotic (DZ) and monozygotic (MZ) twins. Hultkrantz et al. (2017) conclude from these studies that the casual part of the relationship between education and earnings is around 0.5 or somewhat lower, so we use a causality correction factor at 0.5 with 0.35 as a lower alternative.

In a second step, these estimates of high school graduation education premia are used to assess the net present societal value of passing an important threshold at the end of compulsory school, that is, at age 16 (for most pupils). This latter achievement is related to the minimum requirement for being eligible to a national programme in upper secondary school. In Sweden, 99.5 percent of all pupils, except those of special schools for children with intellectual disabilities, continue from compulsory school to upper secondary school, but the 15–20 percent of each cohort that do not meet the eligibility requirements for starting in a national programme start instead in an "Introduction programme" that is meant to prepare them for transfer to a national programme. However, only a quarter of the non-eligible pupils eventually graduate from high school. On the other hand, also some of the eligible pupils drop out before graduation, although this portion is much lower. Therefore, eligibility, which is a measure that is clearly defined and recorded in administrative registers for the whole population, can be used to predict high school graduation and, in turn, life-course earnings. Also, it can be used to predict the total cost of high school education, which is potentially important both in benefit-cost analysis and in cost-offset analysis.

In the second step, therefore, a tree-analysis approach is used to calculate the (average) net present societal value of eligibility. The tree analysis is based on the conditional probabilities of graduation from upper secondary school after three or four to five years, respectively, of eligible and non-eligible pupils, and the annual average costs of education in the national programmes and the introduction programme, respectively.

The final results show that, with base case assumptions on real wage growth (1.5 percent), discount rate (3 percent) and causality correction factor (0.5), the earnings net present value to society of high school graduation is around 160,000 Euros, while eligibility on average is worth 100,000 Euros per individual.

3.5 Value of Statistical Life, Quality of Life and Willingness to Pay

Benefit measures in BCA are ultimately based on the willingness-to-pay (WTP) concept. While cost offsets and gross earnings effects are directly measurable using market prices, many important "human" or "quality-of-life" effects have to be estimated by revealed or stated preference methods for elicitation of non-market priced values.

There are two common approaches to economic evaluation of effects on mortality and morbidity. One is cost-effectiveness analysis where alternative interventions are compared according to their incremental unit cost, that is, the incremental cost of the intervention divided by a one-dimensional measure of the intervention effect. The output measure can be, for instance, a survival or fatality rate, the number of expected life-years gained or the number of quality-adjusted life-years (QALYs) gained. In benefit-cost analysis, benefits are valued in monetary measures based on WTP estimates. Such measures are the Value of Statistical Life (VSL) and Value of Statistical Illness/Injury (VSI). Another approach is the so-called hybrid BCA that extends cost-effectiveness analysis by imposing a monetary value on a QALY.

I have been involved in a couple of recent Swedish-stated preference studies of VSL, VSI and WTP/QALY (for previous studies, see Hultkrantz and Svensson 2012): in one, Olofsson et al. (2016), we use a so-called chained method in a traffic safety context. The chained approach is based on a two-step procedure in which, first, the WTP is estimated for a health state that is relatively easy for respondents to evaluate (low or medium severity, short duration, high frequency/prevalence) and then is scaled up to more severe, longer duration, less frequent health states (severe injury or fatality). This means that all measures can be derived on various paths depending on the nature of the health states in the two steps. For VSL, estimates were held in a range of 3–5 million Euros, and for WTP/QALY estimates were between 0.24–0.32 million Euros. In two other studies, Olofsson et al. (2017), we estimate WTP/QALY for fatal diseases/injuries with varying severity and duration of morbidity before death. A general finding is that these values are slightly higher than those for traffic-related injuries and fatalities. Another approach to estimation of WTP/QALY is a revealed preference study by Svensson et al. (2015) of implicit threshold values of reimbursement decisions for pharmaceuticals in Sweden. Based on decisions made from 2005 to 2011, these threshold values are found to be in the range from 0.07 to 0.12 million Euros.

Early intervention measures for children and youth sometimes target categories of individuals with enhanced suicide risk, for instance, programmes for reducing school bullying or depression treatment. In a state preference study, Persson and Svensson (2013) estimate the aggregate societal WTP for measures to prevent school bullying in a medium-size Swedish city to 0.065–0.093 million Euros per statistical bullying victim. In a recent study, Vimefall et al. (2018) estimate WTP for depression prevention and estimate VSL in both traffic accident and suicide contexts. The main purpose of this study is to find support for value transfer from the well-studied traffic safety context to suicide prevention.

3.6 Summary and Looking Ahead

As of yet (June 2018), some of the groundwork of a Swedish BCA model for evaluation of early intervention and prevention for children and youth has been laid, in particular some data for cost-offset analysis and an education-earnings link. Also, several studies have been conducted for WTP valuation of mortality and morbidity. However, much work remains. Some studies are already underway for improving data sources for cost-offset analysis, especially concerning avoidable costs in compulsory school, high school and costs of placement of young individuals in family homes or institutions.

Another important gap to be filled by on-going work relates to the cost of crime and criminality. The first step is an extension of the education earnings linkage as, based on Swedish longitudinal register data, there is support that societal costs of crime also can be linked to educational attainment (Bergman and Andershed 2009; Nilsson et al. 2014; and, in a natural experiment setting that allows for causal inference, Hjalmarsson et al. 2014 and Åslund et al. 2017). These links can, as in WSIPP (2016), be used for economic assessment based on methods developed by Cohen and Piquero (2009) and McCollister et al. (2010).

However, although more work is needed before all potentially important benefits of intervention and prevention can be assessed, it is already possible to do informative benefit-cost assessments with the available components. This will now be demonstrated by brief summaries of two recent BCA studies.

4 Case Studies

4.1 Supported Employment

People with intellectual disabilities have a low probability of ever getting a job in Sweden. A recent study (Arvidsson et al. 2015) finds that only 22 percent of graduates from special upper secondary schools during the preceding eleven years were employed at least one hour a week by the end 2011. These schools prepare pupils aged 16–20 years who have been considered to have an intellectual disability for a work life, but apparently fail to do so for most. Therefore, 47 percent of the graduates had ended up in day-activity programs organised and funded by the local governments, while the remaining 31 percent were not in any kind of occupation.

In two separate studies, Larsson Tholén et al. (2017) and Persson (2017) have made cost-offset and benefit-cost evaluations of a programme called "Job in Sight" (JiS) that was conducted as a four-year trial including all pupils in the special upper secondary schools of a medium-size Swedish city. JiS was much inspired by so-called Supported Employment strategies developed in the United States that have been found in several studies to be successful in this respect (Marshall et al. 2014; Dowler and Walls 2014). A specific feature of JiS, though, was that it was provided as an integrated part of the last year in special schools, and the institutional context is quite different from the United States.

While there was plenty of previous evidence on effectiveness of this kind of approach, the cost of the programme would have been seen as prohibitive if it was not for a grant from the European Social Fund to this specific project. The cost per pupil of JiS amounted to 30,500 Euros, which corresponds to 114 percent of the cost of a full year of the special school, which is way beyond what the school administration could finance within its regular budget. This aspect is also probably the main reason that Supported Employment approaches have not been used previously in special schools. The objective of the two economic evaluation studies was therefore to find out whether there were economic arguments for permanent funding either by the municipality or through state aid.

Both studies were based on a before-after evaluation design study in which the employment status of the former pupils were followed by administrative registers up to eight years after graduation, in which the first four annual cohorts constituted a control group and the last four the treatment group. Pooled panel probit regression results showed that those treated by the JiS programme had, on average, a 31 percent higher probability of being employed (with controls for age, programme and local unemployment rate in the graduation year).

In cost-offset analysis based on this estimated effect, Hultkrantz et al. (2017) calculate MPP from the implied cost savings by fewer individuals in need of day-activity programmes. The result is a MPP at 7.5 years. This is within a ten-year payback-period requirement, suggesting that a "business case" can be made for municipality funding of the programme. In the second study, Persson (2017) develops the analysis further into a societal BCA. The treatment effect on the employment status of the former pupils is predicted up to age 30 with a Markov model of annual transitions between four states: regular employment, subsidised employment, unemployment and disability pension. Societal (tangible) benefits are then estimated from three sources: avoided cost of day-service programmes, productivity in regular employment and the share of non-subsidised productivity in subsidised employment. In spite of the ignorance of quality-of-life improvement effects, the BCR is estimated to 2.3. A probabilistic sensitivity analysis suggests that the probability of a positive net benefit is 69 percent.

4.2 Parental Training

Over time, several manual-based programmes have been developed for teaching parents of children with externalising behavior problems (Conduct Disorder, ADHD, or combinations) how to support their children. Four such programmes (COPE, Comet, Connect and Incredible Years) and a self-help book targeting parents of children aged 3–12 years were evaluated in a randomised control trial conducted in several Swedish municipalities by Stattin et al. (2015), with a two-year follow up by Högström et al. (2017). All programmes were found to be effective in reducing externalising behavior problems.

Based on these effect studies, two economic evaluations have been made. Sampaio et al. (2016) evaluate and compare the cost-effectiveness of the programmes from estimates of the costs of the programmes and short-term outcomes. As any cost-effectiveness study, this is useful for a decision maker that wants to select one programme, but does not show whether any programme delivers value for the money. However, this is made in a BCA study by Nystrand et al. (2017). They develop a Markov model using population-wide epidemiological data with annual transitions between disease and recovery to predict the intervention effects for the children of the trial samples up to age 20 years. This is then used in the benefit-cost appraisal, where the benefits include avoided costs in compulsory school, avoided cost from clinical treatment of neuropsychiatric problems and the net benefit from passing the eligibility threshold in compulsory school (based on the study by Hultkrantz et al. (2017)). All programmes are found to have BCRs way above unity.

5 Conclusion

In this chapter, I have given a brief overview of the institutional background that motivates the on-going research in Sweden for developing tools for BCA of early intervention and prevention measures for children and young people. The interest in innovative forms for funding of social impact investments in Sweden has been mainly driven by a wish to improve efficiency of local government services in education and social work. The idea is that by taking an investment perspective, some of the shortsightedness and silo mentality of one-year-ahead budget planning can be avoided. Thus, the main motive has not been a search for private funding sources in times of fiscal austerity. However, recently at least one public-private partnership has been set up. Anyway, these developments have revealed a lack of valid tools for making economic evaluations of overall societal returns as well as of financial returns to local governments, which is what have spurred the work on such models that is reviewed here.

I have described the general structure of the models and some work on their empirical content that has been made or is underway. While not all benefits have yet been monetised, as indicated by the summary of two case studies, even partial benefits can be sufficient to show that some early intervention and prevention measures for children and youth have favorable societal returns and cost offsets.

References

Arvidsson, J., Widén, S., & Tideman, M. (2015). Post-school options for young adults with intellectual disabilities in Sweden. *Research and Practice in Intellectual and Developmental Disabilities, 2*(2), 180–193.

Åslund, O., Grönqvist, H., Hall, C., & Vlachos, J. (2017). Education and criminal behavior: Insights from an expansion of upper secondary school. *Labour Economics* (e-published ahead of print).

Bergman, L., & Andershed, A.-K. (2009). Predictors and outcomes of persistent or age-limited registered criminal behaviour: A 30-year longitudinal study of a Swedish urban population. *Aggressive Behaviour, 35*, 164–178.

Cohen, M. A., & Piquero, A. R. (2009). New evidence on the monetary value of saving a high risk youth. *Journal of Quantitative Criminology, 25*, 25–49.

Cunha, F., & Heckman, J. J. (2010). *Investing in our young people*. National Bureau of Economic Research WP 16201. Retrieved from http://www.nber.org/papers/w16201.

Dowler, D. L., & Walls, R. T. (2014). A review of supported employment services for people with disabilities: Competitive employment, earnings, and service costs. *Journal of Rehabilitation, 80*(1), 11–21.

Edovald, T., Bjornstad, G., & Ellis, D. (2013). *Investing in children: Technical report*. The Social Research Unit at Dartington.

Heckman, J. J. (2006). Skill formation and the economics of investing in disadvantaged children. *Science, 312*, 1900–1902.

Hjalmarsson, R., Holmlund, H., & Lindqvist, M. J. (2014). The effect of education on criminal convictions and incarceration: Causal evidence from micro-data. *The Economic Journal, 125*, 1290–1326.

Hogstrom, J., Olofsson, V., Ozdemir, M., Enebrink, P., & Stattin, H. (2017). Two-Year Findings from a national effectiveness trial: Effectiveness of behavioral and non-behavioral parenting programs. *Journal of Abnormal Child Psychology, 45*, 527–542.

Hultkrantz, L. (2014). *Sociala investeringsfonder: motivering, förutsättningar, nuläge och utvecklingsbehov*. Stockholm: SNS Förlag.

Hultkrantz, L., Karpaty, P., & Vimefall, E. (2017). Education-earnings linkage for assessing societal benefits of interventions for children and youth in Sweden. *Psychosocial Intervention, 26*(3), 171–179.

Hultkrantz, L., & Svensson, M. (2012). The value of a statistical life in Sweden: A review of the empirical literature. *Health Policy, 108*, 302–310.

Hultkrantz, L., & Vimefall, E. (2017). Social investment funds in Sweden: Status and design issues. *Scandinavian Journal of Public Administration, 21*(3), 85–108.

Isacsson, G. (2004). Estimating the economic return to educational levels using data on twins. *Journal of Applied Econometrics, 19*, 99–119.

Lång, E., & Nystedt, P. (2016). Learning for life? The effects of schooling on earnings and health-related behavior over the life cycle. Working paper, Department of Management and Engineering – Division of Economics Linköping University.

Larsson Tholén, S., Hultkrantz, L., & Persson, M. (2017). Economic evaluation of supported employment inspired program for pupils with intellectual disabilities. *Nordic Journal of Working Life Studies, 7*(1), 69–86 (open access).

Marshall, T., Goldberg, R. W., Braude, L., Dougherty, R. H., Daniels, A. S., Ghose, S. S., George, P., & Delphin-Rittmon, M. E. (2014). Supported employment: Assessing the evidence. *Psychiatric Services, 65*(1), 16–23. https://doi.org/10.1176/appi.ps.201300262.

McCollister, K. E., French, M. T., & Fang, H. (2010). The cost of crime to society: New crime-specific estimates for policy and program evaluation. *Drug and Alcohol Dependence, 108*, 98–109.

Meghir, C., & Palme, M. (2005). Educational reform, ability and family background. *American Economic Review, 95*(1), 414–425.

Nilsson, A., Estrada, F., & Bäckman, O. (2014). Offending, drug abuse and life chances—A longitudinal study of a Stockholm birth cohort. *Journal of Scand Stud Criminology Crime Prevention, 15*(2), 128–142.

Norrköping. (2010). Riktlinjer för hantering av Norrköping kommuns sociala investeringsfond. KS-605/2010. Ekonomi och Styrningskontoret, Norrköping Municipality Office, Norrköping.

Nystrand, C., Vimefall, E., Hultkrantz, L., & Feldman, I. (2017). *Benefit-cost analysis of indicated parent training programs*. Paper presented at the Social Impact Investment International Conference, 11–12 October, 2017, Sapienza University, Rome.

OECD. (2015). *Improving Schools in Sweden: An OECD perspective*. Paris: OECD.

Olofsson, S., Gerdtham, U.-G., Hultkrantz, L., & Persson, U. (2016). *Value of a QALY and VSI estimated with the chained approach*. Working Paper 2016:33, Nationalekonomiska Institutionen, Ekonomihögskolan vid Lunds Universitet.

Olofsson, S., Gerdtham, U.-G., Hultkrantz, L., & Persson, U. (2017). Measuring the end of life premium in cancer using individual ex ante willingness to pay. *European Journal of Health Economics* (online).

Persson, M., & Svensson, M. (2013). The willingness to pay to reduce school bullying. *Economics of Education Review, 35*, 1–11.

Persson, M. (2017). *A benefit-cost analysis of an individual placement and support program for adoloscents with intellectual disabilities*. Örebro: Örebro University School of Business.

Sampaio, F., Enebrink, P., Mihalopoulos, C., & Feldman, I. (2016). Cost-effectiveness of four parenting programs and bibliotherapy for parents of children with conduct problems: A multicenter randomized controlled trial. *The Journal of Mental Health Policy and Economics, 19*(4), 201–212.

Sarkadi, A., Sampaio, F., Kelly, M. P., & Feldman, I. (2014). A novel approach used outcome distribution curves to estimate the population-level impact of a public health intervention. *Journal of Clinical Epidemiology, 67*, 785–792.

Stattin, H., Enebrink, P., Ozdemir, M., & Giannotta, F. (2015). A national evaluation of parenting programs in Sweden: The short-term effects using an RCT effectiveness design. *Journal of Consulting and Clinical Psychology, 83*, 1069–1084.

Svensson, M., Nilsson, F., & Arnberg, K. (2015). Reimbursement decisions for pharmaceuticals in Sweden: The impact of disease severity and cost effectiveness. *Pharmacoeconomics, 33*, 1229–1236.

Svensson, M., & Hultkrantz, L. (2017). A comparison of cost-benefit and cost effectiveness analysis in practice: Divergent policy practices in Sweden. *Nordic Journal of Health Economics, 5*(2), 41–53.

Vimefall, E., Persson, M., Olofsson, S., & Hultkrantz, L. (2018). *Willingness to pay for suicide prevention.* Paper presented at the Swedish Health Economics Association annual conference, Lund University, March 14–15, 2018.

Wellander, L., Wells, M. B., & Feldman, I. (2016). Does prevention pay? Costs and potential cost-savings of school interventions targeting children with mental health problems. *The Journal of Mental Health Policy and Economics, 19*(2), 91–101.

WSIPP. (2016). *Benefit-cost technical documentation.* Olympia, WA: Washington State Institute of Public Policy.

8

Impact Measurement for Social Innovation: Analysis of the Spanish Third Sector

Marta Solórzano-García, Julio Navío-Marco, and Mercedes Valcárcel-Dueñas

1 Introduction

Contemporary civil societies face challenges that need new approaches, approaches that mainly come from third-sector organizations. These new approaches for solving social problems are called social innovation. In order to generate and develop social innovation, these organizations should enhance their potential and improve their management to address the changes that are occurring in society and strongly affect the way third-sector organizations operate and their way of interacting with other stakeholders. In recent years, the public spotlight on voluntary-sector organizations, and their ability to demonstrate effectiveness, has become intense. Monitoring (collecting information and tracking progress rou-

M. Solórzano-García (✉) • J. Navío-Marco
UNED, Madrid, Spain
e-mail: msolorzano@cee.uned.es

M. Valcárcel-Dueñas
Fundación Tomillo, Madrid, Spain

M. La Torre, M. Calderini (eds.), *Social Impact Investing Beyond the SIB*, Palgrave Studies in Impact Finance, https://doi.org/10.1007/978-3-319-78322-2_8

tinely and systematically) and evaluation (gathering research and other data to make judgments and determine the value of worth of something) has become a critical part of organizational life. The approach taken in this study is to identify "third sector" with "non-profit sector." Inside the category of third sector, the Third Sector of Social Action (TSAS) is distinguished by the intended purpose of its organizations. Through the Second Strategic Plan of the Spanish TSAS, we can confirm the definition of TSAS used in this research: "The Third Sector of Social Action is formed by private voluntary and non-profit entities, arising from free citizens' initiative, that work independently to promote the recognition and exercise of social rights, to achieve social cohesion and inclusion in all its dimensions and to avoid certain social groups exclusion from adequate levels of well-being" (Plataforma de ONG de Acción Social 2013). According to a perspective that takes into account the finalist sense, entities are considered non-profit (not-for-profit organizations) when oriented to meet social needs or, in other words, when the goal of providing services to members or the community prevail over profit. This chapter reports on the range and extent of monitoring and evaluation practices in the TSAS. The research proposed is needed to build an evidence base about monitoring and evaluation practice and its benefits, if any, and to place that practice within the context of funders' requirements and evaluation activity. We want to identify the resources available to Third Sector Organizations (TSOs) as well as the extent to which organizations had learnt the skills and techniques needed to carry out evaluation.

- Had they also acquired the skills necessary not only to manage and interpret data but also to make it useful?
- How had the emphasis on value and on outcomes and impact that were pervading the policy and funding environment affected learning from evaluation and created benefits for users?

This knowledge, that we will have gained from the first two phases of the research, will allow us to develop the third-stage methodology that serves the TSOs to monitor and evaluate their activities systematically over time as well as to serve stakeholders' evaluation requirements.

2 Background and Current Status

During the last three decades, Spanish Third Sector (TS) has gradually gained presence in the social, political and economic Spanish scene. The economic boom lived until 2008 and the emphasis on the welfare state resulted in a dizzying growth of Spanish TSAS organizations during the years before the economic crisis. They received a large amount of public funding, and the diversification and positive evolution of intervention programmes resulted in the creation of a great number of TS entities. Additionally, regulatory framework changes occurred that caused private financing participation in the sector.

The economic relevance of the Spanish TS, according to the TSAS annual report (2015), is revealed by its contribution to the Spanish Gross National Product (1.51%) and its social implication (29,737 organizations that employed 644,979 workers and had 1,272,338 volunteers). Out of all these organizations, the three that are considered "singular entities" (ONCE, the Red Cross and Caritas) employed 77,000 paid staff and managed a total income of €14,470 million, 1.5% of Spanish GDP (Ruiz 2015).

The financial structure of social service TSOs is highly dependent on public funding. The percentage of public funding was already high before the crisis, 61.3% (Ruiz 2015: 94). However, the degree of dependence of the different TSO clusters is very uneven, so the impact of the budgetary austerity policies applied during the crisis years has also been uneven. Public funds accounted for two thirds of the income of medium-sized TSOs. These were the TSOs that had grown and expanded most during the period of economic prosperity that preceded the crisis. They were also those that suffered the greatest reduction in public funding. Another group of very large TSOs and "singular entities" is less dependent on the public purse (around 33%). Lastly, small TSOs also depend less on public funding (33%), which they mainly receive from the regional and municipal levels of government. One major challenge for the TSOs is diversifying their funding and correcting its concentration on a single source. While this dependence has lessened in part, in the boom years it also increased, placing a number of TSOs in a vulnerable position of excessive dependence and consequent financial risk (Fundación Lealtad 2013). External audits continue to be on the to-do list for many TSOs, as 58.45% do not audit their accounts (Ruiz 2015: 92). The major form of funding is subsidies and grants, rather than agreements and contracts with government bodies. The budgetary austerity policy was applied two years after the crisis began, mainly from the end of 2010 onwards. The reduction in public funding had a broad, widespread but uneven impact on the TSOs. The total public funding of Spanish social sector TSOs fell from €10,480.5 million in 2010 to €8002.34 million in 2013, in other words, it fell by an average 23.6% (Ruiz 2015: 95). By level of government, approximately 50% of the funding is from the regional governments, around 30% from the provincial and municipal councils and 10–15% from the central government.

The social service TSOs budget volume has decreased significantly during the last past years. In the boom years, TSOs budgets figures reflected high expenses, placing a number of TSOs in a vulnerable position of excessive dependence and consequent financial risk (Fundación Lealtad 2013) (Fig. 8.1).

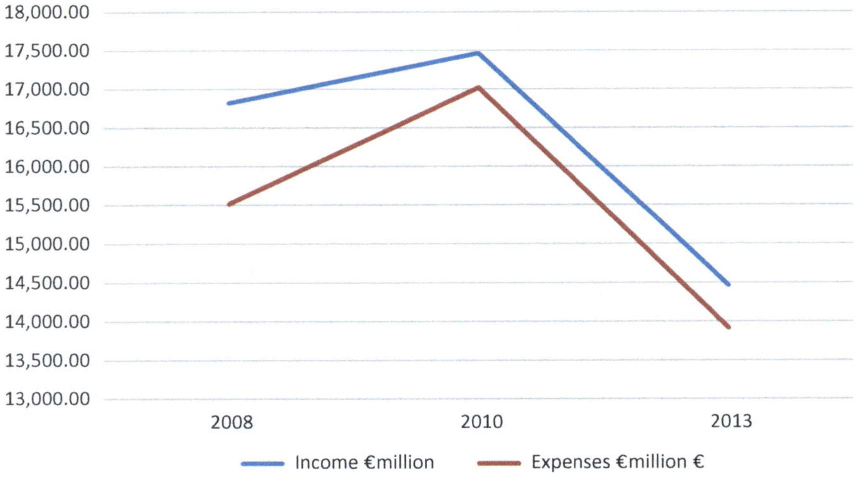

Fig. 8.1 Total Spanish TSAS's income and expenses. Years 2008, 2010, 2013. Source: Authors' own work

The financial structure of social service TSOs has evolved in order to confront the effects of the economic crisis. Although the sector is highly dependent on public funding, a diversification of the funding sources is observed, fundamentally among the singular and largest TSOs. The rest of the organizations are making an attempt at this, but diversifying their funding and correcting its concentration on a single source is still a big challenge to deal with (Fig. 8.2).

The degree of dependence of the different TSO clusters is very uneven, so the impact of the budgetary austerity policies applied during the crisis years has also been uneven. External audits continue to be on the to-do list for many TSOs, as 58.45% do not audit their accounts (Ruiz 2015: 92).

The budgetary austerity policy was applied two years after the crisis began, mainly from the end of 2010 onwards. The reduction in public funding had a broad, widespread but uneven impact on the TSOs. The

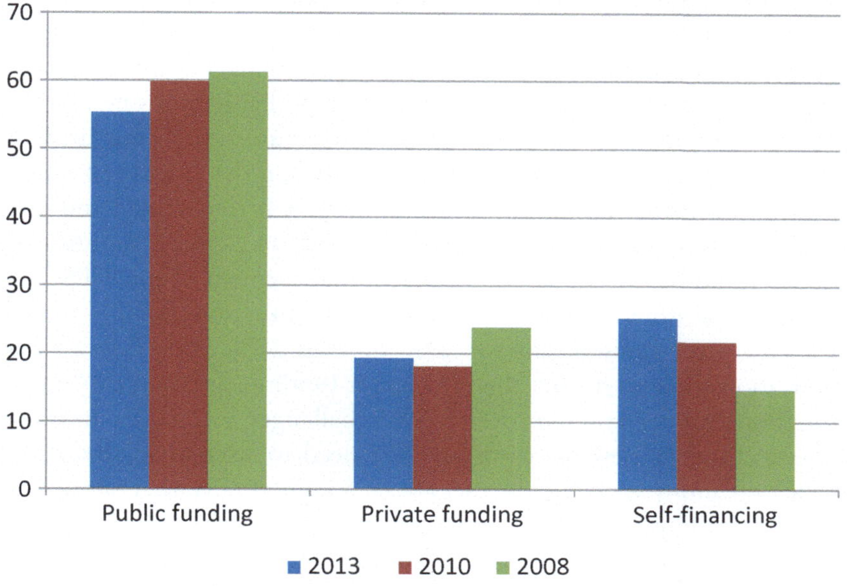

Fig. 8.2 Percentage of each type of funding in relation to the total funding of TSAS entities. 2008, 2010, 2013. Source: Authors' own work

Table 8.1 TSAS's total income per funding source

	2013	2010	2008
Public funding	€8002.34	€10,480.50	€10,313.42
Private funding	€2807.33	€3179.09	€4021.06
Self-financing	€3661.11	€3807.92	€2409.03
Total revenue	€14,470.77	€17,467.50	€16,824.50

Years: 2008, 2010, 2013
Source: Authors' elaboration based on Ruiz (2015)

total public funding of Spanish social sector TSOs fell from €10,480.5 million in 2010 to 8002.34 million in 2013, an average 23.6% (Ruiz 2015: 95). Private funding suffered an overall decrease from €3179.09 to €2807.33 but the percentage that private funding represent relative to the total funding of the sector experienced a relative growth (Table 8.1). Largest TSOs balance their accounts better than the smaller ones, even getting to make a positive difference in their outcome. Smaller companies, on the other hand, normally exhibit an average deficit. The more efficient management of largest entities could be due to the provision of monitoring and control mechanisms of the activity, which help managers to take good decisions that result in end-of-year budgets without deficit. Small entities are in a more difficult position, probably motivated by the multipurpose character of the personnel structure, not being used to adjusting expenses during a period of austerity and the absence of monitoring and control mechanisms of the activity. A better-trained and prepared management staff and implementation of activity monitoring systems could be the key to more efficient management of small TSOs.

Future assessments predict that financing situation for TSOs will aggravate, with funding cuts of 20% or even 30%. This forecast has implications that go further than the sector funding, and make its transformation and overcoming some crucial challenges a necessity. In other respects, funders' new demands and the need to strengthen the sector image will imply a change in the TSOs' accountability that should be based on the impact that these organizations generate in society.

Therefore, one of the biggest challenges the sector faces is how to develop an accurate measurement of the impact it generates and how to monitor, evaluate and control the activities performed to generate that impact. It needs not only to rationalize its management in order to increase its effectiveness but to create adequate information systems leading to the achievement of information transparency about the management of the organization's resources.

To this end, it is essential to develop a methodology that could make impact measurement a tool of efficient management, communication and transparency. An innovative mechanism that permits to show the stakeholders the economic, social and environmental value that the organization is generating should be developed. And to do so, it won't be enough to show the results obtained but how they have been achieved. This will enable the stakeholders of the organization to evaluate the entity's enforcement and value generation capacity, and adopt the appropriate decisions.

3 Improving the Methodology for Monitoring and Evaluating

The analysis and measurement of the social impact is an aspect that directly affects the provision of public services and in many cases the use of public resources. In addition, all the stakeholders committed to social impact seek to be able to know which initiatives provide the best results, in terms of efficiency. Pressure on non-profit organizations for more rigorous impact measurement and reporting can come from a range of involved actors. These include the clients, other social purpose organizations and so-called patrons (Ebrahim 2003). The challenges posed by the measurement of social impact in TS entities arise from their ultimate objective: to know the influence generated by the project, policy, action or activity being analyzed, in aspects related to the development, values and human needs. With the growth of the "social investment state" and the gradual phasing out of grant-giving to the third sector, we anticipate that measures of social impact will become increasingly central for the assessment of policies and social action plans and to resource acquisition in particular. Used properly, it also provides an engaging narrative of the organization's impact.

Social impact assessment serves three principal functions: (1) performance measurement (both for internal and external purposes); (2) to attract funding (and other resources); and (3) to reinforce the organizational mission (Pathak and Dattani 2014). Out of more than 40 approaches that have been developed for measuring social impact (Stevenson et al. 2010), some of the most recognized are: Logic models, Social Accounting and Audit, methods based in Cost-Benefit and Cost-Effectiveness and Social Return on Investment (SROI). Among them, SROI has undoubtedly grown into the pre-eminent means of evaluating net social returns. Although these are the most widely used approaches, there are many others, so it is unlikely to establish a single reference and, in fact, no standard has been agreed upon to measure social impact. Recognizing there are no "one-size-fits-all" solutions, it is important for organizations to choose the approach that best suits their specific environment and requirements. This, far from being an inconvenience, is a positive factor in the objective of pursuing a correct measurement of social impact, since the objective of any organization that takes into account the social impact of its initiatives is to optimize impacts in several dimensions rather than to maximize impacts against any dimension (Maas and Liket 2011); the measurement process can not pose in a uni-directional way. Combined measurements would allow a common framework of comparison, homogenized and benchmarked, that would allow a comparative evaluation of the goodness and virtues of the future projects that are being analyzed. Additionally, using a single approach could ignore the different stages that organizations are at, not only in terms of their size and resources, but in terms of their cultural openness to and capacity for evaluation. Given the diversity of the organizations within the non-profit sector, it is virtually impossible that one single measure of impact or one approach will be suitable for all of them.

The analysis of the different methods of measurement of social impact will allow us to draw some conclusions and set future goals.

The Logic models, such as the Logical Framework Approach (LFA), are, rather than a method, a global project-planning framework that often precedes specific methodologies for measuring social impact. The advantage and attraction of Logic models is that they provide a framework that enables organizations to embed evaluation and performance assessment into the program design and life-cycle process of the program (Zappalà and Lyons 2009). Logic models or the Logic approach to program design and evaluation emerged in the 1970s as a response to the shortcomings of many program evaluations that were being conducted. Since the 1990s, different agencies linked to development cooperation have promoted the application of more advanced approaches than LFA but have taken many elements of this early approach. This included "Results Based Management" (RBM), which focuses the analysis on the achievement of results in the interventions and not only, as before, in the management of invested resources.

In relation to Accounting and Social Audit models (Gibbon and Dey 2011), the internal data collection and analysis procedures (social accounting) are followed by an independent audit of the results (social auditing) before finally disseminating the outcome more widely (reporting). Therefore, it will be important to establish information standards and methodologies and generally accepted accreditation processes, since, as González et al. (2010: 23) indicate "it is true that there are reports commonly and popularly called 'Social Balances', but on the other hand they are very far from what could be expected from a document with that name. None of these tools is really useful to help the knowledge of the generation of social value, communication and transparency of the value generated and, consequently, to win it back." This method has a longer history of innovation and use in the United Kingdom; it has been to some extent eclipsed by the importing and development of the SROI approach, which has been supported by recent UK and Scottish government initiatives.

On the other hand, it would be very useful to design indicators and/or tools that allow us to gain a broader understanding of the reality of projects and their execution, with a focus on social value and impact. In this sense, the Social Balance model could benefit much of the work done in the other methodologies and, in this sense, could serve to offer new analysis to solve different needs.

The methods based on the comparison between costs and benefits have very limited methodological development. The possibilities of use are directed to the adaptation of the concept to the specific casuistry of the projects under analysis and, in particular, for the determination and quantification of those effects of a non-economic nature but that have an evident social impact.

The non-excessive complexity of these models and the intuitive interpretation of the results allow them to be a good initial option for those entities that are not applying more complex procedures in determining the social value of their projects, or for those whose small size limits the implementation of broader and more demanding methodologies.

Based on a more generalized use of Cost-Benefit and Cost-Effectiveness analyses, these methodologies can be taken as a reference for the development of research and new valuation systems (Retolaza and Ramos 2005), allowing to advance in this field towards models of more complex and global management that pursue the maximization of social impact and integrate the entire entity. Cost-benefit analysis has traditionally been used for evaluating the costs and benefits of policies and programmes by government, with more recent work, such as that by Fujiwara and Campbell (2011), looking to incorporate social and well-being considerations into the policy tool. This is the most demanding approach for the analysis of costs and outcomes, as it requires a comprehensive measurement of costs and program impacts. Unfortunately, classical cost-effectiveness analysis and cost-benefit analysis (and therefore any approach that incorporates these methodologies) do not currently incorporate a consistent approach in order to deal with value judgments. Each study reflects the researcher's assessment about how the costs and benefits are distributed among stakeholders and how the various outcomes are valued.

SROI is probably the methodology most widely applied and the most widely analyzed by researchers (Solórzano et al. 2015). SROI's application is a relatively young discipline. As a result, there is great variability in how SROI is applied across projects. This makes robust and consistent comparisons across social ventures difficult while rendering the validity of SROI measures vulnerable to contestation. On the other hand, probably the most widely acknowledged quality of SROI is its effectiveness as a communication tool.

SROI has detractors, as seen in Fujiwara (2015), which synthesizes the ideas of those who consider it a vague concept; that its approach to the stakeholders may be limited, which is based in a methodology that it considers to be obsolete and incomplete; that it does not have a clear normative approach; and that it approaches the principles of equality and equity unduly, giving greater importance to groups that are not the most needy. It also finds that the calculation of the ratio is susceptible to bias and that, since its design has not followed the advances in statistics and econometrics, it does not meet the criteria necessary to raise inference tests, which causes the application of statistical methods to infer causality to be limited or even problematic. It is possible to identify three groups of limitations in connection with SROI analysis (Maier et al. 2015). Firstly, there are certain fundamental and irresolvable issues that have the potential to call the method as a whole into question. Secondly, there are some issues that are also irresolvable but that do not preclude using the method, as long as they are understood and knowingly taken into account. Thirdly, there are a number of technical issues that might be remedied as the method matures.

Methodologically, there are many advances that have been proposed in relation to the SROI, given its quantitative nature, although with important qualitative foundations in its construction. Already in Tuan and Emerson (2000) two challenges were posed: on the one hand, the determination of an adequate discount rate—the social discount rate; and on the other hand, the incorporation of the degree of difficulty to reach the proposed social objectives, implying the calculation in social terms of a traditionally financial magnitude—the beta. Subsequently, other authors have explored the methodological keys and conceptual difficulties of SROI, such as Moody et al. (2013) and Pathak and Dattani (2014), among others. In addition to the importance of the aforementioned, it will be important to make progress in setting standards for the allocation of general costs and methodologies related to weightings, which allow us to know the actual counter-value of the initiatives under assessment.

4 Conclusions

Based on the above, we propose, as main conclusions of this research, the main fronts where we consider that work in the field of social impact measurement must progress:

- The first challenge in measuring and/or estimating social value beyond the lack of common measures is the lack of quality data for these measures overall. Measuring data (social outputs, outcomes, impacts and costs) requires a lot of resources and time. Collecting and analyzing data can be very expensive and this expense is often borne by the grantees of foundations that require such data. Typically, non-profits have limited time and money to pursue activities outside of their mission. Additionally, most non-profits do not have the administrative depth or expertise to track social outcome and cost data.
- Another significant issue is to improve the transparency of the organizations and the structuring of information based on their usefulness and relevance. Under the premise that resources are scarce and social intervention needs are very high, the entities must be transparent. Likewise, it should be possible to demonstrate a certain degree of usefulness in all projects undertaken that may be observable and identifiable by stakeholders.
- It is very relevant to advance in the definition and selection of indicators, given the complexity of this point. On the one hand, because it is difficult to collect the value of qualitative aspects such as well-being, social relations or mental health status and to reflect them in monetary values can be sometimes inappropriate. It is important not to force monetization when this is not possible and in this case, it may be useful to use "financial proxies," ensuring their quality and integrity, in order to avoid the consumption of significant resources for organization and generation of unnecessary or inefficient information.
- The institutional commitment to measuring the impact of its initiatives, on all stakeholders, both the positive and negative effects, direct and indirect, and on the entire temporal scope of the results of these initiatives, constitutes the third overall challenge. It should be noted that sometimes the social impact of the initiatives is not immediate, so the measurements should be made the moment they materialize, and it is necessary to keep track of those results. To date, it is common to stop analyzing the results of the initiatives once they have been finalized, the funding line has been replaced or the associated policy has disappeared, causing loss of information about its real impact in the long term. Social impact should be measured taking into account the

greater good (solution of the social problem) for the greater number of stakeholders (who should be paid attention to and whose problem is solved through the social action implemented) because their interests have intrinsic value. Additionally, in the *Practical Guide for Measurement and Impact Management*, it is recommended that entities focus their calculation on results, as noted by the European Venture Philanthropy Association (2013: 94), "techniques for doing so (i.e. randomized control groups) are very costly in terms of time and can also raise ethical issues in the case in which potential beneficiaries of the Social Project are excluded."
- Another challenge is related to the establishment of adequate communication mechanisms with stakeholders, focused on the information of their interest and in the form and time necessary for decision making, facilitating comparison with other initiatives. And for this, the measurement should be oriented not to the triggers of payment by the promoter, but to the results and impacts actually sought, since its objective is to improve knowledge in the organization and boost its effectiveness and efficiency.

In any case, regardless of the method selected for the measurement of social impact, what is truly relevant for organizations is always to follow a structured methodology, properly reasoned and focused on continuous improvement. And for all those involved—organizations, users, patrons, researchers and public authorities—the important thing is to continue to make progress, so that small progresses continue to be made with the ultimate goal of promoting equitable development, the defence of values and satisfaction of the needs of the disadvantaged.

References

Ebrahim, A. (2003). Accountability in practice: Mechanisms for NGOs. *World Development, 31*(5), 813–829.

EVPA. (2013). *A practical guide to measuring and managing impact*. Brussels: European Venture Philanthropy Association.

Fujiwara, D. (2015). *The seven principle problems of SROI*. London: Simétrica.

Fujiwara, D., & Campbell, R. (2011). *Valuation techniques for social cost-benefit analysis: Stated preference, revealed preference and subjective well-being approaches*. London: HM Treasury and Department for Work and Pensions.

Fundación Lealtad. (2013). *Las ONG españolas ante la crisis (2007–2013). Análisis de la evolución de las ONG de la Guía de la Transparencia*. Madrid: Fundación Lealtad.

Gibbon, J., & Dey, C. (2011). Developments in social impact measurement in the third sector: Scaling up or dumbing down? *Social and Environmental Accountability Journal, 31*(1), 63–72.

González, N., Valcárcel, M., & Contreras, R. (2010). *Valor social*. Valencia: Asociación Nittúa.

Maas, K., & Liket, K. (2011). Social impact measurement: Classification of methods. In R. Burritt et al. (Eds.), *Environmental management accounting, supply chain management, and corporate responsibility accounting*. New York: Springer Publishers.

Maier, F., Schober, C., Simsa, R., & Millner, R. (2015). SROI as a method for evaluation research: Understanding merits and limitations. *VOLUNTAS: International Journal of Voluntary and Nonprofit Organizations, 26*(5), 1805–1830.

Moody, M., Littlepage, L., Marron, J., Payda, N., & McCahill, P. (2013). Valuing SROI: Social Return on Investment Techniques and Organizational Implementation in the Netherlands and United States. *Research and Publications. 6.* Johnson Center at Grand Valley State University; Lilly Family School of Philanthropy at Indiana University.

Pathak, P., & Dattani, P. (2014). Social return on investment: Three technical challenges. *Social Enterprise Journal, 10*(2), 91–104.

Plataforma de ONG de Acción Social. (2006). *Plan Estratégico del Tercer Sector de Acción Social.* Madrid: Plataforma de ONG de Acción Social.

Retolaza, J. L., & Ramos, M. (2005). Modelización del costo de las empresas de inserción para la administración pública. *Revista de Economía Pública, Social y Cooperativa, 52*, 361–385.

Ruiz, R. (dir). (2015). *El Tercer Sector de Acción Social en 2015: impacto de la crisis*. Madrid: Plataforma de ONG de Acción Social.

Solórzano, M., González, N., Contreras, R., & Navío, J. (2015). *Del valor social al impacto social. Aplicación de coeficientes de depuración en el método SROI.* Madrid: INAP Investiga.

Stevenson, N., Taylor, M., Lyon, F., & Rigby, M. (2010). *Joining the dots: Social impact measurement, commissioning from the third sector and supporting social enterprise development*. Norwich: The Guild.

Tuan, M., & Emerson, J. (2000). The Roberts enterprise development fund: A case study on venture philanthropy. In REDF (Ed.), *REDF box set 2 — Social purpose enterprises and venture philanthropy in the New Millenium*. San Francisco: REDF Publications.

Zappalà, G., & Lyons, M. (2009). *Recent approaches to measuring social impact in the third sector: An overview*. Sydney: Centre for Social Impact.

9

Social Impact Investments Beyond Social Impact Bonds: A Research and Policy Agenda

Helen Chiappini

1 The Main Outlines of the Book

This book provides many specific outlines on the social impact investments (SIIs) market. Impact investors seem more aware now than in the past about what social impact investments are and about the main differences between SIIs and other familiar investments, like socially responsible investments (SRIs). The most talked about (and maybe attractive) investment of the SII industry appears to be social impact bonds (SIBs) (Carè and Wendt 2018). SIBs allow public bodies to repay financial return whether the expected social impact is achieved, controlling for social-mission drift. However, the SIB market suffers many limits, including the restricted knowledge of social risk determinants and lack of studies assessing the relationship between social risk and financial return. The study conducted by Scognamiglio et al. (2018) in Chap. 3 constitutes one of the first attempts to fill this gap. Scognamiglio et al. (2018) developed a social risk score and found that SIBs have a medium level of social

H. Chiappini (✉)
G. d'Annunzio University of Chieti and Pescara, Pescara, Italy
e-mail: helen.chiappini@unich.it

M. La Torre, M. Calderini (eds.), *Social Impact Investing Beyond the SIB*, Palgrave Studies in Impact Finance, https://doi.org/10.1007/978-3-319-78322-2_9

risk, mostly driven by social outcome evaluation. Social risk and financial return of a sample of 34 SIBs worldwide appeared not significantly correlated. Thus, future investigations should assess the role played by financial risk in determining SIBs financial return.

The SIB model is also challenging from a regulatory perspective, as shown in Chap. 4 by Rizzello et al. (2018) in which they discuss the Italian market and the complexity of its architecture. In fact, the public-private partnership and the involvement of a social impact independent evaluator provide an advantage in terms of social challenges met, without weighing down the public balance sheet. From another perspective, SIBs can—under some conditions—experience a start delay of a social intervention. An interesting alternative can be considered by the case presented in Chap. 5 by Addarii et al. (2018). They analyzed one of the first infrastructure public partnerships agreed upon for the realization of the hospital in Treviso, Italy.

Another financial alternative available in the SII market is crowdfunding. Crowdfunding bases the success on the crowd: a wide range of people can potentially support a campaign, regardless of the amount of money they invest (Belleflamme et al. 2010; Whitla 2009). Large potential for improving their effectiveness can be driven by the use of a crowdfunding platform within an innovative scheme called 'Social Bond Crowdfunding based,' which is discussed in Chap. 6 (Gallucci et al. 2018).

The measurement of social impact remains a challenging area within the SII framework as is illustrated by the Swedish case in Chap. 7 (Hultkrantz 2018) and the Spanish one in Chap. 8 (Solórzano-García et al. 2018).

Although the SII market appears characterized by a wide range of financial architectures (beyond SIBs) suitable to realize social and (or) environmental impacts, a great market potential is still unexpressed or limited by different kind of barriers.

2 Impact Investments: A Research and Policy Agenda

A research and policy agenda can be formulated for any kind of SII architecture. However, some pillars regard many financial structures as well as geographical areas and political contexts.

Thus, this section assesses research and policy points still open and highly interrelated, like the need for: a hard and soft regulation; a transparent governance; reliable social and financial performance; and the market development.

2.1 Hard and Soft Regulation for the Impact Sector

The SII market is a growing market (Mudaliar et al. 2017b), however, the development of ad hoc regulation did not correspond to the industry growth. Some products, like microcredit, are regulated by pioneering law, as in Italy and France, but the industry as a whole is not regulated by specific law. Thus, on the one hand, the SII industry can be affected by asymmetric information and by the risk of the development of a shadow market. On the other hand, the market functioning can be affected by concerns in terms of investors protection and by reputational and stability risk.

Asymmetric information is related to the concept of impact investment. To date, many international organizations and scholars have spent time discussing what an impact investment is (i.e., Social Impact Investment Taskforce 2014; Organization for Economic Cooperation and Development, OECD 2015), however, no country has regulated by law when we can refer to a financial product as an impact investment. Looking to social impact funds, Chiappini (2017) showed that many funds are far from an impact investment as defined by the OECD (2015) in a report including the consideration of experts and of the Social Impact Investment International Taskforce. Thus, asymmetric information may not only characterize impact funds but also transcend to the larger spectrum of social impact products.

The concatenate concerns regard both the establishment of a shadow market in which many financial actors can be advantaged in their funding by the misuse of the term 'impact investment' and the relative risk for unaware impact investors. By contrast, large impact investors can also experience relevant difficulties in portfolio selection, recognizing an evident difficulty in answering the question: when is an investee organization (really) an impact body?

In Europe, the High-Level Expert Group on Sustainable Finance has recently suggested that the European Commission develop a standard for sustainable assets, including an official European green bond standard, while the Directive 2014/95/UE on non-financial disclosure is already in force in many European countries.

Thus, whether governments can act in order to regulate the impact investment market and their segments (hard regulation), professional bodies can play an important role as well in developing guidelines (soft regulations).

The potential role of professional bodies was recalled by the Independent Advisory Group appointed by the UK government in 2016. The Advisory Group (2017) recognized that trust of UK impact investors can be gained (among others) with the implementation of standards concerning impact investments.

The United Nations Environment Programme Finance Initiative[1] released in January 2017 a standard called 'The Principles for Positive Impact Finance'. Those principles include a definition of impact finance (first principle), the general framework in which the impact finance move (second principle) and the following other two principles:

1. Transparency and disclosure on:
    (a) the process that guided the selection of eligible social impact projects
    (b) projects financed and on their social impact achieved
    (c) the monitoring process of financed projects
2. Assessment of social impact achieved

This standard can be viewed as one of the first attempts to provide a standard for SII. However, it is far from a comprehensive standard. Thus, there is still large space for social impact standards.

[1] United Nations Environment Programme Finance Initiative (UNEP FI 2017) is a partnership between United Nations Environment and the global financial sector created in the wake of the 1992 Earth Summit with a mission to promote sustainable finance. More than 200 financial institutions collaborate with UN Environment.

2.2 Governance, Ownership and the Missing Link with Social and Financial Performance

Ownership and governance of financial institutions are under the lens of regulators and policy makers due to the relevant role played in the stability of the financial sector. At the European level, the concept of governance recently assumed relevance in the field of sustainability. Indeed, the European High-Level Expert Group on Sustainable Finance released a Report in July 2017 including policy recommendations in terms of governance. Specifically, the High-Level Expert Group indicates the need for a sustainability committee for some specific typologies of firms and over some firms' size and recalled that incorporating 'long-term value creation and improving investor governance should be central objectives at the European level. Sustainability needs to be embedded in the objectives and oversight of board directors and investment institutions/funds and their advisers' (p. 26). Thus, those elements appear to be essential aspects also for the impact investment industry devoted to social impact alongside financial return.

In a theoretical perspective, ownership and governance play a critical role in the mission-lock of demand-side organizations and supply-side organizations. Demand-side organizations experience mission drift especially when the funding phase is completed. Indeed, Mudaliar et al. (2017a) report that only 11% of delivery organizations measure social impact after the investors exit. Thus, the impact attitude of some delivery organizations can be driven by funding needs.

Scholars are investigating the governance role in impact finance. Lehner (2016) suggests the study of the impact that crowdfunding can have on corporate governance of social enterprises due to the large number of stakeholders involved. Chiappini (2017) recognized that there is no evidence about the mission-lock clauses used by social impact funds, governance structures and boards composition of those investors, and the link between those elements and social and financial performance are opaque areas.

Governance is also relevant for other impact actors such as foundations, banks, microfinance institutions and governance bodies. Many central and local government bodies have been involved in the SII field, however, those impact projects have been governed in different ways. For instance, the United Kingdom established a specific unit in the prime minister's cabinet office: the Social Impact Finance Team, while other countries have not established a specific unit. Are there implications in terms of social impact investment development emerging from different projects' governance?

Moreover, in terms of governance of social impact actors there are no evidences about whether demographic features of impact committees or of the board of directors drive a more effective mission and mission-lock than others do. Thus, while many studies recognized that a more diversified board of directors can have a positive role in firms' and banks' risk-taking and performance (i.e., Berger et al. 2014; Adams and Ferreira 2009) or that CEO features can impact firms' performance (i.e., Palvia et al. 2015; Faccio et al. 2016) in the social impact investment field those elements are under-investigated.

2.3 Reliable Social and Financial Performance Track Records

Case studies support the in-depth analysis of specific impact projects, impact institutions or financial architecture active in the social impact industry. However, the sector suffers from a lack of mainstream research assessing social and financial performance.

With regard to social performance, the proliferation of impact metrics and the large amount of social areas (i.e., health, education, justice) did not support the development of a univocal or restricted set of social impact metrics. Indeed, the TRASI Foundation (2015) has recognized more than 150 metrics to measure social impact. Therefore, the overall estimation of social impact generated through many years of impact investments is not currently assessed. By contrast, we know the state of measurement practices through the lens of proxy institutions, as discussed by Mudaliar et al. (2017a) in the Global Impact Investment Network (GIIN) report.

Regarding financial performance, another recent report of the GIIN has summarized the widest research analyzing SII financial performance. Indeed, Mudaliar and Bass (2017) recognized the following widest studies of financial performance.

Cambridge Associates (CA) and the GIIN since 2015 update quarterly a performance report of 71 social impact funds targeting market-rate-returns and investing mostly in Africa and the United States, and marginally (17%) in other emerging economies (Bouri et al. 2015). The Wharton Social Impact Initiative (WSI) analyzed 32 market-rate-seeking private equity impact funds (Gray et al. 2016), while Symbiotics (2017) analyzed 98 microfinance impact vehicles (MIVs). Other research—restricted in terms of sector and geographical area—have been recognized by Mudaliar and Bass (2017), such as the research conducted by EngagedX and the Social Investment Research Council (2015) and the Boston Consulting Group (BCG).

Research conducted by scholars are limited due to the lack of public time series and public available benchmarks. An illustration of these phenomena is provided by the London Social Stock Exchange (SSX) and its 36 member companies[2] (SSX 2017b). Among these organizations, only 14 are publicly listed securities; nine are traded on the London Stock Exchange's Alternative Investment Market (AIM) and five on the Social Stock Exchange segment of the ICAP Securities and Derivatives Exchange (ISDX).

Impact Indexes have been recently created. For instance, the MSCI ACWI Sustainable Impact Index—including listed companies 'whose core business addresses at least one of the world's social and environmental challenges, as defined by the United Nations Sustainable Development Goals (UN SDGs)' and meeting some minimum ESG standards (MSCI 2017a)—was established in November 2015. Thus, time series are no longer than two years (MSCI 2017b) and they are not suitable for financial investigation and comparisons.

This makes it challenging to study performance, risk-adjusted performance and the portfolio contribution to performance and risk of social impact investments as shown in preliminary investigation by La Torre et al. (2017a, b).

[2] The London Social Stock Exchange (SSX) promoted in 2013 to foster the fundraising of delivery organizations. Specifically, 'it offers access to funding to impact organizations and a framework for impact assessment through the Impact Reporting Process which is the key milestone for achieving membership at the Social Stock Exchange. It offers access to the world's first regulated market dedicated to impact businesses of all sizes and investors, meaning that the SSX is a platform where accredited member companies can be traded publicly' (SSX 2017a).

Thus, the SII funding of financial-first (and impact-first) investors remains challenging due to the absence of resilient (and independent) information about social and financial performance. Working in this direction can contribute to market development and to the attraction of investments, meeting the funding needs of demand-side organizations. In contrast, a reverse causality can be found: the SII market growth can drive both the establishment of impact indexes and of scholars' research exploring financial and social performance.

2.4 Market Development

The demand for SIIs and SRIs is progressively growing. Schroders (2017) published results of research conducted on 22,100 retail investors in 30 countries. The research shows that younger generations are more inclined to invest in products aiming at social impact and sustainability. Among Millennials (18 to 35 years of age), 52% 'often or always invest in sustainable investment funds', compared to 40% of people aged 36 to 50 years (Generation X) and 31% of people aged 51 to 69 years (Baby Boomers) (p. 8).

Those results have been confirmed by Union Bank of Switzerland (UBS) (2017): Millennials are proactively interested in SIIs instead of the investments barriers that they face, among which is the limited information on impact investments. Barriers to the investment in the SII market have also been recognized in the United Kingdom, one of the most developed markets for SII. Research conducted by Barclays (2015) showed that the investment gap between people that would like invest in the industry (56%) and people investing in it (9%) is consistent.

Governments and professional bodies can actively work in order to build up a trustable market. Aspects recalled in previous sections can drive the market development, but other aspects are also relevant. The increasing availability of financial products incorporating social impact aims and possibly certified by independent evaluators as 'impact investments' can also contribute to fill the gap between demand and supply of SIIs.

The Independent Advisory Group to the UK government (2017) recalled three elements useful in order to 'make it easier for people to invest' (p. 6): improve the social finance education of people through coordinated actions of governments, professional bodies and organizations involved in the field; boost the trustee of investors through standards; and develop more products embodying impact finance concerns.

2.5 Concluding Remarks

The impact finance market faces many research and policy paths still open. This chapter assesses some of the most relevant ones. However, other aspects can drive the market development, such as the partnership between private and public entities, favourable fiscal policies and reliable market infrastructures. The space for research is large and worldwide scholars can significantly contribute to the development of the impact finance discipline.

References

Adams, R., & Ferreira, D. (2009). Women in the boardroom and their impact on governance and performance. *Journal of Financial Intermediation, 94*(2), 291–309.

Addarii, F., Lipparini, F., & Medda, F. (2018). Impact investing to transform PPP for infrastructures of public interest: The case of the new hospital of Treviso. In M. La Torre & M. Calderini (Eds.), *Social impact investing beyond the SIB: Evidence from the market*. London: Palgrave Macmillan.

Barclays. (2015). *The value of being human: A behavioral framework for impact investing and philanthropy*. Retrieved from https://wealth.barclays.com/content/dam/bwpublic/global/documents/wealth_management/wp-a-behavioural-framework-for-impact-investing-and-philanthropy.pdf.

Belleflamme, P., Lambert, T., & Schwienbacher, A. (2010). *Crowdfunding: Tapping the right crowd*. CORE discussion paper no. 2011/32. Retrieved from http://ssrn.com/abstract=1578175.

Berger, A. N., Kick, T., & Schaeck, K. (2014). Executive board composition and bank risk taking. *Journal of Corporate Finance, 28*(C), 48–65.

Bouri, A., Mudaliar, A., Schiff, H., Matthews, J., & Sternlicht, D. (2015). *Introducing the impact investing benchmark*. Cambridge Associates and the Global Impact Investment Network; updates through December 2016.

Retrieved from https://40926u2govf9kuqen1ndit018su-wpengine.netdna-ssl.com/wp-content/uploads/2017/08/Impact-Investing-Benchmark-Statistics_3.31.2017.pdf.

Carè, R., & Wendt, K. (2018). Investing with impact: An integrated analysis between academics and practitioners. In M. La Torre & M. Calderini (Eds.), *Social impact investing beyond the SIB: Evidence from the market*. London: Palgrave Macmillan.

Chiappini, H. (2017). *Social impact funds: Definition, assessment, performance*. London: Palgrave Macmillan.

EngagedX and Social Investment Research Council. (2015). *The social investment market through a data lens*. Retrieved from www.engagedx.com/downloads/SIRC_EngagedX_The_Social_Investment_Market_Through_a_Data_Lens_FINAL.pdf.

European High-Level Expert Group on Sustainable Finance. (2017). *Interim report*. Retrieved from https://ec.europa.eu/info/sites/info/files/170713-sustainable-finance-report_en.pdf.

Faccio, M., Marchica, M. T., & Mura, R. (2016). CEO gender, corporate risk-taking and efficiency of capital allocation. *Journal of Corporate Finance, 39*, 193–209.

Gallucci, C., Modina, M., & Minguzzi, A. (2018). The evolution of a social service crowdfunding platform towards an impact investing logic: The meridonare case study. In M. La Torre & M. Calderini (Eds.), *Social impact investing beyond the SIB: Evidence from the market*. London: Palgrave Macmillan.

Gray, J., Ashburn, N., Douglas, H., & Jeffers, J. (2016). *Great expectations: Mission preservation and financial performance in impact investing*. Wharton Social Impact Initiative. Retrieved from https://socialimpact.wharton.upenn.edu/wp-content/uploads/2016/09/Great-Expectations-Mission-Preservation-and-Financial-Performance-in-Impact-Investing.pdf.

Hultkrantz, L. (2018). Benefit-cost evaluation of prevention and early intervention measures for children and youth in Sweden. In M. La Torre & M. Calderini (Eds.), *Social impact investing beyond the SIB: Evidence from the market*. London: Palgrave Macmillan.

Independent Advisory Group to the United Kingdom Government. (2017). *Growing a culture of social impact investing in the UK*. Retrieved from www.gov.uk/government/uploads/system/uploads/attachment_data/file/664321/Full_Report_Growing_a_Culture_of_Social_Impact_Investing_in_the_UK.pdf.

La Torre, M., Chiappini, H., & Mango, F. (2017a). *Impact-oriented microfinance investment vehicles: A preliminary investigation on the controversial link between performance and stability*. Accepted by Journal of Business and Economics.

La Torre, M., Mango, F., & Chiappini, H. (2017b). *Do impact investments contribute to portfolio performance? A preliminary investigation*. Accepted by Journal of Business and Economics.

Lehner, O. M. (2016). Crowdfunding in social finance. In A. Nicholls, R. Paton, & J. Emerson (Eds.), *Social finance* (pp. 521–542). Oxford: Oxford University Press.

MSCI. (2017a). *MSCI ACWI Sustainable Impact Index methodology*. Retrieved from www.msci.com/eqb/methodology/meth_docs/MSCI_ACWI_Sustainable_Impact_Index_June2017.pdf.

MSCI. (2017b). *MSCI ACWI Sustainable Impact Index factsheet*. Retrieved from www.msci.com/documents/10199/6d2b3e68-90e0-448e-bd52-eaf0397539d1.

Mudaliar, A., & Bass, R. (2017). *Evidence on the financial performance of impact investments*. New York: The Global Impact Investing Network. Retrieved from https://thegiin.org/assets/2017_GIIN_FinancialPerformanceImpactInvestments_Web.pdf.

Mudaliar, A., Pineiro, A., Bass, R., & Dithrich, H. (2017a). *The state of impact measurement and management practice*. New York: The Global Impact Investing Network. Retrieved from https://thegiin.org/knowledge/publication/imm-survey.

Mudaliar, A., Schiff, H., Bass, R., & Dithrich, H. (2017b). *Annual impact investor survey 2017*. New York: The Global Impact Investing Network. Retrieved from https://thegiin.org/research/publication/annualsurvey2017.

OECD. 2015. Social impact investment. Building the evidence base. Paris. http://www.oecd.org/publications/social-impact-investment-9789264233430-en.htm.

Palvia, A., Vähämaa, E., & Vähämaa, S. (2015). Are female CEOs and Chairwomen more conservative and risk averse? Evidence from banking industry during the financial crisis. *Journal of Business Ethics, 131*(3), 577–594.

Rizzello, A., Caridà, R., Trotta, A., Ferraro, G., & Carrè, R. (2018). The use of payment by results in healthcare: A review and a proposal. In M. La Torre & M. Calderini (Eds.), *Social impact investing beyond the SIB: Evidence from the market*. London: Palgrave Macmillan.

Schroders. (2017). *Global investor study*. Global perspectives on sustainable investing 2017. Retrieved from http://www.schroders.com/en/sysglobalassets/digital/insights/2017/pdf/global-investor-study-2017/schroders_report_sustainable-investing_final.pdf.

Scognamiglio, E., Rizzello, A., & Chiappini, H. (2018). Social risk and financial return: Evidences from social impact bonds. In M. La Torre & M. Calderini (Eds.), *Social impact investing beyond the SIB: Evidence from the market*. London: Palgrave Macmillan.

Social Impact Investment Taskforce. 2014. Impact investment: e invisible heart of markets. London. http://www.socialimpactinvestment.org/.

Solórzano-García, M., Valcárcel-Dueñas, M., & Navío-Marco, J. (2018). Impact measurement for social innovation: Analysis of the Spanish third sector. In M. La Torre & M. Calderini (Eds.), *Social impact investing beyond the SIB: Evidence from the market*. London: Palgrave Macmillan.

SSX. (2017a). *The world's only public social stock exchange*. Impact Report 2016. Retrieved from http://socialstockexchange.com/worlds-public-social-stock-exchange/.

SSX. (2017b). *Member companies making a positive impact*. Retrieved from http://socialstockexchange.com/membership/member-profiles/.

Symbiotics. (2017, September). *Symbiotics MIV survey*. Retrieved from http://symbioticsgroup.com/wp-content/uploads/2017/09/Symbiotics-2017-MIV-Survey.pdf.

Trasi Foundation. (2015). *Tool and resource to measure social impact*. Retrieved from http://foundationcenter.org/gain-knowledge/foundation-ideas/trasi.

UBS. (2017). *Millennials – The global guardians of capital*. Retrieved from https://www.ubs.com/global/en/wealth-management/chief-investment-office/key-topics/2017/millennials.html#par_textimage_1327286662.

UNEP FI. (2017). *Principles for positive impact finance*. Retrieved from www.unepfi.org/publications/banking-publications/principles-for-positive-impact-finance/.

Whitla, P. (2009). Crowdsourcing and its application in marketing activities. *Contemporary Management Research, 5*(1), 15–28.

Index[1]

[1] Note: Page numbers followed by 'n' refer to notes.

M. La Torre, M. Calderini (eds.), *Social Impact Investing Beyond the SIB*, Palgrave Studies in Impact Finance, https://doi.org/10.1007/978-3-319-78322-2

The manufacturer's authorised representative in the EU is Springer Nature Customer Service Centre GmbH, Europaplatz 3, 69115 Heidelberg, Germany. If you have any concerns regarding our products, please contact ProductSafety@springernature.com

Printed and bound by CPI Group (UK) Ltd, Croydon, CR0 4YY

01/10/2026

02225955-0001